The Best
AMERICAN
ESSAYS
1986

The Best
AMERICAN
ESSAYS
1986

Edited and with an Introduction
by ELIZABETH HARDWICK

ROBERT ATWAN,
Series Editor

TICKNOR & FIELDS   NEW YORK   1986

ISSN 0888-3742
ISBN 0-89919-467-2
ISBN 0-89919-474-5 (pbk.)

Printed in the United States of America

v 10 9 8 7 6 5 4 3 2 1

"The Follies of Writer Worship" by Julian Barnes. First published in *The New York Times Book Review*. Copyright © 1985 by Julian Barnes. Reprinted by permission of the author.

"Not-Knowing" by Donald Barthelme. First published in *The Georgia Review*. Copyright © 1985 by Donald Barthelme. Reprinted by permission of the author.

"Flight from Byzantium" by Joseph Brodsky. First published in *The New Yorker*. Copyright © 1985 by Joseph Brodsky. Reprinted from his volume *Less Than One* by permission of Farrar, Straus & Giroux, Inc.

"Heatherdown" by Alexander Cockburn. First published in *Grand Street*. Copyright © 1985 by Grand Street Publications, Inc. Reprinted by permission of the publisher.

"The Passing of Jazz's Old Guard: Remembering Charles Mingus, Thelonious Monk, and Sonny Stitt" by Gerald Early. First published in *The Kenyon Review*. Copyright © 1985 by Gerald Early. Reprinted by permission of the author.

"Of Accidental Judgments and Casual Slaughters" by Kai Erikson. First published in *The Nation*. Copyright © 1985 by *The Nation* magazine, Nation Associates, Inc. Reprinted by permission of the publisher.

"When the Cockroach Stood by the Mickle Wood" by Robert Fitzgerald. First published in *The Yale Review*. Copyright © 1985 by Yale University. Reprinted by permission of Penelope Laurans Fitzgerald.

"China Still Lifes" by William Gass. First published in *House & Garden*. Copyright © 1985 by William Gass. Reprinted by permission of the author.

"Nasty Little Facts" by Stephen Jay Gould. First published in *Natural History*, Vol. 94, No. 2. Copyright © 1985 by The American Museum of Natural History. Reprinted by permission of the publisher.

"Dressed to Thrill" by Anne Hollander. First published in *The New Republic*. Copyright © 1985 by Anne Hollander. Reprinted by permission of the author.

"Morality and Foreign Policy" by George F. Kennan. First published in *Foreign*

Contents

Foreword by Robert Atwan   ix

Introduction by Elizabeth Hardwick   xiii

Julian Barnes. THE FOLLIES OF WRITER WORSHIP   1
    from The New York Times Book Review

Donald Barthelme. NOT-KNOWING   9
    from The Georgia Review

Joseph Brodsky. FLIGHT FROM BYZANTIUM   25
    from The New Yorker

Alexander Cockburn. HEATHERDOWN: A LATE IMPERIALIST
    MEMOIR   66
    from Grand Street

Gerald Early. THE PASSING OF JAZZ'S OLD GUARD:
    REMEMBERING CHARLES MINGUS, THELONIOUS MONK,
    AND SONNY STITT   93
    from The Kenyon Review

Kai Erikson. OF ACCIDENTAL JUDGMENTS AND CASUAL
    SLAUGHTERS   116
    from The Nation

Robert Fitzgerald. WHEN THE COCKROACH STOOD BY THE
    MICKLE WOOD   130
    from The Yale Review

William Gass. CHINA STILL LIFES   152
   from House & Garden

Stephen Jay Gould. NASTY LITTLE FACTS   161
   from Natural History

Anne Hollander. DRESSED TO THRILL   174
   from The New Republic

George F. Kennan. MORALITY AND FOREIGN POLICY   188
   from Foreign Affairs

Joyce Carol Oates. ON BOXING   204
   from The New York Times Magazine

Cynthia Ozick. THE FIRST DAY OF SCHOOL: WASHINGTON
   SQUARE, 1946   219
   from Harper's Magazine

Edward Rothstein. THE BODY OF BACH   227
   from The New Republic

Frederick Turner. VISIONS OF THE PACIFIC   240
   from Southwest Review

Gore Vidal. ON ITALO CALVINO   254
   from The New York Review of Books

John Wain. JULIA   268
   from The American Scholar

Biographical Notes   283

Notable Essays of 1985   287

Foreword

THIS IS THE INAUGURAL VOLUME of *The Best American Essays*. Such a collection has been long overdue. E. B. White — whose death last year deprived the American essay of one of its most respected practitioners — once observed that essayists don't receive the same literary attention as novelists, poets, and dramatists. The essayist, said White, "must be content in his self-imposed role of second-class citizen." Ten years ago, Edward Hoagland, another excellent essayist, also commented on the odd status of the essay: "It's strange that though two fine anthologies remain that publish the year's best stories, no comparable collection exists of essays." That collection finally exists.

This new series calls attention to the essay as a vital and remarkably versatile literary form. The modern American essay has adapted to a reading public's imperious demand for information, while retaining the personal, fluid, and speculative manner that has long characterized the form. Consider how many physicians and medical researchers have recently discovered the essay — not the technical article but the genuine literary form — as an especially effective way of bridging science and literature, of uniting what Stephen Jay Gould calls "nasty little facts" with humanistic values. Perhaps this should come as no surprise, since the essay began in aphorism, and the aphorism — Hippocrates was the first to use the word — grew out of medical science: "Life is short," he admonished, "the Art long, opportunity fleeting, experiment treacherous, judgment difficult."

Hippocrates was speaking of the art of medicine; but he might as well have been describing the art of the essay. Certainly those writers for whom the essay is not the occasional piece of prose, but rather what Annie Dillard calls the "real work," know that the essay — like fiction, poetry, and drama — has its own special challenges, its own opportunities for individual craft and style. Essayists are not people inspired to write nonfiction — whatever that nonword means — but to write essays.

But what are essays? One of my favorite definitions comes from a well-known student's *Handbook to Literature*. An essay, it starts confidently, is "a moderately brief prose discussion of a restricted topic." But by the next sentence that encyclopedic self-assurance has completely vanished, and we are informed that "no satisfactory definition can be arrived at." Even Montaigne, who named the genre four hundred years ago, stopped short of defining it. He saw the strange, eccentric stuff he wrote mainly in terms of literary production, as an active verb — he attempts, he tests, he tries, he *essays* — and not in terms of literary consumption — the finished composition. The writing spirit, not the reading matter. Montaigne may have been the first writer to invite the reader to catch him in the act: *Watch me thinking. Watch me writing.*

Thought and expression, substance and style: the essayist shuttles between these fuzzy boundaries, now settling down with ideas and exposition, now searching for eloquence and charm. Drift too far in one direction and you get an article — informative, impersonal, subject-bound; but move too far to the other side and you get a literary pose — arch, impressionistic, overwritten. Robert Louis Stevenson was one of those brilliant young essayists always willing to sacrifice substance to style. David Daiches found a way to pin down that tendency: "Stevenson wanted to be a writer before he had anything to say." But no one has expressed the modern essay's need to balance craft and concept better than Virginia Woolf: "The art of writing has for backbone some fierce attachment to an idea."

So many things go under the name of essay — celebrity profiles, interviews, political commentary, reviews, reportage, scientific papers, scholarly articles, snippets of humor, and those thin 750-word rectangles appropriately called "columns." Much of this day-to-day prose — though often informative and entertaining — loses its appeal as soon as whatever occasioned it loses its power to command attention. Flip through the pages of old magazines and you are more likely to read the ads than the articles.

Yet essays appear every year that transcend the daily newspaper and the monthly magazine. For various reasons of craft, or insight, or feeling, these essays leave a permanent impression. They become — as did E. B. White's essays in the forties, James Baldwin's in the fifties, Joan Didion's in the sixties, and Annie Dillard's in the seventies — a vital part of contemporary literature. They deserve to be collected; to be read again and again.

The Best American Essays will feature a selection of the year's outstanding essays, essays of literary achievement that show an awareness of craft and a forcefulness of thought. Roughly a hundred essays will be screened from a wide variety of regional and national publications. (Fine essays have a way of turning up in unexpected places, as the reading public discovered when it learned that Lewis Thomas's prize-winning essays had regularly appeared in *The New England Journal of Medicine*.) These hundred or so essays will be turned over to a distinguished guest editor, who may add a few personal favorites to the list and who will make the final selections.

To qualify for selection, the essays must be works of respectable literary quality intended as fully developed, independent essays (not excerpts or reviews) on subjects of general interest (not specialized scholarship), originally written in English (or translated by the author) for first appearance in an American periodical during the calendar year. Publications that want to make sure their contributions will be considered each year should include the series on their subscription list (Robert Atwan, *The Best American Essays*, P.O. Box 1074, Maplewood, New Jersey 07040).

For this inaugural volume, I would like to thank my friend Laurance Wieder, who helped me get the project started. Corlies Smith and Katrina Kenison at Ticknor & Fields gave the plan a warm and instantaneous reception. The many magazine editors I spoke with were generous in their support and unanimous in their belief that this was an idea whose time had come. I think the series is immensely fortunate in having one of America's premier authors, Elizabeth Hardwick, as its first guest editor.

R.A.

Introduction

THE ESSAY? Thousands of pages of prose are published each month and not many of them are given to fiction. Perhaps most of the pages are information about the events of the day or the week and are not to be thought of as essays. What is this thunder and hail of newsprint felling the forests of the world? Journalism? Not quite, not nowadays. The knowing would not restrict the word *journalism* to mere information, if information can be thought of as *mere*. Nowadays journalism is a restless and predatory engagement, having established its imperial mandate under the phrase *new journalism*, established its claim with such occupying force that the phrase itself is no longer needed, no longer defining.

If we cannot be sure we are reading journalism according to the rules of the professional schools, we are even less certain that we are reading the elevated essay. Still, there is something called the essay, and volumes by individual writers are published under the title. Even then the term does not provide a serenity of precision; it is not altogether genuine in its shape, like fiction or poetry. It does not even have the advantage of pointing to scale since some essays are short and many are long and most incline to a condition of unexpressed hyphenation: the critical essay, the autobiographical essay, the travel essay, the political — and so on and so on.

There is a self-congratulatory sense in the word *essay*. It wants to signify that what has been offered is not a lesser offering, not just a review, a sketch, a "piece" — odd, useful word — summoned to feed the hungry space of periodicals. Sometimes the vagrant coinage *essayistic* appears in the press, and this is bad news for the language since it indicates an extension of murky similarity to what is itself more than a little cloudy. Of course, we always know what a barbarism is trying to say; its nature is to indicate the struggle for definition.

To be like an essay, if not quite the real thing, means that, in a practical bit of prose, attention has been paid to expressiveness and that to gain expressiveness certain freedoms have been exercised, freedoms illicit in the minds of some readers, freedoms not so much exercised as seized over the border. Essays are aggressive even if the mind from which they come is fair, humane, and, when it is to the point, disinterested. Hazlitt, in an essay on the poets living in his own time, writes: "Mrs. Hannah More is another celebrated modern poetess, and I believe still living. She has written a great deal which I have never read." It might take Mrs. More, if indeed she lived still, some time to figure out just what was being said.

The aggressiveness of the essay is the assumption of the authority to speak in one's own voice and usually the authority is earned by previous performance. We see a name on the cover or inside the pages and we submit to the reading with some eagerness, which may be friendly eagerness or not. One of the assumptions of the essayist is the right to make his own mistakes, since he speaks only for himself, allowing for the philosopher's cunning observation that "in my opinion" actually asserts "all reasonable men will agree." This claim is sometimes disputed by an elected authority, the editor, who may think too many villages have been overrun by the marauder. Since the freedom of the open spaces is the condition of the essay, too much correction and surgical intervention turns the composition into something else, perhaps an article, that fertile source of profit and sometimes pleasure in the cultural landscape.

William Gass, in what must be called an essay, a brilliant one, about Emerson, an essayist destined from the cradle, makes a distinction between the article and the essay. Having been employed by the university and having heard so many of his colleagues "doing an article on," Gass has come to think of the article as "that awful object" because it is under the command of defensiveness in footnote, reference, coverage, and would also pretend that all must be useful and certain, even if it is "very likely a veritable Michelin of misdirection." If the article has a certain sheen and professional polish, it is the polish of "the scrubbed step" — practical economy and neatness. The essay, in Gass's view, is a great meadow of style and personal manner, freed from the need for defense except that provided by an individual intelligence and sparkle. We consent to watch a mind at work, without agreement often, but only for pleasure. Knowledge hereby attained, great indeed, is again wanted for the pleasure of itself.

We would not want to think of the essay as the country of old men, but it is doubtful that the slithery form, wearisomely vague and as chancy as trying to catch a fish in the open hand, can be taught. Already existing knowledge is so often required. Having had mothers and fathers and the usual miserable battering of the sense of self by life may arouse the emotional pulsations of a story or a poem; but feeling is not sufficient for the essay. Comparisons roam about it, familiarity with those who have plowed the field before, shrewdness concerning the little corner or big corner that may remain for the intrusion of one's own thoughts. Tact and appropriateness play a part. How often we read a beginner's review that compares a thin thing to a fat one. "John Smith, like Tolstoy, is very interested in the way men interact under the conditions of battle." Well, no.

Fortunately, the essay is not a closed shop, and the pages do vibrate again and again with the appearance of a new name with no credentials admired or despised. An unknown practitioner of the peculiar animation of the prose of an essay takes up the cause. It is an occasion for happiness since it is always astonishing that anyone will write an essay. Some write them not once but more or less regularly. To wake up in the morning under a command to animate the stones of an idea, the clods of research, the uncertainty of memory, is the punishment of the vocation. And all to be done without the aid of end-rhyme and off-rhyme and buried assonance; without an imagined character putting on a hat and going into the street.

Those with the least gift are most anxious to receive a commission. It seems to them that there lies waiting a topic, a new book, a performance, and that this is known as material. The true prose writer knows there is nothing given, no idea, no text or play seen last evening until an assault has taken place, the forced domination that we call "putting it in your own words." Talking about, thinking about a project bears little relation to the composition; enthusiasm boils down with distressing speed to a paragraph, often one of mischievous banality. To proceed from musing to writing is to feel a robbery has taken place. And certainly there has been a loss; the loss of the smiles and ramblings and discussions so much friendlier to ambition than the cold hardship of writing.

Essays are addressed to a public in which some degree of equity exists between the writer and the reader. Shared knowledge is a necessity, although the information need not be concrete. Perhaps it is more to be thought of as a sharing of the experience of reading certain kinds of texts, texts with omissions and elisions, leaps. The essayist does not stop to identify the common ground; he will not write, "Picasso, the great Spanish painter who lived long in France." On the other hand, essays are about something, something we may not have had reason to study and master, often matters about which we are quite ignorant. Elegance of presentation, reflection made interesting and significant, easily lead us to engage our reading minds with Zulus, herbaceous borders in the English garden, marriage records in eighteenth-century France, Japanese scrolls.

In the contemporary essay, as in contemporary fiction, the use of the first-person narrator or expositor has become so widespread it must be seen as a convenience. This is a puzzle having to do, perhaps, not with self-assertion to fill every available silence, but with modesty, a fear of presumption. In fiction a loss of movement is accepted by the choice of "I" in order to gain relief from knowing and imagining without the possibility of being there to know. That at least may be one of the aesthetic considerations. Also, the dominance of the first-person narrator in current fiction seems to reflect uncertainty about the classical conception of character; often the contemporary psyche is not seen as a lump of traits so much as a mist of inconsistencies, flights, constant improvisations. It is more agreeable to this sense of things to write "It seemed to me" rather than "It was."

In the essay we find the intrusion of the "I" even where little is autobiographical. In my mind I imagine a quite obscure reflection beginning, "I pulled into the filling station with my wife in the front seat and the kids restless and hungry in the back, and there I saw an interesting commercial logo, a sort of unicorn-horse that recalled to me certain medieval illuminated texts." What will follow is as it is, learned, perhaps difficult. How to account for the filling station, except as a fear of presumption about the subject, a search for immediacy, a loosening of the boundaries of prose? Of course it doesn't always work. There are many things worth knowing that cannot be made familiar.

De Quincy in his memoir about the Lake Poets tells of a Mr. Wedgewood, a gifted, loved, quite rich young man, patron of Samuel Coleridge, the tormented genius who very much needed a patron. Mr. Wedgewood sought to distract himself from feelings of depression and lassitude by buying a butcher shop, where the wrangling abuse would force him to a high level of response. The experiment was not happy. There is a certain kind of polemical essay around that is a butcher shop of raw, hacked opinion which arouses a sure relief from torpor by encouraging dissent and violent rebuttal.

Intemperance in political writing has its hacks and its celebrated practitioners. As Trevor-Roper writes in his introduction to a volume of essays by the great Macaulay, "Macaulay could be very unjust to persons. He could also be vindictive. His essay on Boswell's *Life of Johnson* is both. He is unjust to Johnson, unjust to Boswell, and positively vindictive to the editor, Croker, who was not only a Tory but a member of parliament who enraged Macaulay by opposing him in the debates on parliamentary reform." Macaulay was a Whig. It is nearly always useful to be aware of the mind-set of essayists because a determined coloration of belief may spread itself far and wide and land not only on the political field but on the head of the novelist, the film maker, the historian. So it has been; so it is yet. The mastery of expository prose, the rhythm of sentences, the pacing, the sudden flash of unexpected vocabulary, redeem polemic, and, in any case, no one is obliged to agree. But ill-written, pompously self-righteous, lamely jocular forays offend because an air of immature certainty surrounds them. Too great a degree of exhortation and corrective insistence makes us wish for the tones of the earlier English "familiar essay," with its calm love of nature and tolerance of human frailty.

The selections in the present volume are under the domination of the year 1985, the year just past. That is the way with selections. Many of the outstanding writers in the form are missing, the year not having caught them on the run. To list the lamented absences would be lengthy and then there would be the regret of having, no matter the length, forgotten just the ones wished to be present. And yet 1985 was surely a year like any other for the essay; that is, a year filled with gifts that arrived without expectation. In a sense, every interesting essay is a surprise. The weeks, the months turn over; subscriptions come in the mail, magazine covers in the store arrest the attention and lead us to want to *find out*. Find out what is in the minds of critics of books and art and federal budgets and city scandals. Often we read something unexpected by writers whose work we know. Each month, somewhere, one or another will have written about subjects we had not thought to connect them with. We discover journeys, side-lines of passionate interest, peculiar bits of knowledge, confessions quite new. In this volume a certain range was desirable, a distribution showing the variety of the element and a variety of publications. The book might be three times as long and, in fact, was almost twice as long when the final selection itself turned out to have many more words than practical. In the essay, the "best" is to be thought of as "some of the best." The form exists in so many shapes and sizes and is directed to every point of the compass. The essay is nothing less than the reflection of all there is: art, personal experience, places, literature, portraiture, politics, science, music, education — and just thought itself in orbit. Roland Barthes has written an essay on wrestling, the spectacle of it; Hazlitt composed "The Fight": "Reader, have you ever seen a fight? If not you have pleasure to come, at least if it is a fight between the Gas-man and Bill Neate." Proust wrote an essay "On Reading"; Sartre has written two essays on Faulkner and thousands have been written on Proust and Sartre and again on Faulkner.

There is nearly always a time when the novelist and poet will stand aside to create something other. This will be an imaginative essay and they are among the most beautiful and arresting we know. They tend to be offhand and intuitive, flashing and yet exacting — D. H. Lawrence's, for example. Knowing how to write — there is no substitute for that. The writer may be said to precede the material, and that is why academic writing, where the material is the fundamental capital, is so often like hoeing a hard field in winter. However, being a professor and knowing a great deal about some things does not make one an academic writer. Only the withholding gods can accomplish that.

So there is no end to the essay, and no beginning. Walter Benjamin makes a visit to Moscow: "Each thought, each day, each life lies here as on a laboratory table." The poet, Jules LaForgue, goes to Berlin to be in the service of the Empress: "She has been bored, she is still bored, and she still dreams." Joan Didion has been to Alcatraz Island in California: "Alcatraz Island is covered with flowers now: orange and yellow nasturtiums, geraniums, sweet grass, blue iris, black-eyed Susans. Candytuft springs up through the cracked concrete in the exercise yard."

The essay, at least in reduction, is to be thought of as popular. Think of the number published. In the lightest examples — short sentences, short altogether, with photographs surrounding the shortness — it appears that words here and there about celebrities are gratifying in the gross. This cannot be the search for information, since there is little information in them. Libel is the handmaiden of information about the living. The appeal of celebrity journalism seems to rest upon a promise and to accept the fact that the promise will again and again be unfilled. To know the sanitized items, in almost infinite repetition, about the famous indicates an overwhelming appetite. Born somewhere, lives somewhere, may have a "wonderful" child, possibly a mate to whom, for the time being, everything is owed. Parents somewhere and, nearer, the career itself. "I want to improve my acting." All of this is prose of some kind, a commission arranged and concluded.

The true essay, making as it does a contribution to the cultural life, is not so simple. Its celebrities are likely to be long-dead painters, writers, and thinkers; living ones not memorable in photographs, and not a synopsis. Insofar as essays give information, and of course they do in their way, a peculiar condition of reciprocity, reader participation, prevails. Wit, the abrupt reversal, needs to strike a receptive ear or eye or else the surprise is erased, struck down. Expressiveness is an addition to statement, and hidden in its clauses is an intelligence uncomfortable with dogmatism, wanting to make allowances for the otherwise case, the emendation.

A well-filled mind itself makes the composition of essays more thorny rather than more smooth, with everything readily available. There is seldom absolute true assertion unless one is unaware. Words and phrases, ideas and opinions, invading the vast area of even the narrowest topic must fall back on a fluency of reference, reference sometimes merely hinted, if the convincing is to be achieved. Conviction itself is partial and the case is never decided. The essay is not the ground of verdicts. It rests on singularity rather than consensus.

Montaigne: can there be a reflection upon the essay without the dropping of this sacred name? Emerson finds Montaigne a "representative man" under the description the skeptic, as Shakespeare is the poet. A close reading of the essay will show that Emerson writes around Montaigne rather than about him. However much he may admire the French master's candor and "uncanonical levity," the men are not attuned, differences in temperament being too great. Gass, in his essay on Emerson, slides into a diversion on Montaigne and notes, "Have we digressed, however? I hope so." Hannah Arendt in her writing on the great modern essayist, Walter Benjamin, remarks upon the difference in the social station of the modern essayist when compared to the world of the classical European man of letters.

The world of the American essay is a democratic one, a meritocracy. And much more so now than in the time of Emerson, a man from the old Harvard, well-educated in a nation commonly much less so. The tones of "Self-Reliance" and even of "Compensation" would not appear to be suitable orchestration today. Confidence it has, if very different from the given, worldly self-confidence of Montaigne. Emerson's confidence, his attraction to enlightened sermonizing, is addressed to an audience still small enough for instruction. "The man must be so much, that he must make all circumstances indifferent."

Modes of conduct — except for that of foreign policy, which is impersonal in spite of pleas to view it as a burning pan on the stove in the kitchen of every citizen — commend themselves as a subject mostly to cranks and uplifters and health fiends. If we would in the manner of Lord Chesterfield tell a young gentleman how to behave, the pages might take the form of case histories of drug addicts, dropouts, and statistics on earning power. The American essay, the contemporary one, is personal in its manners, as a display, and also as a wrestling with means, how to shape the exposition. Little is proposed as a model. The personality of the literary critic is sharp and — with the most gifted — eccentric, but it wishes to reveal a difference in itself, not to promote imitation in manner, but only imitation in opinion, since every opinion loves a follower.

We have here seventeen essays published in the year 1985, seventeen humours, as Montaigne said he had a thousand within himself. Most gathered here are self-propelled, and a few are responses to an occasion. All have knowledge, casually at hand, the knowledge of a free and unbound intelligence and sensibility. None reflects expertise, a more mechanical acquisition suggesting usefulness rather than passion. Some are straightforward and some wind through the paths of memory, the unmapped individual experience. Such is the way in the art of the essay.

ELIZABETH HARDWICK

The Best
AMERICAN
ESSAYS
1986

JULIAN BARNES

The Follies of Writer Worship

FROM THE NEW YORK TIMES BOOK REVIEW

I ONCE OWNED a piece of Somerset Maugham's gate. Well, not exactly Somerset Maugham's gate — it wasn't pillaged from the Villa Mauresque — but near enough. My chunk of literary wood came from the vicarage at Whitstable where Maugham spent part of his unhappy boyhood. Decades later local gray-beards with lips untouched by a lie would assure you that they had often seen the future novelist swinging on the vicarage gate. When it fell into disrepair some twenty years ago, I greedily acquired a section of it — a spar about a yard long, with a nail at each end and a thick carapace of white paint. I kept it under the stairs, alongside other pointless yet favored items — the half-finished brass rubbing, the broken typewriter, the tennis racquet with strings burst into a mad spaghetti. From time to time I would take out my private trophy, examine it with half-embarrassed fondness, then put it back.

Those who admire Maugham will understand this attach-ment, while those who don't may find it pathetic and miscon-ceived: other people's tastes in art can seem as mysterious and trivial as their tastes in love. Ford Madox Ford, in the course of his engagingly unreliable memoirs, tells the story of a distant relation, a lady-in-waiting at the court of Saxe-Weimar, who always exuded a faint and disagreeable smell. When she died they discovered round her neck a sachet containing half a cigar. The other half had been smoked by Liszt at a lunch some thirty years earlier; after the composer's departure, she had raided the ashtray for the token she had worn ever since. Was she a

foolish old woman or a devoted lover of art? Of course it depends partly on whether we believe Ford. Do cigar butts retain
their odor for thirty years? An unsentimental reader of the story
might wonder if its subject wasn't, sadly, just an old lady who
smelled.

In many ways readers must be a severe disappointment to
writers. Why don't they just get on with it — buy the books and
read the words? That's what the business is about, after all. But
instead, they want autographs, cigar ends, bits of hair, bits of
your gate, bits of your time, bits of your life. Fandom, obse-
quious yet demanding, is not confined to the music business.

Did the gate-spar increase my understanding of Maugham's
fiction? No more than the cigar butt sharpened its rescuer's appreciation of Liszt's piano technique. Yet such reverent souvenir-
hunting is often deeply installed in those who love art. It seems
like proof of proper intent: if you preserve the trivial, then you
must truly value the serious. Take the case of Robert Louis
Stevenson's hair. When the novelist died at forty-four, he was
survived by his old Scottish nurse, who would regularly be
sought out by literary enthusiasts. Asked if she had any memen-
toes of the young genius, she would admit to possessing a single
lock of hair she had cut from Louis's head some forty years
earlier. She was naturally unwilling to part with it, but, well,
perhaps . . . By the time the canny nanny had finished trading,
all the fans were satisfied. If there are enough pieces of the
True Cross in circulation to keep an Eskimo family in log fires
for a decade, there is enough Stevenson hair around to open a
wig-shop.

A few years ago I was driving round northern France on a
studious pilgrimage — Michelet's château at Vascoeuil, Monet's
garden at Giverny, Balzac's retreat at Saché, Anatole France's
house at Tours and so on. The trip culminated at Rouen, hometown of the writer I had idolized unswervingly for twenty years
or so — Gustave Flaubert. I didn't expect there would be very
much to see: the writer's house had been demolished a century
ago, and most of his possessions were scattered or lost. But a
few scraps of memorabilia had survived, and their aura would
be enhanced by their scarcity.

I went first to the Hôtel-Dieu, the hospital where Flaubert's father was chief surgeon. There is a small museum here: you are shown the novelist's first magazine article, his *eau de Cologne* pot, the room in which he was born. Toward the end of the visit I came across the unlikeliest exhibit — a stuffed green parrot. The label explained that this was the very parrot that Flaubert had borrowed from the local natural history museum when he was writing his story "A Simple Heart." It appears there as Félicité's parrot Loulou, a bird that increases in symbolic significance as its owner gets older and more fuddled. "A Simple Heart" is one of the most perfect short stories ever written: the combination of this, the strangeness of the relic before me and the improbability of its survival seemed very touching. It was a small epiphany. This parrot had once stood on the writer's desk; now, a century later, it stood in front of me. It was as though the parrot were a relay runner who had just passed on some invisible baton. I felt closer to Flaubert.

Two days later I visited the second Flaubert shrine, at Croisset, on the outskirts of the city. Here, in the middle of the Rouen waterfront, stands a one-room pavilion, all that remains of the original family estate. Again, there is a small collection of Flaubertian relics, exerting their disproportionate power. You can examine a lock of hair (not of a Stevensonian provenance), the crumpled handkerchief with which the writer mopped his brow as he lay dying and the glass from which he took his last drink of water. I gazed at them with due deference, and then looked up. Perching on top of a cupboard was another stuffed parrot. Also green, and also entirely authentic: yes, yes, they assured me, this was definitely the parrot borrowed by Flaubert when he was writing "A Simple Heart." No doubt at all.

It was a droll, deflating moment, part Monty Python, part moral tale. The first parrot had made me feel in touch with the master. The second parrot mocked me with a satirical squawk. What makes you think you can seize hold of a writer that easily, it asked, and pecked me sharply on the wrist for my presumption.

Many writers learn to handle the idolatry of their fans with a measure of grace, but if you are a writer who has the misfortune to be dead as well as famous, matters are less under your control.

"He became his admirers," wrote Auden on the death of Yeats. The dead poet has been ingested by his readers; from now on he will be read, admired and loved in a different way — owned without opposition:

> Now he is scattered among a hundred cities
> And wholly given over to unfamiliar affections,
> To find his happiness in another kind of wood
> And be punished under a foreign code of conscience.

Writers, as they grow older, anticipate and increasingly fear those unfamiliar affections, that foreign code of conscience. In the present century, more than ever before, their punishment is likely to include betrayal by biography. And the more famous you are, the more likely that betrayal. After all, you belong to the world, not to yourself — don't you? You can't expect loyalty now.

Auden asked that after his death all his letters be burned, but nobody obeyed: not his old friend Stephen Spender, nor even Faber & Faber, the British publishers he had helped enrich. The poet requested that no biography be written of him: three have already appeared. George Orwell's similar wish has also been ignored; so has T. S. Eliot's, despite the stout rear guard of his widow Valerie. Do such requests indicate naïveté about the literary world? Are they no more than a vain attempt to exercise power from beyond the grave — a final, failing arrogance? Perhaps the most chilling betrayal of our times has been that of Somerset Maugham, who instructed his literary executor, Spencer Curtis Brown, that no biography be written of him. Gradually, however, the force of this instruction waned: Brown authorized Ted Morgan's biography, and explained his own disobedience in a preface: "Many people may think I have acted wrongly. Only one man could have given me a clear decision, and he was the man who had sufficient confidence in me to place his reputation in my hands."

It is curious reasoning. You might think that Maugham had already made "a clear decision." You might also think that if the novelist had been able to read Ted Morgan's sour and prurient work, it would only have endorsed the correctness of his original resolution.

The wider public assumes that writers don't want their biographies written because they don't want the gossip to come out — that mad wife, the taste for young men, that embarrassing disease, the booze, the laziness. Doubtless this element exists (though no more than with other categories of biographee), but the main motive is usually larger: it's a defiant attempt to concentrate the reader's mind on the work. The writer's life usually isn't (as it seems to the writer) an especially interesting or instructive one. It is full of frailty and defeat like any other life. What counts is the work. Yet the work can quite easily be buried, or half-buried, by the life. Think of Byron, Wilde, Robert Lowell, Samuel Johnson. And even the biography that glorifies the life, that styles itself as homage, may be just another, less obvious form of betrayal. What novelist, given the choice, wouldn't prefer you to reread one of his novels rather than read his biography?

My encounter with Flaubert's two parrots roosted in my mind. It was a joke, a lesson, a warning. You may feel "close" to a writer when you walk round his house and examine a lock of his hair, but the only time you are truly close is when you are reading words on the page. This is the only pure act: the rest — from fandom to *Festschrift* — is dilution, marginality, betrayal — the higher sentimentality. Biography is only sophisticated hair-collecting.

There seemed other things wrong with the biographical form, especially when applied to someone as long dead and as long famous as Flaubert. Each new biography is another layer of papier-mâché applied to the funeral mask, making the features more stylized. It is another layer of holy turf added to the tumulus, burying the writer even further underground. Worse, the come-lately biographer is forever condemned to that dutiful trudge in the footsteps of his predecessors, reinterpreting here, questioning there, being a little more judicious, being *fair*. I wanted to write about Flaubert, though in quite what form I didn't as yet know. All I knew was that I didn't want to be fair or judicious; I wanted the process, and the result, to be somehow more active, more aggressive. Flaubert himself seemed to approve this stance. In a letter of 1872 to his friend Ernest Feydeau, he urged: "When you write the biography of a friend, you must do it as if you were taking *revenge* for him."

Is there that much revenge to be taken on behalf of someone generally acknowledged to be a great writer? Oh yes; there is always some slack in the rope. For a start, there are those who disparaged, cheated and undervalued him in his lifetime. Listen, for instance, to Maxime Du Camp, one of Flaubert's oldest friends tempering his praise: "I am absolutely convinced that Flaubert was a writer of rare merit, and had he not been attacked by his terrible nervous illness he would have been a writer of genius." Nor do envy and condescension die when the novelist expires. He then becomes vulnerable to the jealous colleague who finds his fame overbearing, to the judicious commentator with a nose for anachronism or mistake, and to that brand of critic who secretly loves to be disappointed.

The two-parrot incident suggested an idea for a short story — the story developed into a novel about a retired English doctor obsessed by Flaubert. And the process of researching the novel led me eventually to solve the tiny mystery as to which bundle of feathers represented the image of the True Parrot. The resulting book felt like an act of revenge, and an act of homage; but also — occasionally — like an act of betrayal. Was this because the writers you love are as capable of inducing unspecific guilt as the people you love? Perhaps. But it's also the case that Flaubert instills a certain wariness in those who write about him. He didn't issue prohibitions like Auden, Eliot and the rest, but you are made to feel that your activities are under scrutiny.

He despised critics, for instance: criticism, he wrote to Louise Colet in 1853, is "lower than rhyming games and acrostics, which at least demand a modicum of invention." If he didn't express quite the same scorn for biography, he certainly considered it a principle of fiction that the personality of the writer, and the expression of subjective opinion, were irrelevant: "Man is nothing, the work of art everything . . . . It would be very pleasant for me to say what I think and relieve Monsieur Gustave Flaubert's feelings by means of such utterances; but what is the importance of the said gentleman?" In Christian doctrine, death destroys the body and allows the soul to fly free; in Flaubertian literary doctrine, death destroys the personality and allows the work of art to fly free. That was his theory, and also his hope.

It didn't work out like that, of course. The child who says, "Don't follow me," and walks away, is always sure to be followed. The writer may repeat, "Don't follow me," but still the critics will play their rhyming games and the biographers will analyze Monsieur Gustave Flaubert's feelings. Perhaps the prohibition makes them even more avid. Sartre, for instance, spent the last ten years of his life on his massive psychobiography of Flaubert: the enterprise that began with less than sympathetic intent, and that ended as something almost comic. Sartre is like some distempered body snatcher who exhumes Flaubert in order to rebury him in a deeper, unmarked grave, but who fails to notice while digging that he is throwing up a huge bank of earth behind him, marking the burial-spot even more clearly.

And in every case, of course, the biographer, the critic, the fan find reasons why the writer's interdictions — or, in Flaubert's case, sardonic discouragements — don't really apply to them. Maugham's literary executor convinced himself that, had the novelist lived, he would surely have come round to the idea of a biography. With "Flaubert's Parrot," I caught myself arguing that while Flaubert disapproved of critics and seemed indifferent to biography, he never said it was forbidden to write a novel about him, did he?

Why do we disobediently pursue? We persuade ourselves that a writer's life helps illuminate his work, but I wonder if we really believe this. The life offers false and easy explanations — Eliot's first marriage went wrong, so he took a glum view of things in "The Waste Land." Only the work can really explain the work. So perhaps we want to approach and touch the writer's life for a more basic, a more magical reason. Parallels between religion and art have generally been much overworked but perhaps literary biography in the twentieth century has come to occupy the place once owned by hagiography except that in these disenchanted times, the instructive lives of saints have been replaced by the instructive lives of sinners: the reader now thrills to the bad life rather than the good life. And just as the saint's relics were kept in a gold casket beneath the altar, so now we preserve the writer's relics, although we expect no miracles from them.

I no longer own my spar of Somerset Maugham's gate. It disappeared in a move, or was burned by mistake or stolen to patch someone else's gate. Besides, I am no longer quite so keen on Maugham. But I have something else now, an odder and more poignant trophy — an unopened packet of Disque Bleu that was found at Arthur Koestler's elbow after his suicide two years ago. The cigarettes sit on a shelf a few feet from my desk. I look across at them from time to time. They still smell of tobacco, though of course have another twenty-eight years to go before rivaling Liszt's aromatic cigar butt. I don't think I'll be smoking them just yet.

DONALD BARTHELME

Not-Knowing

FROM THE GEORGIA REVIEW

LET US SUPPOSE that someone is writing a story. From the world of conventional signs he takes an azalea bush, plants it in a pleasant park. He takes a gold pocket watch from the world of conventional signs and places it under the azalea bush. He takes from the same rich source a handsome thief and a chastity belt, places the thief in the chastity belt and lays him tenderly under the azalea, not neglecting to wind the gold pocket watch so that its ticking will, at length, awaken the now-sleeping thief. From the Sarah Lawrence campus he borrows a pair of seniors, Jacqueline and Jemima, and sets them to walking in the vicinity of the azalea bush and the handsome, chaste thief. Jacqueline and Jemima have just failed the Graduate Record Examination and are cursing God in colorful Sarah Lawrence language. What happens next?

Of course, I don't know.

It's appropriate to pause and say that the writer is one who, embarking upon a task, does not know what to do. I cannot tell you, at this moment, whether Jacqueline and Jemima will succeed or fail in their effort to jimmy the chastity belt's lock, or whether the thief, whose name is Zeno and who has stolen the answer sheets for the next set of Graduate Record Examinations, will pocket the pocket watch or turn it over to the nearest park employee. The fate of the azalea bush, whether it will bloom or strangle in a killing frost, is unknown to me.

A very conscientious writer might purchase an azalea at the

Downtown Nursery and a gold watch at Tiffany's, hire a hand-some thief fresh from Riker's Island, obtain the loan of a chastity belt from the Metropolitan, inveigle Jacqueline and Jemima in from Bronxville, and arrange them all under glass for study, writing up the results in honest, even fastidious prose. But in so doing he places himself in the realm of journalism or sociology. The not-knowing is crucial to art, is what permits art to be made. Without the scanning process engendered by not-knowing, without the possibility of having the mind move in unanticipated directions, there would be no invention.

This is not to say that I don't know anything about Jacqueline or Jemima, but what I do know comes into being at the instant it's inscribed. Jacqueline, for example, loathes her mother, whereas Jemima dotes on hers — I discover this by writing the sentence that announces it. Zeno was fathered by a — what? Polar bear? Roller skate? Shower of gold? I opt for the shower of gold, for Zeno is a hero (although he's just become one by virtue of his golden parent). Inside the pocket watch there is engraved a legend. Can I make it out? I think so: *Drink me*, it says. No no, can't use it, that's Lewis Carroll's. But could Zeno be a watch swallower rather than a thief? No again, Zeno'd choke on it, and so would the reader. There are rules.

Writing is a process of dealing with not-knowing, a forcing of what and how. We have all heard novelists testify to the fact that, beginning a new book, they are utterly baffled as to how to proceed, what should be written and how it might be written, even though they've done a dozen. At best there's a slender intuition, not much greater than an itch. The anxiety attached to this situation is not inconsiderable. "Nothing to paint and nothing to paint with," as Beckett says of Bram van Velde. The not-knowing is not simple, because it's hedged about with prohibitions, roads that may not be taken. The more serious the artist, the more problems he takes into account and the more considerations limit his possible initiatives — a point to which I shall return.

What kind of a fellow is Zeno? How do I know until he's opened his mouth?

"*Gently, ladies, gently,*" says Zeno, as Jacqueline and Jemima bash away at the belt with a spade borrowed from a friendly

park employee. And to the park employee: "Somebody seems
to have lost this-here watch."

Let us change the scene.

Alphonse, the park employee from the preceding episode, he
who lent the spade, is alone in his dismal room on West Street
(I could position him as well in a four-story townhouse on East
Seventy-second, but you'd object, and rightly so, verisimilitude
forbids it, nothing's calculated quicker than a salary). Alphonse,
like so many toilers in the great city, is not as simple as he seems.
Like those waiters who are really actors and those cab drivers
who are really composers of electronic music, Alphonse is sun-
lighting as a Parks Department employee although he is, in
reality, a literary critic. We find him writing a letter to his friend
Gaston, also a literary critic although masquerading pro tem as
a guard at the Whitney Museum. Alphonse poises paws over his
Smith-Corona and writes:

Dear Gaston,
    Yes, you are absolutely right — Postmodernism is dead. A stun-
ning blow, but not entirely surprising. I am spreading the news as
rapidly as possible, so that all of our friends who are in the Postmod-
ernist "bag" can get out of it before their cars are repossessed and
the insurance companies tear up their policies. Sad to see Postmodernism go (and so quickly!). I was fond of it. As fond, almost, as I
was of its grave and noble predecessor, Modernism. But we cannot
dwell in the done-for. The death of a movement is a natural part of
life, as was understood so well by the partisans of Naturalism, which
is dead.
    I remember exactly where I was when I realized that Postmodern-
ism had bought it. I was in my study with a cup of tequila and William
Y's new book, *One-Half*. Y's work is, we agree, good — *very* good. But
who can make the leap to greatness while dragging after him the
burnt-out boxcars of a dead aesthetic? Perhaps we can find new
employment for him. On the roads, for example. When the insight
overtook me, I started to my feet, knocking over the tequila, and
said aloud (although there was no one to hear), "What? Postmodernism, too?" So many, so many. I put Y's book away on a high
shelf and turned to the contemplation of the death of Plainsong, A.D.
958.
    By the way: Structuralism's tottering. I heard it from Gerald, who

is at Johns Hopkins and thus in the thick of things. You don't have to tell everybody. Frequently, idle talk is enough to give a movement that last little "push" that topples it into its grave. I'm convinced that's what happened to the New Criticism. I'm persuaded that it was Gerald, whispering in the corridors.

On the bright side, one thing that is dead that I don't feel too bad about is Existentialism, which I never thought was anything more than Phenomenology's bathwater anyway. It had a good run, but how peeving it was to hear all those artists going around talking about "the existential moment" and similar claptrap. Luckily, they have stopped doing that now. Similarly, the Nouveau Roman's passing did not disturb me overmuch. "Made dreariness into a religion," you said, quite correctly. I know this was one of your pared-to-the-bone movements and all that, but I didn't even like what they left out. A neat omission usually raises the hairs on the back of my neck. Not here. Robbe-Grillet's only true success, for my money, was with *Jealousy,* which I'm told he wrote in a fit of.

Well, where are we? Surrealism gone, got a little sweet toward the end, you could watch the wine of life turning into Gatorade. Sticky. Altar Poems — those constructed in the shape of an altar for the greater honor and glory of God — have not been seen much lately: missing and presumed dead. The Anti-Novel is dead; I read it in the *Times.* The Anti-Hero and the Anti-Heroine had a thing going which resulted in three Anti-Children, all of them now at M.I.T. The Novel of the Soil is dead, as are Expressionism, Impressionism, Futurism, Imagism, Vorticism, Regionalism, Realism, the Kitchen Sink School of Drama, the Theatre of the Absurd, the Theatre of Cruelty, Black Humor, and Gongorism. You know all this; I'm just totting up. To be a Pre-Raphaelite in the present era is to be somewhat out of touch. And, of course, Concrete Poetry — sank like a stone.

So we have a difficulty. What shall we call the New Thing, which I haven't encountered yet but which is bound to be out there somewhere? Post-Postmodernism sounds, to me, a little lumpy. I've been toying with the Revolution of the Word, II, or the New Revolution of the Word, but I'm afraid the Jolas estate may hold a copyright. It should have the word *new* in it somewhere. The New Newness? Or maybe the Post-New? It's a problem. I await your comments and suggestions. If we're going to slap a saddle on this rough beast, we've got to get moving.

Yours,
Alphonse

If I am slightly more sanguine than Alphonse about Post-modernism, however dubious about the term itself and not altogether clear as to who is supposed to be on the bus and who is not, it's because I locate it in relation to a series of problems, and feel that the problems are durable ones. Problems are a comfort. Wittgenstein said, of philosophers, that some of them suffer from "loss of problems," a development in which everything seems quite simple to them and what they write becomes "immeasurably shallow and trivial." The same can be said of writers. Before I mention some of the specific difficulties I have in mind, I'd like to at least glance at some of the criticisms that have been leveled at the alleged Postmodernists — let's say John Barth, William Gass, John Hawkes, Robert Coover, William Gaddis, Thomas Pynchon, and myself in this country, Calvino in Italy, Peter Handke and Thomas Bernhard in Germany, although other names could be invoked. The criticisms run roughly as follows: that this kind of writing has turned its back on the world, is in some sense not about the world but about its own processes, that it is masturbatory, certainly chilly, that it excludes readers by design, speaks only to the already tenured, or that it does not speak at all, but instead, like Frost's Secret, sits in the center of a ring and Knows.

I would ardently contest each of these propositions, but it's rather easy to see what gives rise to them. The problems that seem to me to define the writer's task at this moment (to the extent that he has chosen them as his problems) are not of a kind that make for ease of communication, for work that rushes toward the reader with outflung arms — rather, they're the reverse. Let me cite three such difficulties that I take to be important, all having to do with language. First, there is art's own project, since Mallarmé, of restoring freshness to a much-handled language, essentially an effort toward finding a language in which making art is possible at all. This remains a ground theme, as potent, problematically, today as it was a century ago. Secondly, there is the political and social contamination of language by its use in manipulation of various kinds over time and the effort to find what might be called a "clean" language, problems associated with the Roland Barthes of *Writing*

Degree Zero but also discussed by Lukács and others. Finally, there is the pressure on language from contemporary culture in the broadest sense — I mean our devouring commercial culture — which results in a double impoverishment: theft of complexity from the reader, theft of the reader from the writer.

These are by no means the only thorny matters with which the writer has to deal, nor (allowing for the very great differences among the practitioners under discussion) does every writer called Postmodern respond to them in the same way and to the same degree, nor is it the case that other writers of quite different tendencies are innocent of these concerns. If I call these matters "thorny," it's because any adequate attempt to deal with them automatically creates barriers to the ready assimilation of the work. Art is not difficult because it wishes to be difficult, but because it wishes to be art. However much the writer might long to be, in his work, simple, honest, and straightforward, these virtues are no longer available to him. He discovers that in being simple, honest, and straightforward, nothing much happens: he speaks the speakable, whereas what we are looking for is the as-yet unspeakable, the as-yet unspoken.

With Mallarmé the effort toward mimesis, the representation of the external world, becomes a much more complex thing than it had been previously. Mallarmé shakes words loose from their attachments and bestows new meanings upon them, meanings which point not toward the external world but toward the Absolute, acts of poetic intuition. This is a fateful step; not for nothing does Barthes call him the Hamlet of literature. It produces, for one thing, a poetry of unprecedented difficulty. You will find no Mallarmé in Bartlett's *Familiar Quotations*. Even so ardent an admirer as Charles Mauron speaks of the sense of alienation enforced by his work. Mauron writes: "All who remember the day when first they looked into the *Poems* or the *Divagations* will testify to that curious feeling of *exclusion* which put them, in the face of a text written with *their* words (and moreover, as they could somehow feel, magnificently written), suddenly outside their own language, deprived of their rights in a common speech, and, as it were, rejected by their oldest

friends." Mallarmé's work is also, and perhaps most importantly, a step toward establishing a new ontological status for
the poem, as an object in the world rather than a representation
of the world. But the ground seized is dangerous ground. After
Mallarmé the struggle to renew language becomes a given for
the writer, his exemplary quest an imperative. Mallarmé's work,
"this whisper that is so close to silence," as Marcel Raymond calls
it, is at once a liberation and a loss to silence of a great deal of
territory.

The silencing of an existing rhetoric (in Harold Rosenberg's
phrase) is also what is at issue in Barthes's deliberations in *Writing Degree Zero* and after — in this case a variety of rhetorics
seen as actively pernicious rather than passively inhibiting. The
question is, what is the complicity of language in the massive
crimes of Fascism, Stalinism, or (by implication) our own policies
in Vietnam? In the control of societies by the powerful and their
busy functionaries? If these abominations are all in some sense
facilitated by, made possible by, language, to what degree is that
language ruinously contaminated (considerations also raised by
George Steiner in his well-known essay "The Hollow Miracle"
and, much earlier, by George Orwell)? I am sketching here,
inadequately, a fairly complex argument; I am not particularly
taken with Barthes's tentative solutions but the problems command the greatest respect. Again, we have language deeply sus-
picious of its own behavior; although this suspicion is not
different in kind from Hemingway's noticing, early in the century, that words like *honor, glory,* and *country* were perjured,
bought, the skepticism is far deeper now, and informed as well
by the investigations of linguistic philosophers, structuralists,
semioticians. Even conjunctions must be inspected carefully. "I
read each word with the feeling appropriate to it," says Wittgenstein. "The word 'but' for example with the but-feeling. . . ." He
is not wrong. Isn't the but-feeling, as he calls it, already sending
us headlong down a greased slide before we've had the time to
contemplate the proposition it's abutting? Quickly now, quickly
— when you hear the phrase "our vital interests" do you stop to
wonder whether you were invited to the den, Zen, Klan, or
coven meeting at which these were defined? Did you speak?

In turning to the action of contemporary culture on language, and thus on the writer, the first thing to be noticed is a loss of reference. If I want a world of reference to which all possible readers in this country can respond, there is only one universe of discourse available, that in which the Love Boat sails on seas of passion like a Flying Dutchman of passion and the dedicated men in white of *General Hospital* pursue, with evenhanded diligence, triple bypasses and the nursing staff. This limits things somewhat. The earlier newspaper culture, which once dealt in a certain amount of nuance and zestful, highly literate hurly-burly, has deteriorated shockingly. The newspaper I worked for as a raw youth, thirty years ago, is today a pallid imitation of its former self. Where once we could put spurious quotes in the paper and attribute them to Ambrose Bierce and be fairly sure that enough readers would get the joke to make the joke worthwhile, from the point of view of both reader and writer, no such common ground now exists. The situation is not peculiar to this country. Steiner remarks of the best current journalism in Germany that, read against an average number of the *Frankfurter Zeitung* of pre-Hitler days, it's difficult at times to believe that both are written in German. At the other end of the scale much of the most exquisite description of the world, discourse about the world, is now being carried on in mathematical languages obscure to most people — certainly to me — and the contributions the sciences once made to our common language in the form of coinages, new words and concepts, are now available only to specialists. When one adds the ferocious appropriation of high culture by commercial culture — it takes, by my estimate, about forty-five minutes for any given novelty in art to travel from the Mary Boone Gallery on West Broadway to the display windows of Henri Bendel on Fifty-seventh Street — one begins to appreciate the seductions of silence.

Problems in part define the kind of work the writer chooses to do, and are not to be avoided but embraced. A writer, says Karl Kraus, is a man who can make a riddle out of an answer.

Let me begin again.

Jacqueline and Jemima are instructing Zeno, who has returned the purloined GRE documents and is thus restored to dull respectability, in Postmodernism. Postmodernism, they tell him, has turned its back on the world, is not about the world but about its own processes, is masturbatory, certainly chilly, excludes readers by design, speaks only to the already tenured, or does not speak at all, but instead —

Zeno, to demonstrate that he too knows a thing or two, quotes the critic Perry Meisel on semiotics. "Semiotics," he says, "is in a position to claim that no phenomenon has any ontological status outside its place in the particular information system from which it draws its meaning" — he takes a large gulp of his Gibson — "and therefore, all language is finally groundless." I am eavesdropping and I am much reassured. This insight is one I can use. Gaston, the critic who is a guard at the Whitney Museum, is in love with an IRS agent named Madelaine, the very IRS agent, in fact, who is auditing my return for the year 1982. "Madelaine," I say kindly to her over lunch, "semiotics is in a position to claim that no phenomenon has any ontological status outside its place in the particular information system from which it draws its meaning, and therefore, all language is finally groundless, including that of those funny little notices you've been sending me." "Yes," says Madelaine kindly, pulling from her pocket a large gold pocket watch that Alphonse has sold Gaston for twenty dollars, her lovely violet eyes atwitter, "but some information systems are more enforceable than others." Alas, she's right.

If the writer is taken to be the work's way of getting itself written, a sort of lightning rod for an accumulation of atmospheric disturbances, a St. Sebastian absorbing in his tattered breast the arrows of the Zeitgeist, this changes not very much the traditional view of the artist. But it does license a very great deal of critical imperialism.

This is fun for everyone. A couple of years ago I received a letter from a critic requesting permission to reprint a story of mine as an addendum to the piece he had written about it. He attached the copy of my story he proposed to reproduce, and I was amazed to find that my poor story had sprouted a set of tiny numbers — one to eighty-eight, as I recall — an army of tiny numbers marching over the surface of my poor distracted text. Resisting the temptation to tell him that all the tiny numbers were in the wrong places, I gave him permission to do what he wished, but I did notice that by a species of literary judo the status of my text had been reduced to that of footnote.

There is, in this kind of criticism, an element of aggression that gives one pause. Deconstruction is an enterprise that announces its intentions with startling candor. Any work of art depends upon a complex series of interdependences. If I wrench the rubber tire from the belly of Rauschenberg's famous goat to determine, in the interest of a finer understanding of same, whether the tire is a B. F. Goodrich or a Uniroyal, the work collapses, more or less behind my back. I say this not because I find this kind of study valueless but because the mystery worthy of study, for me, is not the signification of parts but how they come together, the tire wrestled over the goat's hind legs. Calvin Tomkins tells us in *The Bride and the Bachelors* that Rauschenberg himself says that the tire seemed "something as unavoidable as the goat." To see both goat and tire as "unavoidable" choices, in the context of art-making, is to illuminate just how strange the combinatorial process can be. Nor was the choice a hasty one; Tomkins tells us that the goat had been in the studio for three years and had appeared in two previous versions (the final version is titled "Monogram") before it met the tire.

Modern-day critics speak of "recuperating" a text, suggesting an accelerated and possibly strenuous nursing back to health of a basically sickly text, very likely one that did not even know itself to be ill. I would argue that in the competing methodologies of contemporary criticism, many of them quite rich in implications, a sort of tyranny of great expectations obtains, a rage for final explanations, a refusal to allow a work that mystery which is essential to it. I hope I am not myself engaging in mystification if I say, not that the attempt should not be made, but that the mystery exists. I see no immediate way out of the paradox — tear a mystery to tatters and you have tatters, not mystery — I merely note it and pass on.

We can, however, wonder for a moment why the goat girdled with its tire is somehow a magical object, rather than, say, only a dumb idea. Harold Rosenberg speaks of the contemporary artwork as "anxious," as wondering: Am I a masterpiece or simply a pile of junk? (If I take many of my examples here from the art world rather than the world of literature it is because the issues are more quickly seen in terms of the first: "goat" and "tire" are standing in for pages of prose, pounds of poetry.) What precisely is it in the coming together of goat and tire that is magical? It's not the surprise of seeing the goat attired, although that's part of it. One might say, for example, that the tire *contests* the goat, *contradicts* the goat, as a mode of being, even that the tire *reproaches* the goat, in some sense. On the simplest punning level, the goat is *tired.* Or that the unfortunate tire has *been caught by* the goat, which has been fishing in the Hudson — goats eat anything, as everyone knows — or that the goat is being *consumed by* the tire; it's outside, after all, mechanization takes command. Or that the goateed goat is protesting the fatigue of its friend, the tire, by wearing it as a sort of STRIKE button. Or that two contrasting models of infinity are being presented, tires and goats both being infinitely reproducible, the first depending on the good fortunes of the B. F. Goodrich company and the second upon the copulatory enthusiasm of goats — parallel production lines suddenly met. And so on. What is magical about the object is that it at once invites and resists interpretation. Its artistic worth is measurable by the degree to which it remains, after interpretation, vital — no interpretation or cardiopulmonary push-pull can exhaust or empty it.

In what sense is the work "about" the world, the world that Jacqueline and Jemima have earnestly assured Zeno the work has turned its scarlet rump to? It is to this vexing question that we shall turn next.

Let us discuss the condition of my desk. It is messy, mildly messy. The messiness is both physical (coffee cups, cigarette ash) and spiritual (unpaid bills, unwritten novels). The emotional life of the man who sits at the desk is also messy — I am in love with a set of twins, Hilda and Heidi, and in a fit of enthusiasm I have joined the Bolivian army. The apartment in which the desk is located seems to have been sublet from Moonbeam McSwine. In the streets outside the apartment melting snow has revealed a choice assortment of decaying et cetera. Furthermore, the social organization of the country is untidy,

the world situation in disarray. How do I render all this messiness, and if I succeed, what have I done?

In a common-sense way we agree that I attempt to find verbal equivalents for whatever it is I wish to render. The unpaid bills are easy enough. I need merely quote one: FINAL DISCONNECT NOTICE. Hilda and Heidi are somewhat more difficult. I can say that they are beautiful — why not? — and you will more or less agree, although the bald statement has hardly stirred your senses. I can describe them — Hilda has the map of Bolivia tattooed on her right cheek and Heidi habitually wears, on her left hand, a set of brass knuckles wrought of solid silver — and they move a step closer. Best of all, perhaps, I can permit them to speak, for they speak much as we do.

> "On Valentine's Day," says Hilda, "he sent me oysters, a dozen and a half."
> "He sent me oysters too," said Heidi, "two dozen."
> "Mine were long-stemmed oysters," says Hilda, "on a bed of the most wonderful spinach."
> "Oh yes, spinach," says Heidi, "he sent me spinach too, miles and miles of spinach, wrote every bit of it himself."

To render "messy" adequately, to the point that you are enabled to feel it — it should, ideally, frighten your shoes — I would have to be more graphic than the decorum of the occasion allows. What should be emphasized is that one proceeds by way of particulars. If I know how a set of brass knuckles feels on Heidi's left hand it's because I bought one once, in a pawnshop, not to smash up someone's face but to exhibit on a pedestal in a museum show devoted to cultural artifacts of ambivalent status. The world enters the work as it enters our ordinary lives, not as world-view or system but in sharp particularity: a tax notice from Madelaine, a snowball containing a résumé from Gaston.

The words with which I attempt to render "messy," like any other words, are not inert, rather they are furiously busy. We do not mistake the words *the taste of chocolate* for the taste of chocolate itself, but neither do we miss the tease in *taste*, the shock in *chocolate*. Words have halos, patinas, overhangs, echoes.

The word *halo,* for instance, may invoke St. Hilarius, of whom we've seen too little lately. The word *patina* brings back the fine pewtery shine on the saint's halo. The word *overhang* reminds us that we have, hanging over us, a dinner date with St. Hilarius, that crashing bore. The word *echo* restores us to Echo herself, poised like the White Rock girl on the overhang of a patina of a halo — infirm ground, we don't want the poor spirit to pitch into the pond where Narcissus blooms eternally, they'll bump foreheads, or maybe other parts closer to the feet, a scandal. There's chocolate smeared all over Hilarius' halo — messy, messy. . . .

The combinatorial agility of words, the exponential generation of meaning once they're allowed to go to bed together, allows the writer to surprise himself, makes art possible, reveals how much of Being we haven't yet encountered. It could be argued that computers can do this sort of thing for us, with critic-computers monitoring their output. When computers learn how to make jokes, artists will be in serious trouble. But artists will respond in such a way as to make art impossible for the computer. They will redefine art to take into account (that is, to exclude) technology — photography's impact upon painting and painting's brilliant response being a clear and comparatively recent example.

The prior history of words is one of the aspects of language the world uses to smuggle itself into the work. If words can be contaminated by the world, they can also carry with them into the work trace elements of world which can be used in a positive sense. We must allow ourselves the advantages of our disadvantages.

A late bulletin: Hilda and Heidi have had a baby, with which they're thoroughly displeased, it's got no credit cards and can't speak French, they'll send it back. . . . Messy.

Style is not much a matter of choice. One does not sit down to write and think: Is this poem going to be a Queen Anne poem, a Biedermeier poem, a Vienna Secession poem, or a Chinese Chippendale poem? Rather it is both a response to constraint and a seizing of opportunity. Very often a constraint is an opportunity. It would seem impossible to write *Don Quixote* once again, yet Borges has done so with great style, improving on the original (as he is not slow to tell us) while remaining faithful to it, faithful as a tick on a dog's belly. I don't mean that whim does not intrude. Why do I avoid, as much as possible, using the semicolon? Let me be plain: the semicolon is ugly, ugly as a tick on a dog's belly. I pinch them out of my prose. The great German writer Arno Schmidt, punctuation-drunk, averages eleven to a page.

Style is of course *how*. And the degree to which *how* has become *what* — since, say, Flaubert — is a question that men of conscience wax wroth about, and should. If I say of my friend that on this issue his marbles are a little flat on one side, this does not mean that I do not love my friend. He, on the other hand, considers that I am ridden by strange imperatives, and that the little piece I gave to the world last week, while nice enough in its own way, would have been vastly better had not my deplorable aesthetics caused me to score it for banjulele, cross between a banjo and a uke. Bless Babel.

Let us suppose that I am the toughest banjulele player in town and that I have contracted to play "Melancholy Baby" for six hours before an audience that will include the four next-toughest banjulele players in town. We imagine the smoky basement club, the hustling waiters (themselves students of the jazz banjulele), Jacqueline, Jemima, Zeno, Alphonse, Gaston, Madelaine, Hilda, and Heidi forming a congenial group at the bar. There is one thing of which you may be sure: I am not going to play "Melancholy Baby" as written. Rather I will play something that is parallel, in some sense, to "Melancholy Baby," based upon the chords of "Melancholy Baby," made out of "Melancholy Baby," *having to do with* "Melancholy Baby" — commentary, exegesis, elaboration, contradiction. The interest of my construction, if any, is to be located in the space between the new entity I have constructed and the "real" "Melancholy Baby," which remains in the mind as the horizon which bounds my efforts.

This is, I think, the relation of art to world. I suggest that art is always a meditation upon external reality rather than a representation of external reality or a jackleg attempt to "be" external reality. If I perform even reasonably well, no one will accuse me of not providing a true, verifiable, note-for-note reproduction of "Melancholy Baby" — it will be recognized that this was not what I was after. Twenty years ago I was much more convinced of the autonomy of the literary object than I am now, and even wrote a rather persuasive defense of the proposition that I have just rejected: that the object is itself world. Beguiled by the rhetoric of the time — the sculptor Phillip Pavia was publishing a quite good magazine called *It Is,* and this was typical — I felt that the high ground had been claimed and wanted to place my scuffed cowboy boots right there. The proposition's still attractive. What's the right answer? Bless Babel.

A couple of years ago I visited Willem de Kooning's studio in East Hampton, and when the big doors are opened one can't help seeing — it's a shock — the relation between the rushing green world outside and the paintings. Precisely how de Kooning manages to distill nature into art is a mystery, but the explosive relation is there, I've seen it. Once when I was in Elaine de Kooning's studio on Broadway, at a time when the metal sculptor Herbert Ferber occupied the studio immediately above, there came through the floor a most horrible crashing and banging. "What in the world is that?" I asked, and Elaine said, "Oh, that's Herbert thinking."

Art is a true account of the activity of mind. Because consciousness, in Husserl's formulation, is always consciousness *of* something, art thinks ever of the world, cannot not think of the world, could not turn its back on the world even if it wished to. This does not mean that it's going to be honest as a mailman; it's more likely to appear as a drag queen. The problems I mentioned earlier, as well as others not taken up, enforce complexity. "We do not spend much time in front of a canvas whose intentions are plain," writes Cioran, "music of a specific character, unquestionable contours, exhausts our patience, the over-explicit poem seems . . . incomprehensible." Flannery O'Connor, an artist of the first rank, famously disliked anything that looked funny on the page, and her distaste has widely been taken as a tough-minded put-down of puerile experimentalism. But did she also dislike anything that looked funny on the wall? If so, a severe deprivation. Art cannot remain in one place. A certain amount of movement, up, down, across, even a gallop toward the past, is a necessary precondition.

Style enables us to speak, to imagine again. Beckett speaks of "the long sonata of the dead" — where on earth did the word *sonata* come from, imposing as it does an orderly, even exalted design upon the most disorderly, distressing phenomenon known to us? The fact is not challenged, but understood, momentarily, in a new way. It's our good fortune to be able to imagine alternative realities, other possibilities. We can quarrel with the world, constructively (no one alive has quarreled with the world more extensively or splendidly than Beckett). "Belief in progress," says Baudelaire, "is a doctrine of idlers and Belgians." Perhaps. But if I have anything unorthodox to offer here, it's that I think art's project is fundamentally meliorative. The aim of meditating about the world is finally to change the world. It is this meliorative aspect of literature that provides its ethical dimension. We are all Upton Sinclairs, even that Hamlet, Stéphane Mallarmé.

JOSEPH BRODSKY

Flight from Byzantium

FROM THE NEW YORKER

Translated, from the Russian, by Alan Myers and the author.

1

BEARING IN MIND that every observation suffers from the observer's personal traits — that is, it too often reflects his psychological state rather than that of the reality under observation — I suggest that what follows be treated with a due measure of skepticism, if not with total disbelief. The only thing the observer may claim by way of justification is that he, too, possesses a modicum of reality, inferior in extent, perhaps, but conceding nothing in quality to the subject under scrutiny. A semblance of objectivity might be achieved, no doubt, by way of a complete self-awareness at the moment of observation. I do not think I am capable of this; in any event, I did not aspire to it. All the same, I hope that something of the sort took place.

2

My desire to get to Istanbul was never a genuine one. I am not even sure whether such a word — *desire* — should be used here. On the other hand, it could hardly be called a mere whim or a subconscious urge. Let it be a desire, then, and let's note that it came about partly as the result of a promise I made to myself in 1972, on leaving my hometown, that of Leningrad, for good — to circumnavigate the inhabited world along the latitude and along the longitude (i.e., the Pulkovo meridian) on which Leningrad is situated. By now, the latitude has been more or less

taken care of; as to the longitude, the situation is anything but
satisfactory. Istanbul, though, lies only a couple of degrees west
of that meridian.

The aforementioned motive is only marginally more fanciful
than the serious — indeed, the chief — reason, about which I
will say something a bit later, or than a handful of totally frivo-
lous secondary or tertiary ones, which I'll broach at once, it
being now or never with such trivia: (a) it was in this city that
my favorite poet, Constantine Cavafy, spent three momentous
years at the turn of the century; (b) I always felt, for some
reason, that here, in apartments, shops, and coffeehouses, I
should find intact an atmosphere that at present seems to have
totally vanished everywhere else; (c) I hoped to hear in Istanbul,
on the outskirts of history, that "overseas creak of a Turkish
mattress" which I thought I discerned one night some twenty
years ago in the Crimea; (d) I wanted to find myself addressed
as "effendi"; (e) — But I'm afraid the alphabet isn't long enough
to accommodate all these ridiculous notions (though perhaps
it's better if you are set in motion precisely by some such non-
sense, for it makes final disappointment so much easier to bear).
So let us get on to the promised "chief" reason, even though to
many it may seem deserving of at best the "f" in my catalogue
of bêtises.

This "chief" reason represents the pinnacle of fancifulness.
It has to do with the fact that several years ago, while I was
talking to a friend of mine, an American Byzantinist, it occurred
to me that the cross that Constantine beheld in his dream on
the eve of his victory over Maxentius — the cross that bore the
legend "In this sign, conquer" — was not in fact a Christian
cross but an urban one, the basic element of any Roman settlement. According to Eusebius and others, Constantine, inspired
by his vision, at once set off for the East. First at Troy and then,
having abruptly abandoned Troy, at Byzantium he founded the
new capital of the Roman Empire — that is, the Second Rome.
The consequences of this move of his were so momentous that,
whether I was right or wrong, I felt an urge to see this place.
After all, I spent thirty-two years in what is known as the Third
Rome, about a year and a half in the First. Consequently, I
needed the Second, if only for my collection.

But let us handle all this in an orderly fashion, so far as this is feasible.

3

I arrived in Istanbul, and left it, by air, having thus isolated it in my mind like some virus under a microscope. If one considers the infectious nature of any culture, the comparison does not seem irresponsible. Writing this note in the Hotel Aegean in the little place called Sounion — at the southeast corner of Attica, forty miles from Athens, where I landed four hours ago — I feel like the carrier of a specific infection, despite constant inoculations of the "classical rose" of the late Vladislav Khodasevich, to which I have subjected myself for the greater part of my life. I really do feel feverish from what I have seen; hence a certain incoherence in all that follows. I believe that my famous namesake experienced something of the sort as he strove to interpret the pharaoh's dreams — though it's one thing to bandy interpretations of sacred signs when the trail is hot (or warm, rather) and quite another a thousand and a half years later.

4

About dreams. This morning, in the wee hours, in Istanbul's Pera Palace, I, too, beheld something — something utterly monstrous. The scene was the Department of Philology of Leningrad University, and I was coming downstairs with someone I took to be Professor D. E. Maximov, except that he looked more like Lee Marvin. I can't recall what we were talking about, but that's not the point. My attention was caught by a scene of furious activity in a dark corner of the landing where the ceiling came down extremely low. I saw there three cats fighting with an enormous rat, which quite dwarfed them. Glancing over my shoulder, I noticed one of the cats ripped apart by the rat and writhing convulsively in agony on the floor. I chose not to watch the battle's outcome — I recall only that the cat became still — and, exchanging remarks with Marvin-Maximov, I kept going down the staircase. I woke up before I reached the hall.

To begin with, I adore cats. Then it should be added that I can't abide low ceilings; that the place only seemed like the Department of Philology, which is just two stories high anyway; that its grubby gray-brown color was that of the façades and interiors of Istanbul, especially the offices I had visited in the last few days; that the streets there are crooked, filthy, dreadfully cobbled, and piled up with refuse, which is constantly rummaged through by ravenous local cats; that the city, and everything in it, strongly smells of Astrakhan and Samarkand; and that the night before I had made up my mind to leave — But of that later. There was enough, in short, to pollute one's subconscious.

5

Constantine was, first and foremost, a Roman emperor — in charge of the Western part of the Empire — and for him "In this sign, conquer" was bound to signify, above all, an extension of his own rule, of his control over the whole empire. There is nothing novel about divining the most immediate future by roosters' innards, or about enlisting a deity as your own captain. Nor is the gulf between absolute ambition and utmost piety so vast. But even if he had been a true and zealous believer (a matter on which various doubts have been cast, especially in view of his conduct toward his children and in-laws) "conquer" must have had for him not only the military, sword-crossing meaning but also an administrative one — that is, settlements and cities. And the plan of any Roman settlement is precisely a cross: a central highway running north and south (like the Corso in Rome) intersects a similar road running east and west. From Leptis Magna to Castricum, an imperial subject always knew where he was in relation to the capital.

Even if the cross of which Constantine spoke to Eusebius was that of the Redeemer, a constituent part of it in his dream was, un- or subconsciously, the principle of settlement planning. Besides, in the fourth century the symbol of the Redeemer was not the cross at all; it was the fish, a Greek acrostic for the name of Christ. And as for the Cross of the Crucifixion itself, it resembled the Russian (and Latin) capital "T," rather than what Michelangelo depicted on that staircase in St. Peter's, or what we nowadays imagine it to have been. Whatever Constantine may or may not have had in mind, the execution of the instructions he received in a dream took the form in the first place of a territorial expansion toward the East, and the emergence of a Second Rome was a perfectly logical consequence of this eastward expansion. Possessing, by all accounts, a dynamic personality, he considered a forward policy perfectly natural. The more so if he was in actual fact a true believer.

Was he or wasn't he? Whatever the answer might be, it is the genetic code that laughed the last laugh. For his nephew happened to be no one else than Julian the Apostate.

6

Any movement along a plane surface which is not dictated by physical necessity is a spatial form of self-assertion, be it empire-building or tourism. In this sense, my reason for going to Istanbul differed only slightly from Constantine's. Especially if he really did become a Christian — that is, ceased to be a Roman. I have, however, rather more grounds for reproaching myself with superficiality; besides, the results of my displacements are of far less consequence. I don't even leave behind photographs taken "in front of" walls, let alone a set of walls themselves. In this sense, I am inferior even to the almost proverbial Japanese. (There is nothing more appalling to me than to think about the family album of the average Japanese: smiling and stocky, he/she/both against a backdrop of everything vertical the world contains — statues, fountains, cathedrals, towers, mosques, ancient temples, etc. Least of all, I presume, Buddhas and pagodas.) *Cogito ergo sum* gives way to *Kodak ergo sum*, just as *cogito* in its day triumphed over "I create." In other words, the ephemeral nature of my presence and my motives is no less absolute than the physical tangibility of Constantine's activities and his thoughts, real or supposed.

7

The Roman elegiac poets of the end of the first century B.C. — especially Propertius and Ovid — openly mock their great contemporary Virgil and his Aeneid. This may be explicable in terms of personal rivalry or professional jealousy or opposition of their idea of poetry as a personal, private art to a conception of it as something civic, as a form of state propaganda. (This last may ring true, but it is a far cry from the truth, nonetheless, since Virgil was the author not only of the Aeneid but also of the Bucolics and the Georgics.) There may also have been considerations of a purely stylistic nature. It is quite possible that from the elegists' point of view the epic — any epic, including Virgil's — was a retrograde phenomenon. The elegists, all of them, were disciples of the Alexandrian school of poetry, which had given birth to a tradition of short lyric verse such as we are familiar with in poetry today. The Alexandrian preference for brevity, terseness, compression, concreteness, erudition, didacticism, and a preoccupation with the personal was, it seems, the reaction of the Greek art of letters against the surplus forms of Greek literature in the Archaic peroid: against the epic, the drama; against mythologizing, not to say mythmaking itself. A reaction, if one thinks about it — though it's best not to — against Aristotle. The Alexandrian tradition absorbed all these things and fitted them to the confines of the elegy or the eclogue: to the almost hieroglyphic dialogue in the latter, to an illustrative function of myth *(exempla)* in the former. In other words, we find a certain tendency toward miniaturization and condensation (as a means of survival for poetry in a world less and less inclined to pay it heed, if not as a more direct, more immediate means of influencing the hearts and minds of readers and listeners) when, lo and behold, Virgil appears with his hexameters and gigantic "social order."

I would add here that the elegists, almost without exception, were using the elegiac distich, a couplet combining dactylic hexameter and dactylic pentameter; also, that they, again almost without exception, came to poetry from the schools of rhetoric, where they had been trained for a juridical profession (as advocates: arguers in the modern sense). Nothing corresponds better to the rhetorical system of thought than the elegiac distich, which provided a means of expressing, at a minimum, two points of view, not to mention a whole palette of intonational coloring permitted by the contrasting meters.

All this, however, is in parentheses. Outside the parentheses lie the elegists' reproaches directed at Virgil on ethical rather than metrical grounds. Especially interesting in this regard is Ovid, in no way inferior to the author of the Aeneid in descriptive skills, and psychologically infinitely more subtle. In "Dido to Aeneas," one of his Heroides — a collection of made-up correspondence from love poetry's standard heroines to their either perished or unfaithful beloveds — the Carthaginian queen, rebuking Aeneas for abandoning her, does so in approximately the following fashion: "I could have understood if you had left me because you had resolved to return home, to your own kinfolk. But you are setting out for unknown lands, a new goal, a new, as yet unfounded city, in order, it seems, to break yet another heart."And so on. She even hints that Aeneas is leaving her pregnant and that one of the reasons for her suicide is the fear of disgrace. But this is not germane to the matter in hand. What matters here is that in Virgil's eyes Aeneas is a hero, directed by the gods. In Ovid's eyes, he is an unprincipled scoundrel, attributing his mode of conduct — his movement along a plane surface — to Divine Providence. (As for Providence, Dido has her own teleological explanations as well, but that is of small consequence, as is our all too eager assumption of Ovid's anti-civic posture.)

8

The Alexandrian tradition was a Grecian tradition: one of order (the cosmos), of proportion, of harmony, of the tautology of cause and effect (the Oedipus cycle) — a tradition of symmetry and the closed circle, of *return to the origin*. And it is Virgil's concept of linear movement, his linear model of existence, that the elegists find so exasperating in him. The Greeks should not be idealized overmuch, but one cannot deny them their cosmic principle, informing celestial bodies and kitchen utensils alike.

Virgil, it appears, was the first — in literature, at least — to apply the linear principle: his hero never returns; he always departs. Possibly, this was in the air; more likely, it was dictated by the expansion of the Empire, which had reached a scale in which human displacement had indeed become irreversible. This is precisely why the Aeneid is unfinished: it must not — indeed, could not — be completed. And the linear principle has nothing to do with the "feminine" character of Hellenism or with the "masculinity" of Roman culture — or with Virgil's own sexual tastes. The point is that the linear principle, detecting in itself a certain irresponsibility vis-à-vis the past — irresponsibility linked with the linear idea of existence — tends to balance this with a detailed projection of the future. The result is either a "retroactive prophecy," like Anchises' conversations in the Aeneid, or social utopianism or the idea of eternal life — i.e., Christianity. There is not much difference between these. In fact, it is their similarity, and not the "messianic" Fourth Eclogue, that practically allows one to consider Virgil the first Christian poet. Had I been writing "The Divine Comedy," I would have placed this Roman in Paradise: for outstanding services to the linear principle, into its logical conclusion.

9

The delirium and horror of the East. The dusty catastrophe of Asia. Green only on the banner of the Prophet. Nothing grows here except mustaches. A black-eyed, overgrown-with-stubble-before-supper part of the world. Bonfire embers doused with urine. That smell! A mixture of foul tobacco and sweaty soap and the underthings wrapped around loins like another turban. Racism? But isn't it only a form of misanthropy? And that ubiquitous grit flying in your muzzle even in the city, poking the world out of your eyes — and yet one feels grateful even for that. Ubiquitous concrete, with the texture of turd and the color of an upturned grave. Ah, all that nearsighted scum — Corbusier, Mondrian, Gropius — who mutilated the world more effectively than any Luftwaffe! Snobbery? But it's only a form of despair. The local population in a state of total stupor whiling its time away in squalid snack bars, tilting its heads as in a *namaz*

in reverse toward the television screen, where somebody is permanently beating somebody else up. Or else they're dealing out
cards, whose jacks and nines are the sole accessible abstraction,
the single means of concentration. Misanthropy? Despair? Yet
what else could be expected from one who has outlived the
apotheosis of the linear principle? From a man who has nowhere to go back to? From a great turdologist, sacrophag, and
the possible author of "Sadomachia"?

10

A child of his age — that is, the fourth century A.D., or, better,
P.V. (Post-Virgil) — Constantine, a man of action, if only because he was emperor, could regard himself as not only the
embodiment but also the instrument of the linear principle of
existence. Byzantium was for him not only symbolically but literally a cross, an intersection of trade routes, caravan roads, etc.
— both from east to west and from north to south. This alone
might have drawn his attention to the place, which had given to
the world (in the seventh century B.C.) something that in all
tongues means the same: money.

Money certainly interested Constantine exceedingly. If he did
possess a measure of greatness, it was most likely financial. A
pupil of Diocletian, having failed to learn his tutor's high art of
delegating authority, he nonetheless succeeded in a by no
means inferior art: to use the modern term, he stabilized the
currency. The Roman solidus, introduced in his reign, played
the role of our dollar for over seven centuries. In this sense, the
transfer of the capital to Byzantium was a movement of the bank
to the mint.

One should perhaps also bear in mind that the philanthropy
of the Christian Church at this time was, if not an alternative to
the state economy, then at least a recourse for a considerable
part of the population, the have-nots. To a large extent, the
popularity of Christianity was based not so much on the idea of
the equality of souls before the Lord as on the tangible — for
the have-nots — fruits of an organized system of mutual assistance. It was in its way a combination of food stamps and the

Red Cross. Neither Neoplatonism nor the cult of Isis organized anything of the kind. In this, frankly, lay their mistake.

One may muse at length on what went on in Constantine's heart and mind with regard to the Christian faith, but as an emperor he could not fail to appreciate the organizational and economic effectiveness of this particular church. Besides, the transferring of the capital to the extreme rim of the Empire transforms that rim into the center, as it were, and implies an equally extensive space on the other side. On the map, this is equivalent to India: the object of all imperial dreams known to us, before and after the birth of Christ.

11

Dust! This weird substance, driving into your face! It merits attention; it should not be concealed behind the word *dust*. Is it just agitated dirt, incapable of finding its own place but constituting the very essence of this part of the world? Or is it the earth striving to rise into the air, detaching itself from itself, like mind from body, like the body yielding itself to the heat? Rain betrays the nature of this substance when brown-black rivulets of it go snaking beneath your feet, beaten back to the cobbles and away down the undulating arteries of this primeval *kışlak*, and yet unable to amass themselves enough to form puddles, because of the countless splashing wheels, numerically superior to the faces of the inhabitants, that bear this substance off, to the sound of blaring horns, across the bridge into Asia, Anatolia, Ionia, to Trebizond and Smyrna.

As everywhere in the East, there are vast numbers of shoe shiners here of all ages, with their exquisite brass-bound boxes housing their kit of boot creams in round, thinnest-of-copper containers with cupola lids. Like little mosques without the minarets. The ubiquity of the profession is explained by the dirt, by that dust which covers your dazzling, reflecting-the-entire-universe-just-five-minutes-ago loafer with a gray, impenetrable powder. Like all shoe shiners, these people are great philosophers. Or, better, all philosophers are but shiners of great shoes. For this reason, it isn't so very important whether you know Turkish.

12

Who these days really examines maps, studies contours, reckons distances? Nobody, except perhaps vacationers or drivers. Since the invention of the push button, even the military don't do it anymore. Who writes letters listing the sights he has seen and analyzing the feelings he had while doing so? And who reads such letters? After us, nothing will remain that is worthy of the name of correspondence. Even young people, seemingly with plenty of time, make do with postcards. People of my age usually resort to those either in a moment of despair in some alien spot or just to kill time. Yet there are places examination of which on a map makes you feel for a brief moment akin to Providence.

13

There are places where history is inescapable, like a highway accident — places whose geography provokes history. Such is Istanbul, alias Constantinople, alias Byzantium. A traffic light gone haywire, with all three colors flaring up at once. Not red-amber-green but white-amber-brown. Also, of course, blue: for the water, for the Bosporus-Marmara-Dardanelles, which separates Europe from Asia — or does it? Ah, all these natural frontiers, these straits and Urals of ours! How little they have ever meant to armies or cultures, and even less to noncultures — though for nomads they may actually have signified a bit more than for princes inspired by the linear principle and justified in advance by an entrancing vision of the future.

Did not Christianity triumph precisely because it provided an end that justified the means, because it temporarily — i.e., for the whole of one's life — absolved one from responsibility? Because the next step, any step at all, in any direction, was becoming logical? Wasn't it — Christianity — in the spiritual sense, at least, an anthropological echo of nomadic existence, its metastasis in the psychology of man the settler? Or, better still, hasn't it simply coincided with purely imperial needs? Pay alone could hardly be enough to stir a legionary (whose career's meaning lay precisely in a long-service bonus, demobilization, and getting a farm plot) from the spot. He should be inspired, too; otherwise, the legions turn into that wolf which only Tiberius could haul back by the ears.

14

A consequence can rarely look back at its cause with anything like approval. Still less can it suspect the cause of anything. The relations between effect and cause lack, as a rule, the rational, analytic element. As a rule, they are tautological and, at best, tinged with the incoherent enthusiasm the latter feels for the former.

It should not be forgotten, therefore, that the belief system called Christianity came from the East, and, for the same reason, it shouldn't be forgotten that one of the ideas that overpowered Constantine after the victory over Maxentius and the vision of the cross was the desire to come at least physically closer to the source of that victory and that vision: to the East. I have no clear notion of what was going on in Judaea at that time, but it is obvious, at least, that if Constantine had set off by land to go there he would have encountered a good many obstacles. In any event, to found a capital overseas would have contradicted plain common sense. Also, one shouldn't rule out a dislike of Jews, quite possible on Constantine's part.

There is something amusing, and even a bit alarming, isn't there, in the idea that the East is actually the metaphysical center of mankind? Christianity had been only one of a considerable number of sects within the Empire — though, admittedly, the most active. By Constantine's reign, the Roman Empire, in no small measure because of its sheer size, had been a veritable country fair or bazaar of creeds. With the exception of the Copts and the cult of Isis, however, the source of all the belief systems on offer was in fact the East.

The West was offering nothing. Essentially, the West was a customer. Let us treat the West with tenderness, then, precisely for its lack of this sort of inventiveness, for which it has paid quite heavily, that pay including the reproaches of excessive rationality one hears to this day. Is this not the way a vender inflates the price of his wares? And where will he go once his coffers are overflowing?

15

If the Roman elegists reflected the outlook of their public in any way at all, one might suppose that by Constantine's reign — i.e., four centuries after the elegists — arguments like "The motherland is in danger" or "Pax Romana" had lost their spell and cogency. And if Eusebius' assertions are correct then Constantine turns out to be neither more nor less than the first Crusader. One should not lose sight of the fact that the Rome of Constantine was no longer the Rome of Augustus, or even that of the Antonines. It was, generally speaking, not ancient Rome anymore: it was Christian Rome. What Constantine brought to Byzantium no longer denoted classical culture: it was already the culture of a new age, brewed in the concept of monotheism, which now relegated polytheism — i.e., its own past, with all its spirit of law, and so forth — to the status of idolatry. This, to be sure, was already progress.

16

Here I should like to admit that my ideas concerning antiquity seem somewhat wild even to me. I understand polytheism in a simple, and therefore no doubt incorrect, fashion. For me, it is a system of spiritual existence in which every form of human activity, from fishing to contemplating the constellations, is sanctified by specific deities. An individual possessing appropriate will and imagination is thus able to discern in his activity its metaphysical, infinite lining. Alternatively, one or another god may, as the whim takes him, appear to a man at any time and possess him for a period. The only thing required of the latter, should he wish this to happen, is for him to "purify" himself, so as to enable the visit to take place. This process of purification (catharsis) varies a great deal and has an individual character (sacrifice, pilgrimage, a vow of some kind) or a public one (theater, sporting contests). The hearth is no different from the amphitheater, the stadium from the altar, the statue from the stewing pan.

A world view of this kind can exist, I suppose, only in settled conditions: when the god knows your address. It is not surprising that the culture we call Greek arose on islands. It is no surprise, either, that its fruits hypnotized for a millennium the entire Mediterranean, including Rome. And it is not surprising, again, that, as its Empire grew, Rome — which was not an island — fled from that culture. The flight began, in fact, with the Caesars and with the idea of absolute power, since in that intensely political sphere polytheism was synonymous with democracy. Absolute power — autocracy — was synonymous, alas, with monotheism. If one can imagine an unprejudiced man, then polytheism must seem far more attractive to him than monotheism, if only because of the instinct of self-preservation.

But there is no such person; even Diogenes, with his lamp, would fail to find him in broad daylight. Bearing in mind the culture we call ancient or classical, rather than the instinct of self-preservation, I can only say that the longer I live the more this idol worship appeals to me, and the more dangerous seems to me monotheism in its pure form. There's little point, I suppose, in laboring the matter, in calling the spade the spade, but the democratic state is in fact the historical triumph of idolatry over Christianity.

17

Naturally, Constantine could not know this. I assume he intuited that Rome was no more. The Christian in him combined with the ruler in a natural and, I am afraid, prophetic manner. In that very "In this sign, conquer" of his, one's ear discerns the ambition of power. And it was "conquer" indeed — more even than he imagined, since Christianity in Byzantium lasted ten centuries. But this victory was, I am sorry to say, a Pyrrhic one. The nature of this victory was what compelled the Western Church to detach itself from the Eastern. That is to say, the geographical Rome from the projected one, from Byzantium. The Church the bride of Christ from the Church the spouse of the State. And it is quite possible that in his drive eastward

Constantine was in fact guided by the East's political climate — by its despotism without any experience of democracy, congenial to his own predicament. The geographical Rome, one way or another, still retained some memories of the role of the senate. Byzantium had no such memory.

18

Today, I am forty-five years old. I am sitting stripped to the waist in the Lykabettos Hotel, in Athens, bathed in sweat, absorbing vast quantities of Coca-Cola. In this city, I don't know a soul. In the evening, when I went out looking for a place to have supper, I found myself in the thick of a highly excited throng shouting something unintelligible. As far as I can make out, elections are imminent. I was shuffling along some endless main street blocked by people and vehicles, with car horns wailing in my ears, not understanding a word, and it suddenly dawned on me that this, essentially, is the afterlife — that life had ended but movement was still continuing; that this is what eternity is all about.

Forty-five years ago, my mother gave me life. She died the year before last. Last year, my father died. I, their only child, am walking along the evening streets in Athens, streets they never saw and never will. The fruit of their love, their poverty, their slavery in which they lived and died — their son walks free. Since he doesn't bump into them in the crowd, he realizes that he is wrong, that this is not eternity.

19

What did Constantine see and not see as he looked at the map of Byzantium? He saw, to put it mildly, a tabula rasa. An imperial province settled by Greeks, Jews, Persians, and such — a population he was used to dealing with, typical subjects of the eastern part of his Empire. The language was Greek, but for an educated Roman this was like French for a nineteenth-century Russian nobleman. Constantine saw a town jutting out into the Sea of Marmara, a town that would be easy to defend if a wall was just thrown around it. He saw the hills of this city, somewhat reminiscent of Rome's, and if he pondered erecting, say, a palace or a church he knew that the view from the windows would be really smashing: on all Asia. And all Asia would gape at the crosses that would crown that church. One may also imagine him toying with the idea of controlling the access of those Romans he had dropped behind him. They would be compelled to trail across the whole of Attica to get here, or to sail around the Peloponnesus. "This one I'll let in, that one I won't." In these terms, no doubt, he thought of his version of the earthly Paradise. Ah, all these excise man's dreams! And he saw, too, Byzantium acclaiming him as her protector against the Sassanids and against our — your and my, ladies and comrades — ancestors from that side of the Danube. And he saw a Byzantium kissing the cross.

What he did not see was that he was dealing with the East. To wage wars against the East — or even to liberate the East — and actually to live there are very different things. For all its Greekness, Byzantium belonged to a world with totally different ideas about the value of human existence from those current in the West: in — however pagan it was — Rome. For Byzantium, Persia, for example, was far more real than Hellas, if only in a military sense. And the differences in degree of this reality could not fail to be reflected in the outlook of these future subjects of their Christian lord. Though in Athens Socrates could be judged in open court and could make whole speeches — three of them! — in his defense, in Isfahan, say, or Baghdad such a Socrates would simply have been impaled on the spot, or flayed, and there the matter would have ended. There would have been no Platonic dialogues, no Neoplatonism, nothing: as there wasn't. There would have been only the monologue of the Koran: as there was. Byzantium was a bridge into Asia, but the traffic across it flowed in the opposite direction. Of course, Byzantium accepted Christianity, but there this faith was fated to become Orientalized. In this, too, to no small degree lies the root of the subsequent hostility of the Roman Church toward the Eastern. Certainly Christianity nominally lasted a thousand years in Byzantium, but what kind of Christianity it was and what sort of Christians these were is another matter.

Oh, I am afraid I am going to say that all the Byzantine

scholastics, all Byzantium's scholarship and ecclesiastical ardor,
its Caesaro-papism, its theological and administrative assertive-
ness, all those triumphs of Photius and his twenty anathemas —
all these came from the place's inferiority complex, from the
youngest patriarchy's grappling with its own ethnic incoherence. Which in the far end, where I find myself standing, has
spawned its dark-haired, leveling victory over that incredibly
high-pitched spiritual quest which took place here, and reduced
it to a matter of wistful yet reluctant mental archeology. And —
oh, again — I am afraid I am going to add that it is for this
reason, and not just because of mean, vengeful memory, that
Rome, which doctored the history of our civilization anyway,
deleted the Byzantine millennium from the record. Which is
why I find myself standing here in the first place. And the dust
stuffs my nostrils.

20

How dated everything is here! Not old, ancient, antique, or even
old-fashioned, but dated. This is where old cars come to die,
and instead become *dolmuşlar*, public taxis; a ride in one is
cheap, bumpy, and nostalgic to the point of making you feel
that you are moving in the wrong, unintended direction — in
part, because the drivers rarely speak English. The United
States naval base near here presumably sold all these Dodges
and Plymouths of the fifties to some local entrepreneur, and
now they prowl the mud roads of Asia Minor, rattling, throt-
tling, and wheezing in evident disbelief in this so taxing afterlife. So far from Dearborn; so far from the promised junkyard!

21

And also Constantine did not see — or, more precisely, did not
foresee — that the impression produced on him by the geographical position of Byzantium was a natural one. That if Eastern potentates should also glance at a map they were bound to
be similarly impressed. As, indeed, was the case — more than
once — with consequences grievous enough for Christianity.
Up until the seventh century, friction between East and West in

Byzantium was of a standard, I'll-skin-you-alive military sort and was resolved by force of arms, usually in the West's favor. If this did not increase the popularity of the cross in the East, at all events it inspired respect for it. But by the seventh century what had risen over the entire East and started to dominate it was the crescent of Islam. Thereafter, the military encounters between East and West, whatever their outcome, resulted in a gradual but steady erosion of the cross and in a growing relativism of the Byzantine outlook as a consequence of too close and too frequent contact between the two sacred signs. (Who knows whether the eventual defeat of iconoclasm shouldn't be explained by a sense of the inadequacy of the cross as a symbol and by the necessity for some visual competition with the anti-figurative art of Islam? Whether it wasn't the nightmarish Arabic lace that was spurring John Damascene?)

Constantine did not foresee that the anti-individualism of Islam would find the soil of Byzantium so welcoming that by the ninth century Christianity would be more than ready to flee to the north. He, of course, would have said that it was not flight but, rather, the expansion of Christianity which he had — in theory, at least — dreamed of. And many would nod to this in agreement: yes, an expansion. Yet the Christianity that was received by Rus from Byzantium in the ninth century already had absolutely nothing in common with Rome. For, on its way to Rus, Christianity dropped behind it not only togas and statues but also Justinian's Civil Code. No doubt in order to facilitate the journey.

22

Having decided to leave Istanbul, I set about finding a steamship company serving the route from Istanbul to Athens or, better still, from Istanbul to Venice. I did the rounds of various offices, but, as always happens in the East, the nearer you get to the goal the more obscure become the means of its attainment. In the end, I realized that I couldn't sail from either Istanbul or Smyrna for two more weeks, whether by passenger ship, freighter, or tanker. In one of the agencies, a corpulent Turkish lady, puffing a frightful cigarette like an ocean liner, advised

me to try a company bearing the Australian — as I at first imagined — name Boomerang. Boomerang turned out to be a
grubby office smelling of stale tobacco, with two tables, one
telephone, a map of — naturally — The World on the wall, and
six stocky, pensive, dark-haired men, torpid from idleness. The
only thing I managed to extract from the one sitting nearest the
door was that Boomerang dealt with Soviet cruises in the Black
Sea and the Mediterranean, but that that week there were no
sailings. I wonder where that young Lubyanka lieutenant who
dreamed up that name came from. Tula? Chelyabinsk?

23

Dreading a repetition, I will nonetheless state again that if Byzantine soil turned out to be so favorable for Islam it was most
likely because of its ethnic texture — a mixture of races and
nationalities that had neither local nor, moreover, overall memory of any kind of coherent tradition of individualism. Dreading
generalizations, I will add that the East means, first of all, a
tradition of obedience, of hierarchy, of profit, of trade, of
adaptability: a tradition, that is, drastically alien to the principles
of a moral absolute, whose role — I mean the intensity of the
sentiment — is fulfilled here by the idea of kinship, of family. I
foresee objections, and am even willing to accept them, in whole
or in part. But no matter what extreme of idealization of the
East we may entertain we'll never be able to ascribe to it the least
semblance of democracy.

And I am speaking here of Byzantium before the Turkish
domination: of the Byzantium of Constantine, Justinian, Theo-
dora — of Christian Byzantium, anyway. Still, Michael Psellus,
the eleventh-century Byzantine historian, describing in his
"Chronographia" the reign of Basil II, tells us about Basil's
prime minister, also Basil, who was the Emperor's uncle and,
because of that, was simply castrated in childhood to eliminate
any possible claim to the throne. "A natural precaution," comments the historian, "since as a eunuch he would not attempt to
usurp the throne from the legitimate heir." Psellus adds, "He
was completely reconciled to his fate, and was sincerely dedicated to the ruling house. After all, it was his family." Let's make

a note that this was written about the time of the reign of Basil
II (A.D. 976–1025), and that Psellus mentions the incident very
much in passing, as a routine affair — as, indeed, it was — at
the Byzantine court. If this was A.D., what, then, of B.C.?

24

And how do we measure an age? And is an age susceptible to
measurement? We should also note that what Psellus describes
takes place before the arrival of the Turks. There are no Baja-
zet-Muhammad-Suleimans about, none of that. For the time
being, we are still interpreting sacred texts, warring against her-
esy, gathering at universal councils, erecting cathedrals, com-
posing tracts. That's with one hand. With the other, we are
castrating a bastard, so that when he grows up there will be no
extra claim to the throne. That, indeed, is the Eastern attitude
toward things — toward the human body in particular — and
whatever era or millennium it is is irrelevant. So it is hardly
surprising that the Roman church turned its nose away from
Byzantium.

But something needs to be said here about that church, too.
It was natural for it to shun Byzantium, both for the reasons
given above and because Byzantium — this new Rome — had
abandoned Rome proper completely. With the exception of Justinian's short-lived efforts to restore imperial coherence, Rome
was left solely to its own devices and to its fate, which meant to
the Visigoths, the Vandals, and whoever else felt inclined to
settle old and new scores with the former capital. One can understand Constantine: he was born, and spent his entire childhood, in the Eastern empire, at Diocletian's court. In this sense,
Roman though he was, he wasn't a Westerner, except in his
administrative designation or through his mother. (Believed to
be born in Britain, she was the one who was interested in Christianity first — to the extent that she traveled later in her life to
Jerusalem and discovered there the True Cross. In other words,
in that family it was the mom who was a believer. And although
there is ample reason to regard Constantine as a true mama's
boy, let's avoid the temptation — let's leave it to the psychia-

trists, as we don't hold a license.) One, let's repeat, can understand Constantine.

As for the attitude of the subsequent Byzantine emperors toward the genuine Rome, it is more complex and rather less explicable. Surely, they had their fill of problems right there in the East, both with their subjects and with their immediate neighbors. Yet the title of Roman emperor, it would seem, should have implied certain geographical obligations. The whole point, of course, was that the Roman emperors after Justinian came for the most part from provinces farther and farther East, from the Empire's traditional recruiting grounds: Syria, Armenia, and so on. Rome was for them, at best, an idea. Several of them, like the majority of their subjects, knew no word of Latin and had never set foot in the city that even by then was quite Eternal. And yet they all regarded themselves as Romans, called themselves so and signed themselves as such. (Something of the sort may be observed even today in the many and varied dominions of the British Empire, or let's recall — so that we don't twist our necks looking for examples — the Evenki, who are Soviet citizens.)

In other words, Rome was left to itself, as was the Roman Church. It would be too lengthy a haul to describe the relations between the Eastern and Western churches. It may be noted, however, that in general the abandonment of Rome was to a certain degree to the Roman Church's advantage, but not entirely to its advantage.

25

I did not expect this note on my trip to Istanbul to expand so much, and I am beginning to feel irritated both with myself and with the material. On the other hand, I am aware that I won't have another chance to discuss all these matters, or if I do I will consciously miss it. From now on, I do promise myself and anyone who has got this far a greater compression — though what I would like to do right now is drop the whole business.

If one must resort to prose, a procedure utterly hateful to the author of these lines, for the very reason that it lacks any form of discipline aside from that generated in the process — if one must use prose, it would be better to concentrate on details, descriptions of places and character: i.e., on things the reader presumably may not have a chance to come across. For the bulk of the aforesaid, as well as everything that follows, is sooner or later bound to occur to anybody, since we are all, one way or another, dependent on history.

26

The advantage of the Roman Church's isolation lay above all in the natural benefits to be derived from any form of autonomy. There was almost nothing and nobody, with the exception of the Roman Church itself, to prevent its developing into a defined, fixed system. Which is what indeed took place. The combination of Roman law, reckoned with more seriously in Rome than in Byzantium, and the specific logic of the Roman Church's inner development evolved into the ethico-political system that lies at the heart of the so-called Western conception of the state and of individual being. Like almost all divorces, the one between Byzantium and Rome was by no means total; a great deal of property stayed shared. But in general one can insist that this Western conception drew around itself a kind of circle, which the East, in a purely conceptual sense, never crossed, and within whose ample bounds was elaborated what we term, or understand as, Western Christianity and the world view it implies.

The drawback of any system, even a perfect one, is that it is a system — i.e., that it must by definition exclude certain things, regard them as alien to it, and as far as possible relegate them to the nonexistent. The drawback of the system that was worked out in Rome — the drawback of Western Christianity — was the unwitting reduction of its notions of evil. Any notions about anything are based on experience. For Western Christianity, the experience of evil was the experience reflected in the Roman law, with the addition of firsthand knowledge of the persecution of Christians by the emperors before Constantine. That's a lot, of course, but it is a long way from exhausting the reality of evil. By divorcing Byzantium, Western Christianity consigned the East to nonexistence, and thus reduced its own notion of human negative potential to a considerable, perhaps even a perilous, degree.

Today, if a young man climbs up a university tower with an automatic rifle and starts spraying passersby, a judge — this is assuming, of course, that the young man has been disarmed and brought to court — will class him as mentally disturbed and lock him up in a mental institution. Yet in essence the behavior of that young man cannot be distinguished from the castration of the royal by-blow as related by Psellus. Nor can it be told apart from the Iranian Imam's butchering tens of thousands of his subjects in order to confirm his version of the will of the Prophet. Or from Dzhugashvili's maxim, uttered in the course of the Great Terror, that "with us, no one is irreplaceable." The common denominator of all these deeds is the anti-individualistic notion that human life is essentially nothing — i.e., the absence of the idea that human life is sacred, if only because each life is unique.

I am far from asserting that the absence of this concept is a purely Eastern phenomenon; it is not, and that is what's indeed scary. But Western Christianity, along with developing all its ensuing ideas about the world, law, order, the norms of human behavior, and so forth, made the unforgivable error of neglecting, for the sake of its own growth and eventual triumph, the experience supplied by Byzantium. After all, that was a short-cut. Hence all these daily — by now — occurrences that surprise us so much; hence that inability on the part of states and individuals to react to them adequately, which shows itself in their dubbing the aforementioned phenomena mental illness, religious fanaticism, and whatnot.

27

In Topkapi, the former palace of the sultans, which has been turned into a museum, are now displayed in a special chamber the objects, most sacred to every Muslim's heart, associated with the life of the Prophet. Exquisitely encrusted caskets preserve the Prophet's tooth, locks from the Prophet's head. Visitors are asked to be quiet, to keep their voices down. All about hang swords of all kinds, daggers, the moldering pelt of some

48 *Flight from Byzantium*

animal bearing the discernible letters of the Prophet's missive to some real historical character, along with other sacred texts. Contemplating these, one feels like thanking fate for one's ignorance of the language. For me, I thought, Russian will do. In the center of the room, inside a gold-rimmed cube of glass, lies a dark-brown object, which I was unable to identify without the assistance of the label. This, in bronze inlay, read, in Turkish and English, "Impress of the Prophet's footprint." Size 18 shoe minimum, I thought as I stared at the exhibit. And then I shuddered: Yeti!

28

Byzantium was renamed Constantinople during Constantine's lifetime, if I am not mistaken. So far as simplicity of vowels and consonants goes, the new name was presumably more popular among the Seljuk Turks than Byzantium had been. But Istanbul also sounds reasonably Turkish — to the Russian ear, at any rate. The fact is, however, that Istanbul is a Greek name, deriving, as any guidebook will tell you, from the Greek *stin poli,* which means simply town. *Stin? Poli?* A Russian ear? Who here hears whom? Here, where *bardak* (brothel in Russian) means glass, where *durak* (fool) means stop. *Bir bardak çay* — one glass of tea; *otobüs durağı* — a bus stop. Good thing "*otobüs,*" at least, is only half Greek.

29

For anyone suffering from shortness of breath, there's nothing to do here — unless he hires a taxi for the day. For anyone coming to Istanbul from the West, the city is remarkably cheap. With the price converted into dollars, marks, or francs, several things here actually cost nothing at all. Those shoe shiners again, for example, or tea. It's an odd sensation to watch human activity that has no monetary expression: it cannot be evaluated. It feels like a sort of heaven, an ur-world; it's probably this otherworldliness that constitutes that celebrated "fascination" of the East for the northern Scrooge.

Ah, this battle cry of the graying blonde: "Bargain!" Doesn't it sound guttural even to an English ear? And, ah, these "Isn't that cute, dearie?"s in a minimum of three European languages, and the rustle of worthless banknotes under the scrutiny of dark, apprehensive eyes, otherwise doomed to the TV set's interference and the voluminous family. Ah, this middle age dispatched all over the world by its suburban mantelpieces! And yet, for all its vulgarity and crassness, this quest is markedly more innocent, and of better consequence for the locals, than that of some talkative smart-ass Parisienne, or of the spiritual lumpen fatigued by yoga, Buddhism, or Mao and now digging into the depths of Sufi, Sunni, Shia "secret" Islam, etc. No money changes hands here, of course. Between the actual and the mental bourgeois, one is better off with the former.

30

What happened next everybody knows: from out of who knows where appeared the Turks. There seems to be no clear answer to where they actually came from; obviously, a very long way off. What drew them to the shores of the Bosporus is also not terribly clear. Horses, I guess. The Turks — more precisely, *tuyrks* — were nomads, so we were taught at school. The Bosporus, of course, turned out to be an obstacle, and here, all of a sudden, the Turks made up their minds not to wander back the way they had come but, instead, to settle. All this sounds rather unconvincing, but let's leave it the way we got it. What they wanted from Byzantium-Constantinople-Istanbul is, at any rate, beyond argument: they wanted to be in Constantinople — i.e., more or less the same thing that Constantine himself wanted. Before the eleventh century, the Turks had no shared symbol. Then it appeared. As we know, it was the crescent.

In Constantinople, however, there were Christians; the city churches were crowned with the cross. The *tuyrks'* — gradually becoming the Turks' — love affair with Byzantium lasted approximately three centuries. Persistence brought its rewards, and in the fifteenth century the cross surrendered its cupolas to the crescent. The rest is well documented, and there is no need to expand upon it. What is worth noting, however, is the striking similarity between "the way it was" and "the way it became." For the meaning of history lies in the essence of structures, not in the character of décor.

31

The meaning of history! How, in what way, can the pen cope with this aggregation of races, tongues, creeds: with the vegetative — nay, zoological — pace of the crumbling down of the tower of Babel, at the end of which one fine day, among the teeming ruins, an individual catches himself gazing in terror and alienation at his own hand or at his procreative organ, not in Wittgensteinian fashion but possessed, rather, by a sensation that these things don't belong to him at all, that they are but components of some do-it-yourself toy set: details, shards in a kaleidoscope through which it is not the cause that peers at the effect but blind chance squinting at the daylight. Unobscured by the blowing dust.

32

The difference between spiritual and secular power in Christian Byzantium wasn't terribly striking. Nominally, the Emperor was obliged to take the views of the Patriarch into account, and, indeed, this often happened. On the other hand, the Emperor frequently appointed the Patriarch and on occasion was, or had grounds for supposing himself to be, a superior Christian vis-à-vis the Patriarch. And, of course, we need not mention the concept of the Lord's anointed, which of itself could relieve the Emperor of the necessity of reckoning with anyone's metaphysics at all. This also happened, and, in conjunction with certain mechanical marvels, of which Theophilus was greatly enamored, played a decisive role in the adoption of Eastern Christianity by Rus in the ninth century. (Incidentally, these marvels — the throne ascending into the air, the metal nightingale, the roaring lions of the same material, and so on — were borrowed by the Byzantine ruler, with minor modifications, from his Persian neighbors.)

Something very similar also occurred with the Sublime Porte, which is to say the Ottoman Empire, alias Muslim Byzantium.

Once again, we have an autocracy, heavily militarized and somewhat more despotic. The absolute head of the state was the
Padishah, or Sultan. Alongside him, however, existed the Grand
Mufti, a position combining — indeed, equating — spiritual and
administrative authority. The whole state was run by a vastly
complex hierarchical system, in which the religious — or, to put
it more conveniently, staunchly ideological — element predom-
inated.

In purely structural terms, the difference between the Second
Rome and the Ottoman Empire is accessible only in units of
time. What is it, then? The spirit of place? Its evil genius? The
spirit of bad spells — *porcha* in Russian? Where, incidentally, do
we get this word *porcha* from? Might it not derive from *porte*? It
doesn't matter. It's enough that both Christianity and *bardak*
with *durak* came down to us from this place where people were
becoming converted to Christianity in the fifth century with the
same ease with which they went over to Islam in the fifteenth
(even though after the fall of Constantinople the Turks did not
persecute the Christians in any way). The reason for both con-
versions was the same: pragmatism. Not that this is connected
with the place, however; this has to do with the species.

33

Oh, all these countless Osmans, Muhammads, Murads, Bajazets,
Ibrahims, Selims, and Suleimans slaughtering their predecessors, rivals, brothers, parents, and offspring — in the case of
Murad II, or III (who cares?), eighteen brothers in a row —
with the regularity of a man shaving in front of a mirror. Oh,
all these endless, uninterrupted wars: against the infidel, against
their own but Shiite Muslims, to extend the Empire, to avenge
a wrong, for no reason at all, and in self-defense. And, oh, those
Janissaries, the élite of the army, dedicated at first to the Sultan,
then gradually turning into a separate caste, with only its own
interests at heart. How familiar it all, including the slaughter,
is! All these turbans and beards, that uniform for heads possessed by one idea only — massacre — and because of that, and
not at all because of Islam's ban on the depiction of anyone or
anything living, totally indistinguishable from one another! And

perhaps "massacre" precisely because all are so much alike that there is no way to detect a loss. "I massacre, therefore I exist."

And, broadly speaking, what, indeed, could be nearer to the heart of yesterday's nomad than the linear principle, than movement across a surface, in whatever direction? Didn't one of them, another Selim, say during the conquest of Egypt that he, as Lord of Constantinople, was heir to the Roman Empire and therefore had a right to all the lands that had ever belonged to it? Do these words sound like justification or do they sound like prophecy, or both? And does not the same note ring four hundred years later in the voice of Ustryalov and the Third Rome's latter-day Slavophiles, whose scarlet, Janissary's-cloaklike banner neatly combined a star and the crescent of Islam? And that hammer, isn't it a modified cross?

These nonstop, lasting-a-thousand-years wars, these endless tracts of scholastic interpretation of the art of archery — might not these be responsible for the development in this part of the world of a fusion between army and state, for the concept of politics as the continuation of war by other means, and for the phantasmagoric, though ballistically feasible, fantasies of Konstantin Tsiolkovsky, the grandfather of the missile?

A man with imagination, especially an impatient one, may be sorely tempted to answer these questions in the affirmative. But perhaps one shouldn't rush; perhaps one should pause and give them the chance to turn into "accursed" ones, even if that may take several centuries. Ah, these centuries, history's favorite unit, relieving the individual of the necessity of personally evaluating the past, and awarding him the honorable status of victim of history.

34

Unlike the Ice Age, civilizations, of whatever sort, move from south to north, as if to fill up the vacuum created by the retreating glacier. The tropical forest is gradually ousting the conifers and mixed woodland — if not through foliage, then by way of architecture. One sometimes gets the feeling that baroque, rococo, and even the Schinkel style are simply a species' unconscious yearning for its equatorial past. Fernlike pagodas also fit this idea.

As for latitudes, it's only nomads who move along them, and usually from east to west. The nomadic migration makes sense only within a distinct climatic zone. The Eskimos glide within the Arctic Circle, the Tartars and Mongols in the confines of the black-earth zone. The cupolas of yurts and igloos, the cones of tents and tepees.

I have seen the mosques of Central Asia, of Samarkand, Bukhara, Khiva: genuine pearls of Muslim architecture. As Lenin didn't say, I know nothing better than the Shah-i-Zinda, on whose floor I passed several nights, having nowhere else to lay my head. I was nineteen then, but I retain tender memories of these mosques not at all for that reason. They are masterpieces of scale and color; they bear witness to the lyricism of Islam. Their glaze, their emerald and cobalt get imprinted on your retina, not least because of the contrast with the yellow-brown hues of the surrounding landscape. This contrast, this memory of a coloristic (at least) alternative to the real world, may also have been the main pretext for their birth. One does, indeed, sense in them an idiosyncrasy, a self-absorption, a striving to accomplish, to perfect themselves. Like lamps in the darkness. Better: like corals in the desert.

35

Whereas Istanbul's mosques are Islam triumphant. There is no greater contradiction than a triumphant church — or greater tastelessness, either. St. Peter's in Rome suffers from this as well. But the Istanbul mosques! These enormous toads in frozen stone, squatting on the earth, unable to stir. Only the minarets, resembling more than anything (prophetically, alas) ground-to-air batteries — only they indicate the direction the soul was once about to take. Their shallow domes, reminiscent of saucepan lids or cast-iron kettles, are unable to conceive what they are to do with the sky: they preserve what they contain, rather than encourage one to set eyes on high. Ah, this tent complex! This complex of spreading on the ground. Of *namaz*.

Silhouetted against the sunset, on the hilltops, they create a powerful impression: the hand reaches for the camera, like that of a spy spotting a military installation. There is, indeed, something menacing about them — eerie, otherworldly, galactic, totally hermetic, shell-like. And all this in a dirty-gray color, like most of the buildings in Istanbul, and all set against the turquoise of the Bosporus.

And if one's pen does not poise to chide their nameless true-believing builders for being aesthetically dumb it is because the tone for these ground-hugging, toad- and crablike constructions was set by the Hagia Sophia, an edifice in the utmost degree Christian. Constantine, it is asserted, laid the foundations; it was erected, though, in the reign of Justinian. From the outside, there is no way to tell it from the mosques, or them from it, for fate has played a cruel (or was it cruel?) joke on the Hagia Sophia. Under Sultan Whatever-His-Redundant-Name-Was, our Hagia Sophia was turned into a mosque.

As transformations go, this one didn't require a great deal of effort: all the Muslims had to do was to erect four minarets, one on each side of the cathedral. Which they did; and it became impossible to tell the Hagia Sophia from a mosque. That is, the architectural standard of Byzantium was taken to its logical end, for it was exactly the squat grandeur of this Christian shrine that the builders of Bajazet, Suleiman, and the builders of the Blue Mosque, not to mention their lesser brethren, sought to emulate. And yet they shouldn't be reproached for that, partly because by the time of their arrival in Constantinople it was the Hagia Sophia that loomed largest over the entire landscape; mainly, however, because in itself the Hagia Sophia was not a Roman creation. It was an Eastern — or, more precisely, Sassanid — product. And, similarly, there is no point in blaming that Sultan What's-His-Name — was it Murad? — for converting a Christian church into a mosque. This transformation reflected something that one may, without giving the matter much thought, take for profound Eastern indifference to problems of a metaphysical nature. In reality, though, what stood behind this, and stands now, in much the same way as the Hagia Sophia, with her minarets and with her Christian-Muslim décor inside, is a sensation, instilled by both history and the Arabic lace, that everything in this life intertwines — that everything is, in a sense, but a pattern in a carpet. Trodden underfoot.

36

It is a monstrous idea, but not without a measure of truth. So let us try to grapple with it. At its source lies the Eastern principle of ornamentation, whose basic element is a verse from the Koran, a quotation from the Prophet: sewn, engraved, carved in stone or wood, and graphically coincident with this very process of sewing, engraving, carving if one bears in mind the Arabic form of writing. In other words, we are dealing with the decorative aspect of calligraphy, the decorative use of sentences, words, letters — with a purely visual attitude to them. Let us, disregarding here the unacceptability of this attitude toward words (and letters, too), point out only the inevitability of a literally spatial — because conveyed by distinctly spatial means — perception of any sacred locution. Let us note the dependence of this ornament on the length of the line and on the didactic character of the locution, often ornamental enough in itself. Let us remind ourselves: the unit of Eastern ornament is the sentence, the word, the letter.

The unit — the main element — of ornamentation that arose in the West was the notch, the tally, recording the passage of days. Such ornament, in other words, is temporal. Hence its rhythm, its tendency toward symmetry, its essentially abstract character, subordinating graphic expression to a rhythmic sense. Its extreme nonantididacticism. Its persistence — by means of rhythm, or repetition — in abstracting from its unit, from that which has already been once expressed. In short, its dynamism.

I would also remark that the unit of this ornamentation — the day, or the idea of the day — absorbs into itself any experience, including that of the sacred locution. From this follows the suggestion that the natty little bordure on a Grecian urn is superior to a pattern in a carpet. Which, in turn, leads us to consider who is more the nomad, the one who wanders in space or the one who migrates in time. However overwhelming (literally, too) the notion that all is interwoven, that everything is merely a pattern in a carpet, trodden underfoot, it frankly yields to the idea that everything gets left behind — the carpet and one's own foot upon it included.

37

Oh, I foresee objections! I see an art historian or an ethnologist preparing to wage battle, figures or potsherds in his hands, over everything stated above. I can see a bespectacled someone carrying in an Indian or Chinese vase with a meander or epistyle just like the natty little Greek bordure and exclaiming, "Well, what about this? Isn't India (or China) the East?" Worse still, that vase or dish may turn out to be from Egypt or elsewhere in Africa, from Patagonia, or from Central America. Then out will gush a downpour of proofs and incontrovertible facts that pre-Islamic culture was figurative, that, thus, in this area the West simply lags behind the East, that ornament is by definition nonfunctional, and that space is greater than time. Or that I, for no doubt political reasons, am substituting anthropology for history. Something like that, or worse.

What can I say to this? And need I say anything? I'm not sure, but, all the same, I will point out that if I hadn't foreseen these objections I wouldn't have taken up my pen — that space to me is, indeed, both lesser and less dear than time. Not because it is lesser but because it is a thing, while time is an idea about a thing. In choosing between a thing and an idea, the latter is always to be preferred, say I.

And I also foresee that there will be no vase, no potsherds, no dish, or bespectacled someone. That no objections will be issued, that silence will reign supreme. Less as a sign of assent than as one of indifference. So let us nastify our conclusion somewhat and add that an awareness of time is a profoundly individual experience. That in the course of his life every person sooner or later finds himself in the position of Robinson Crusoe, carving notches and, having counted, say, seven of them, or ten, crossing them out. Such is the origin of ornament, regardless of preceding civilizations, or of that to which this given person belongs. And these notches are a profoundly solitary activity, isolating the individual and forcing him toward an

understanding, if not of his uniqueness, then at least of the
autonomy of his existence in the world. That is what the basis
of our civilization is, and that is what Constantine walked away
from to the East. To the carpet.

38

A normal hot, dusty, perspiring summer day in Istanbul. Moreover, it is Sunday. A human herd loitering about under the
vaults of the Hagia Sophia. Up there aloft, inaccessible to the
sight, are mosaics representing either kings or saints. Lower
down, accessible to the eye, yet not to the mind, are circular
metallic-looking shields with lacelike quotations from the
Prophet in gold against dark-green enamel. Monumental cam-
eos with coiling characters, evoking shadows of Jackson Pollock
or Kandinsky. And now I become aware of a slipperiness: the
cathedral is sweating. I inquire, and am told it is because of the
sharp jump in temperature. I decide it is because of my presence, and leave.

39

To get a good picture of one's native realm, one needs either to
get outside its walls or to spread out a map. But, as has been
remarked before, who looks at maps nowadays?

If civilizations — of whatever sort they are — do indeed
spread like vegetation in the opposite direction to the glacier,
from south to north, where could Rus, given her geographical
position, possibly tuck herself away from Byzantium? Not just
Kievan Rus but Muscovite Rus as well, and then all the rest of it
between the Donets and the Urals. And one should, frankly,
thank Tamerlane and Genghis Khan for retarding the process
somewhat, by somewhat freezing — or, rather, trampling — the
flowers of Byzantium. It is not true that Rus played a shielding
role for Europe, preserving the West from the Mongol yoke. It
was Constantinople, then still the bulwark of Christendom, that
played the role. (In 1402, incidentally, a situation developed
under the walls of Constantinople which pretty nearly turned
into a total catastrophe for Christianity and, indeed, for the

whole of the then known world: Tamerlane encountered Bajazet. Luckily, they turned their arms against each other: interra-
cial rivalry, it would seem, made itself known. Had they joined
forces against the West — that is, in the direction both were
moving — we would now be looking at the map with an almond-
shaped, predominantly hazel eye.)

There was nowhere for Rus to go to get away from Byzantium
— any more than for the West to get away from Rome. And,
just as the West in age after age became overgrown with Roman
colonnades and legality, Rus happened to become the natural
geographical prey of Byzantium. If in the way of the former
stood the Alps, the latter was impeded only by the Black Sea —
a deep but, in the final analysis, flat thing. Rus received, or took,
from Byzantine hands everything: not only the Christian liturgy
but also the Christian-Turkish system of statecraft (gradually
more and more Turkish, less vulnerable, more militarily ideological), not to mention a significant part of its vocabulary. The
only thing Byzantium shed on its way north was its remarkable
heresies — its Monophysites, its Arians, its Neoplatonists, and
so on — which had constituted the very essence of its literary
and spiritual life. But then its northward expansion took place
at a time of growing domination by the crescent, and the purely
physical power of the Sublime Porte hypnotized the North in
far greater measure than the theological polemics of dying-out
scholiasts.

Still, in the end Neoplatonism triumphed in art, didn't it? We
know where our icons are from, we know the same about our
onion-domed churches. We also know that there is nothing easier for a state than to adapt to its own ends Plotinus' maxim that
an artist's task must be the interpretation of ideas rather than
the imitation of nature. As for ideas, in what way does the late
M. Suslov, or whoever is now scraping the ideological dish, dif-
fer from the Grand Mufti? What distinguishes the General Secretary from the Padishah — or, indeed, the Emperor? And who
appoints the Patriarch, the Grand Vizier, the Mufti, or the Ca-
liph? What distinguishes the Politburo from the Great Divan?
And isn't it only one step from a divan to an ottoman?

Isn't my native realm an Ottoman Empire now — in extent,
in military might, in its threat to the Western world? Aren't we

now by the walls of Vienna? And is not its threat the greater in
that it proceeds from the Easternized, to the point of unrecog-
nizability — no, recognizability! — Christianity? Is it not greater
because it is more seductive? And what do we hear in that howl
of the late Milyukov under the cupola of the short-lived Duma:
"The Dardanelles will be ours!" An echo of Cato? The yearning
of a Christian for his holy place? Or still the voice of Bajazet,
Tamerlane, Selim, Muhammad? And if it comes to this, if we
are quoting and interpreting, what do we discern in that falsetto
of Konstantin Leontiev, the falsetto that pierced the air precisely in these parts, where he served in the Czarist embassy:
"Russia must rule shamelessly"? What do we hear in this putrid,
prophetic exclamation? The spirit of the age? The spirit of the
nation? Or the spirit of the place?

40

God forbid we delve any further into the Turkish-Russian dictionary. Let us just take the word *çay*, meaning "tea" in both
languages, whatever its origins. The tea in Turkey is wonderful
— better than the coffee — and, like the shoe-shining, costs almost nothing in any known currency. It's strong, the color of
transparent brick, but it has no overstimulating effect, because
it is served in a *bardak*, a fifty-gram glass, no more. Of all things
I came across in this mixture of Astrakhan and Stalinabad, it's
the best item. Tea — and the sight of Constantine's wall, which
I would not have seen if I hadn't struck it lucky and got a rogue
taxi-driver who, instead of going straight to Topkapi, bowled
around the whole city.

You can judge the seriousness of the builder's intent by the
wall's height and width and the quality of the masonry. Constantine was thus extremely serious: the ruins where gypsies, goats,
and young people trading in their tender parts may be found
could withstand even today any army, given a positional war.
On the other hand, if civilizations are granted vegetative — in
other words, ideological — character, the erection of the wall
was a sheer waste of time. Against anti-individualism, to say the
least, against the spirit of relativism and obedience, neither wall
nor sea offers a protection.

When I finally reached Topkapi and, having surveyed a good part of its contents — predominantly the *kaftans* of the Sultans, which correspond linguistically and visually to the wardrobe of the Muscovite rulers — headed toward the object of my pilgrimage, the seraglio, I was greeted, sadly, at the door of this most important establishment in the world by a notice in Turkish and English: CLOSED FOR RESTORATION. "Oh, if only!" I exclaimed inwardly, trying to control my disappointment.

41

The quality of reality always leads to a search for a culprit — more accurately, for a scapegoat. Whose flocks graze in the mental fields of history. Yet, a son of a geographer, I believe that Urania is older than Clio; among Mnemosyne's daughters, I think, she is the oldest. So, born by the Baltic, in the place regarded as a window on Europe, I always felt something like a vested interest in this window on Asia with which we shared a meridian. On grounds perhaps less than sufficient, we regarded ourselves as Europeans. By the same token, I thought of the dwellers of Constantinople as Asians. Of these two assumptions, it's only the first that proved to be arguable. I should also admit, perhaps, that East and West vaguely corresponded in my mind to the past and the future.

Unless one is born by the water — and at the edge of an empire at that — one is seldom bothered by this sort of distinction. Of all people, somebody like me should be the first to regard Constantine as the carrier of the West to the East, as someone on a par with Peter the Great: the way he is regarded by the Church itself. If I had stayed longer at that meridian, I would. Yet I didn't, and I don't.

To me, Constantine's endeavor is but an episode in the general pull of the East westward, a pull motivated neither by the attraction of one part of the world for another nor by the desire of the past to absorb the future — although at times and in some places, of which Istanbul is one, it seems that way. This pull, I am afraid, is magnetic, evolutionary; it has to do, presumably, with the direction in which this planet rotates on its axis. It takes the forms of an attraction to a creed, of nomadic thrusts, wars, migration, and the flow of money. The Galata Bridge is not the first to be built over the Bosporus, as your guidebook would claim; the first one was built by Darius. A nomad always rides into a sunset.

Or else he swims. The strait is about a mile wide, and what could be done by a "blond cow" escaping the wrath of Jupiter's spouse could surely have been managed by the dusky son of the steppes. Or by lovesick Leander or by sick-of-love Lord Byron splashing across the Dardanelles. Bosporus! Well-worn strip of water, the only cloth that is properly Urania's, no matter how hard Clio tries to put it on. It stays wrinkled, and on gray days, especially, no one would say that it has been stained by history. Its surface current washes itself off Constantinople in the north — and that's why, perhaps, that sea is called Black. Then it somersaults to the bottom and, in the form of a deep current, escapes back into Marmara — the Marble Sea — presumably to get itself bleached. The net result is that dusted-bottle-green color: the color of time itself. The child of the Baltic can't fail to recognize it, can't rid himself of the old sensation that this rolling, nonstop, lapping substance itself is time, or that this is what time would look like had it been condensed or photographed. This is what, he thinks, separates Europe and Asia. And the patriot in him wishes the stretch were wider.

42

Time to wrap it up. As I said, there were no steamers from Istanbul or Smyrna. I boarded a plane and, after less than two hours' flight over the Aegean, through air that at one time was no less inhabited than the archipelago down below, landed in Athens.

Forty miles from Athens, in Sounion, at the top of a cliff plummeting to the sea, stands a temple to Poseidon, built almost simultaneously — a difference of some fifty years — with the Parthenon in Athens. It has stood here for two and a half thousand years.

It is ten times smaller than the Parthenon. How many times more beautiful it is would be hard to say; it is not clear what should be considered the unit of perfection. It has no roof.

There is not a soul about. Sounion is a fishing village with a couple of modern hotels now, and lies far below. There, on the crest of the dark cliff, the shrine looks from a distance as if it had been gently lowered from Heaven rather than been erected on earth. Marble has more in common with the clouds than with the ground.

Fifteen white columns connected by a white marble base stand evenly spaced. Between them and the earth, between them and the sea, between them and the blue sky of Hellas, there is no one and nothing.

As practically everywhere else in Europe, here, too, Byron incised his name on the base of one of the columns. In his footsteps, the bus brings tourists; later it takes them away. The erosion that is clearly affecting the surface of the columns has nothing to do with weathering. It is a pox of stares, lenses, flashes.

Then twilight descends, and it gets darker. Fifteen columns, fifteen vertical white bodies evenly spaced at the top of the cliff, meet the night under the open skies.

If they counted days, there would have been a million such days. From a distance, in the evening haze, their white vertical bodies resemble an ornament, thanks to the equal intervals between them.

An idea of order? The principle of symmetry? Sense of rhythm? Idolatry?

43

Presumably, it would have been wiser to take letters of recommendation, to jot down two or three telephone numbers at least, before going to Istanbul. I didn't do that. Presumably, it would have made sense to make friends with someone, get into contact, look at the life of the place from the inside, instead of dismissing the local population as an alien crowd, instead of regarding people as so much psychological dust in one's eyes.

Who knows? Perhaps my attitude toward people has in its own right a whiff of the East about it, too. When it comes down to it, where am I from? Still, at a certain age a man gets tired of his own kind, weary of cluttering up his conscious and subconscious. One more, or ten more, tales of cruelty? Another ten, or hundred, examples of human baseness, stupidity, valor? Misanthropy, after all, should also have its limits.

It's enough, therefore, to glance in the dictionary and find that *katorga* (forced labor) is a Turkish word, too. And it's enough to discover on a Turkish map, somewhere in Anatolia, or Ionia, a town called Niğde (Russian for nowhere).

44

I'm not a historian, or a journalist, or an ethnographer. At best, I'm a traveler, a victim of geography. Not of history, be it noted, but of geography. This is what still links me with the country where it was my fate to be born, with our famed Third Rome. So I'm not particularly interested in the politics of present-day Turkey, or in what happened to Atatürk, whose portrait adorns the greasy walls of every last coffeehouse as well as the Turkish lira, unconvertible and representing an unreal form of payment for real labor.

I came to Istanbul to look at the past, not at the future — since the latter doesn't exist here: whatever there was of it has gone north as well. Here there is only an unenviable, third-rate present of the people, industrious yet plundered by the intensity of the local history. Nothing will happen here anymore, apart perhaps from street disorders or an earthquake. Or perhaps they'll discover oil: there's a fearful stench of sulfureted hydrogen in the Golden Horn, crossing whose oily surface you get a splendid panorama of the city. Still, it's unlikely. The stench comes from oil seeping out of rusty, leaking, nearly hole-ridden tankers passing through the Strait. One might squeeze out a living from refining that alone.

A project like that, though, would probably strike a local as altogether too enterprising. The locals are rather conservative by nature, even if they are businessmen or dealers; as for the working class, it is locked, reluctantly but firmly, in a traditional, conservative mentality by the beggarly rates of pay. In his own element, a native finds himself only within the infinitely intertwining — in patterns akin to the carpet's or the mosque walls' — weblike, vaulted galleries of the local bazaar, which is the heart, mind, and soul of Istanbul. This is a city within a city; it, too, is built for the ages. It cannot be transported west, north, or even south. GUM, Bon Marché, Macy's, Harrods taken together and raised to the cube are but child's babble compared with these catacombs. In an odd way, thanks to the garlands of yellow hundred-watt bulbs and the endless wash of bronze, beads, bracelets, silver, and gold under glass, not to mention the very carpets and the icons, samovars, crucifixes, and so on, this bazaar in Istanbul produces the impression of — of all things — an Orthodox Church, though convoluted and branching like a quotation from the Prophet. A laid-out version of the Hagia Sophia.

45

Civilizations move along meridians; nomads (including our modern warriors, since war is an echo of the nomadic instinct) along latitudes. This seems to be yet another version of the cross that Constantine saw. Both movements possess a natural (vegetable or animal) logic, considering which one easily finds oneself in the position of not being able to reproach anyone for anything. In the state known as melancholy — or, more exactly, fatalism. It can be blamed on age, or on the influence of the East, or, with an effort of the imagination, on Christian humility.

The advantages of this condition are obvious, since they are selfish ones. For it is, like all forms of humility, always achieved at the expense of the mute helplessness of the victims of history, past, present, and future; it is an echo of the helplessness of millions. And if you are not at an age when you can draw a sword from a scabbard or clamber up to a platform to roar to a sea of heads about your detestation of the past, the present, and what is to come; if there is no such platform or the sea has dried up, there still remain the face and the lips, which can accommodate your slight — provoked by the vista opening to both your inner and your naked eye — smile of contempt.

46

With it, with that smile on the lips, one may board the ferry and set off for a cup of tea in Asia. Twenty minutes later, one can disembark in Çengelköy, find a café on the very shore of the Bosporus, sit down and order tea, and, inhaling the smell of rotting seaweed, observe without changing the aforesaid facial expression the aircraft carriers of the Third Rome sailing slowly through the gates of the Second on their way to the First.

ALEXANDER COCKBURN

Heatherdown:
A Late Imperialist Memoir

FROM GRAND STREET

ONE BRAVE MORNING in Manhattan, when fall was still holding winter at bay, my daughter Daisy called from London in some excitement. The casting director for a TV movie had been holding some auditions in her school in Hammersmith; she and two schoolmates had been selected for major parts; filming would begin almost at once. Then my former wife came on the phone. She had read the script. Certain scenes could, in the hands of an unscrupulous director, exploit the thirteen-year-old child. Vigilance was necessary. Besides, there was the matter of what Daisy should be paid. . . .

A few days later Daisy called again to report. With the help of a lawyer, proper safeguards had been established and adequate sums guaranteed. It turned out that the director of *Secrets*, one in a series of films generically entitled *First Love*, was to be Gavin Millar. He had been at Oxford at the same time as I had and in my recollection had not seemed then to be an embryonic pornographer.

Daisy added that filming would start in ten days at a recently closed prep school near Ascot. My heart tripped. What was the name of the school? "Hold on while I find the address." The wind outside was stripping golden leaves off the trees in Central Park and I waited, foot poised on the threshold of memory. Daisy picked up the phone again. "Heatherdown. It's called Heatherdown." The past welcomed me in.

In the hard winter of 1947 we moved from London to county Cork, Ireland, and after several months my parents decided that I had better start going to some sort of local school. I would have been happy to go on spending my days playing with Doreen French, the sexton's daughter, and my evenings listening to my father read *Don Quixote*. I was shy and already felt awkward in Ireland, where social divisions were much more transparent than in London. To walk out of the gates of my grandparents' big house and walk along Main Street where the unemployed men lounged all day in front of Farrell's was bad enough. Staring idly at everything, they stared at me too. School meant ridicule at closer quarters.

But my parents were adamant. I was seven and it was time to retrieve the education abandoned when we had left London. They proposed to send me to the Loretto Convent, a large red building overlooking Youghal Bay. My grandmother was horrified. The Loretto Convent was a Roman Catholic institution and we, as members of the Anglo-Irish class were, however notionally, Protestant.

My parents pointed out there was no Protestant school in Youghal. My grandmother was scarcely a bigot but in the late 1940s the gulf between Protestants and Catholics was still fixed and deep — as it is in our town no longer. Brought up in the government houses of varying British colonies from Jamaica to Hong Kong, she took certain social and religious proprieties absolutely for granted. She discovered that there was a tiny parochial school for Protestant children. It was about to close since attendance had just dropped below the quorum of seven children which the Church of Ireland reckoned as the minimum its budget would permit.

There had been, before the achievement of Irish independence, a substantial British garrison in Youghal. St. Mary's Church, whose ancient bell tower loomed behind the wall of my grandparents' equally ancient Tudor house, could hold a congregation of three thousand. Back at the turn of the century certain tradesmen, eager for the business of this garrison, had thought it opportune to convert to Protestantism. They changed ships on a falling tide. The garrison left in 1922 and a quarter of a century later we could see the descendants of the apostates,

beached on the shoals of history. Their stores were ill favored
by the overwhelmingly Catholic population of Youghal and they
had the added misfortune, as members of the shrunken congregation of some sixty-odd souls attending St. Mary's, to have to
endure the Reverend Watts's annual Christmas sermon. Peering down from his pulpit at the shopkeepers who were making
a couple of shillings out of the Christmas buying spree, Watts
would savagely denounce the gross commercialization of a holy
festival celebrating the birth of the Savior. Then he took to
attacking the atom bomb too and the shopkeepers saw their
chance. They complained to the bishop and Watts was demoted
and became curate of Watergrass Hill, a desolate hamlet twenty
miles inland.

The shopkeepers had children, still officially within the Protestant fold, and these were the cannon fodder in my grandmother's campaign. Their parents were told firmly that attendance at the parochial school was essential. A few weeks later
a donkey and trap, purchased by my grandmother, made its
rounds, depositing me and my new companions at the parochial
school, a gray stone building just down the road from the Loretto convent. In the last months of my sojourn at the school
workmen erected a little shrine across the street. There was a
statue of the Virgin and under it some lines, the first of which
read "Dogma of the Ass." The next line continued with "-ump-
tion of the Virgin Mary." The shrine and plaque celebrated the
dogma promulgated by Pope Pius XII in 1950, which asserted
that Mary had been bodily assumed into the bosom of the heavenly father. We used to wonder what archeologists of the future
would make of the plaque, if it got broken and only the top line
survived.

My grandmother rejoiced that I had been saved from priest-
craft and the donkey groaned as he dragged us through the
town. A few months later my parents bought a house of their
own three miles from Youghal, a distance beyond the powers of
the donkey. A new pony, trap and gardener's boy took me to
school in the morning and then would return home. In late
morning my mother would drive the trap in again for shopping
and to take me home for lunch. The gardener's boy would drive
me in again to school after lunch and at the end of the afternoon

make the final trip to take me home once more. Blackie thus
trotted or walked twenty-four miles a day. Once the gardener's
boy forgot to fasten Blackie's reins to the bridle but buckled
them to the shoulder collar instead. It made no difference to
Blackie, who started, stopped and swerved left or right at all the
proper points. A photograph of Main Street in Youghal in 1948
would have shown that eighty percent of all the transportation
was horsedrawn. Fifteen years later the proportions were re-
versed. We got our first car in 1958 when I turned seventeen,
got a license and was thus able to chauffeur our family into the
twentieth century.

Secure from popish influence, my education did not notice-
ably improve. The problem was that though Rome was held at
bay, the Irish state played an important part in our instruction.
It was mandatory that we be taught Gaelic and much time was
set aside for that purpose every day. Thus after two years I was
the regional champion in Scripture knowledge and could say
"Shut the door" and some other useful phrases in Irish.

My parents pondered the alternatives. They could send me
— over my grandmother's undoubted resistance — to the
Christian Brothers school. Its reputation was bad aside from the
brothers' savage recourse to the pandybat. Besides, it would be
of little help in the overall strategic plan of my education, which
was to get me into Oxford.

Though only recently disengaged from the Communist Party
and still — as always — of stout radical beliefs, my father held
true to his class origins in pondering the contours of his plan.
The route march to Oxford or Cambridge was well established:
at the age of eight the raw recruits would go to preparatory —
or prep — schools and there obtain the rudiments of an education sufficient to get them, at the age of fourteen, into a "public"
(that is, private) school such as Eton, Harrow, Winchester, Westminster and so forth.

The alacrity with which parents of the recruits dispatched
them from home at the age of eight has often been noted with
bemused concern by foreigners. From that year forward the
child would be at home for only four months in the year. Of
course many parents are far happier to see the back of a son
than they might care to admit and boarding school was as good

an excuse as any. Besides, these schools allowed the recruits to the system to cluster with members of their own class rather than go to a local school where contact with the lower orders might be inevitable: in sum, these prep and public schools were — and are — the training camps in the long guerrilla war of British social relations.

The form was to put down your child for a prep school as soon as he entered the world. (Girls were less of a problem and might never, at least in those days, be put down for anything at all.) My parents and I had spent a portion of 1941, the year of my birth, sitting in St. John's Wood underground station as the German bombs and rockets rained down overhead. My father was on the Nazi blacklist and in the event of an invasion they certainly would have shot him if his plan to escape by boat to Ireland had failed. The British authorities, scarcely less hostile to Communists than to the Nazis — and in many cases more so — were vacillating on how to deal with Reds. At first they reckoned it best to draft them, send them to the front and hope that the first Panzers they met would do their duty. But then, amid the stunning exhibitions of British military incompetence, it was feared that the Reds would foment discontent and even mutiny. In accord with this dogleg in government policy my father first got a set of peremptory call-up papers and then, almost at once, a countermanding set of instructions. Later a German V-2 rocket landed on our house and reduced it to rubble. Perhaps understandably my father had not got around to the business of putting me down for a prep school. One way or another it did not seem, in the early 1940s, that there would necessarily be prep schools to go to.

But of course the prep schools survived and the "public" schools survived and the British class system survived. For that matter, many of those who had engineered the destruction of our house on Acacia Road survived too. My brother Andrew found one in Washington, D.C., in the late 1970s. He was called Dieter Schwebs. He had been one of the designers of the V-2 and had gone to work for the U.S. after the war. By the time Andrew met him, Schwebs was in the General Accounting Office, rooting out fraud and waste in the Defense Department.

Andrew told him about our house and Schwebs was full of concern: "Oh my heffens, nobody hurt I hope?"

I was nine, already one year late for prep school. It was July 1950 and the start of the school year was menacingly close. No suitable place willing to accept me had been found. Old friends to whom my father had not spoken in years were pressed into action and that filiation of patronage and mutual back-scratching called "the old boy net" was shaken into action. One midsummer day my father dismounted from the bicycle he used to go into the town of Youghal to dispatch articles, make telephone calls and have pleasant conversations in one of Youghal's quiet, dark bars. "Well, we've got you into Heatherdown. It's supposed to be one of the most exclusive and expensive prep schools in England. In a couple of weeks we'll take the boat train to London, and then 'go to Ascot and have a look at the school. If it seems all right we'll get the uniforms and so forth and you'll start there in mid-September.".

The inspection trip was pretty bad. There were no boys about, naturally, but the headmaster described the amenities with a relentless glee which was unnerving. He tried to show my father the cricket pitch, of which he was plainly very proud. My father, who had no views on cricket pitches, tried to offset his lack of interest or knowledge by asking to inspect the kitchens and dormitories. The headmaster, confronted with this aberrant scale of priorities, began to form what became an increasingly dubious opinion of our family's values. There followed an expensive trip to Gorringes, school outfitters, and I was fitted out in the black and red colors that were Heatherdown's motif.

On a grim September morning I stood on the platform at Waterloo Station. Prep schools were clustered thickly around Ascot, perhaps drawn by the magnet of Eton in nearby Windsor, and there was a rainbow of other school uniforms, of Earlywood, Scaitcliffe, Ludgrove and Lambrook. I kept my eyes alert for the red ties and caps of Heatherdown and soon saw these colors adorning a small boy who was sobbing quietly. His equally stricken mother made a lunge to cover his tear-stained face with kisses but he fought her off. Excessive displays of emotion by one's parents were a matter for great dread. In fact any display of originality or character by them, apart from a humdrum sort of parentness or hitting a six at the father's cricket match, was thought to be bad form. The train whistle sounded, my mother began some final gesture of valediction which seemed ominously tinged with sentiment. I scuttled into the same compartment as the sobbing child, the door slammed and we chugged into the home counties.

Daisy called. They had started filming and, "Daddy, we've found your photograph." Every boy leaving Heatherdown had his photograph taken. It was then framed and put up in the corridor outside the classrooms. There were all the boys who had ever been to the school, right back to Hely-Hutchinson, who had his photograph taken in 1914, which meant that he may just have escaped being killed on the Western Front by 1918. About a thousand boys had gone through Heatherdown since his time. In any given year about fifty-five noisy little creatures inhabited the place, along with masters, matron, maids and gardeners.

Daisy reported that my photograph was on the top row, near the music room. I could see in my mind's eye where it was. Next to me there was probably Miller-Mundy and next to him maybe Piggott-Brown or Legge-Bourke. Legge-Bourke's father was a Conservative member of Parliament who once flipped a coin at Prime Minister Attlee during question time, shouting "Next record please." By the time I reached Heatherdown the first post-war Labour government was slipping from power and no one at Heatherdown was particularly upset about this. Parents of boys at Heatherdown were very conservative; masters were very conservative and the boys were very conservative too. Word got around that my father was a Red. This was not quite as bad as being identified as Irish, even though I had no brogue. Six years after a war in which De Valera had kept Ireland neutral, feeling still ran high. In argument the ladder of escalation was soon well known to me: "Cocky's Irish, Cocky's a dirty pig. . . . Cocky helped Hitler in the war. . . ." and so on.

The Attlee government had just survived the election of 1950 but when another election loomed in 1951 excitement ran high. There were endless jocular references to groundnuts — the well-intentioned but ill-fated scheme of the Labour government to cultivate peanuts in west Africa, thus providing employment for the locals and nutrition for British schoolchildren. Cost overruns and mismanagement brought the scheme low and the word "groundnuts" could be guaranteed to arouse derision at any Conservative gathering between the years 1949 and 1964.

The night of the 1951 election a large electoral map of the United Kingdom was placed on an easel in the doorway of our dormitory. As the results came in over the radio a master called Hall would color the relevant constituency blue in the event of a Conservative victory and an unpleasant puce if Labour won. Legge-Bourke was in our dormitory and we naturally rooted for his father Harry, who carried the Isle of Ely by about six thousand votes. When we awoke in the morning an extensive portion of the map was colored blue — some of this being because Conservatives tended to win the large rural constituencies. A rout of Labour and of socialism was proclaimed. Actually Labour won the popular vote by about a quarter of a million, but gerrymandering saw the Conservatives win a clear majority of twenty-six seats over Labour. Thus began thirteen years of Tory rule which lasted clear through the rest of my education and ended only in 1964, just after I had left Oxford. More people, nearly fourteen million, voted for Labour in 1951 than for any British political party before or since, though this was not at all the sense of the situation one got at Heatherdown.

The headmaster was very pleased. At that time the entirely groundless fear that the Labour Party would somehow attack private education was still very great. At each Labour Party conference the rhetorical thunder against it outstripped even the tremendous bellowing against "tied cottages," the feudal system whereby farm workers dwelt in their cottages only at the pleasure of their employers and, at the end of a lifetime of ill-paid labor, were evicted to the local almshouse to make way for younger muscles.

Jokes about the Labour Party were a staple among boys and masters. I was a supporter of the Labour Party — partly because I had the reputation of being Red hell-spawn to maintain and partly because it seemed sensible to oppose anything favored by most of the people at the school. But I felt — amid my support

— the disappointment of a fan who knows that his team is making a bit of an ass of itself and that improvement is unlikely in the near future. The innate conservatism of British schoolboys in private institutions was always impressive. At my next school, sometime in the late fifties, there was a "mock election." My friend Freddy Fitzpayne ran as the Communist and got one vote. I ran as the Labour candidate and got one vote. The Scottish Nationalist got eighty-three and the Conservative ninety-five.

Fitzpayne and I represented that school in debates. Each team had its own topic to which it spoke throughout the debating tournament, no matter what the other team was talking about. Fitzpayne and I used to speak to the motion, Great Britain Must Leave NATO Now. When I sat down after proposing the motion, our opponent would rise and, depending on what school we happened to be debating, would reel off a speech about the monarchy, Scottish independence or, in the case of one debate with Dollar Academy, a spirited defense of some controversial form of pig breeding. Fitzpayne and I got as far as the semifinals with our seditious topic before losing to some polished orators from Edinburgh Academy. We were photographed in the local Blairgowrie paper toasting each other with large pints of beer and narrowly escaped being expelled.

The ground squelched wetly underfoot as I walked across Central Park, brooding about groundnuts, Heatherdown and the autumn reek of Berkshire bonfires. The idea of a quick return flight to yesterday, courtesy of trans-Atlantic standby, was growing on me. If the premise of the voyage was commonplace in one respect — to see how exactly the child had become father to the man — there would be the unusual twist of being there as father of the child.

Three days later I was standing on Waterloo platform, just as I had with my mother over thirty years before. Daisy had been nervous of the idea and I knew well her familiar fear: I would somehow make a fool of myself, embarrass her in front of her friends and the entire production crew of *Secrets*. She reminded me of the Poppy Day Affair, a tale I occasionally told to show what I had had to cope with when I had been a boy worried, just like her, about the embarrassment parents can cause. Even now the memory causes me to sweat and stamp about a bit.

Back in the early 1950s Armistice Day — or Poppy Day — was taken a great deal more seriously than it is now. At precisely 11:00 A.M. there would be two minutes' silence in memory of those killed in the two Great Wars. The service in the little mock Tudor chapel at Heatherdown had an extra piquancy because the headmaster would bring in a small radio, just to make sure that we all fell silent at exactly 11:00 A.M. We didn't associate God with radios, machines that contradicted the high-toned nineteenth-century flavor of our Anglican observances, in which diction was so etherealized that very often it was hard to tell whether we were praying for peace or for good weather on the sports day coming up next week.

As we gathered in the chapel upstairs waiting for the Greenwich Mean Time pips, parents who had traveled to Heatherdown to take their children out for the afternoon would assemble downstairs in the headmaster's study. Since my parents lived in Ireland they rarely appeared. Other boys would occasionally invite me out for tea in Maidenhead, or to their homes if they lived relatively close by. These were the very early days of television and often the parents' idea of an uplifting yet amusing afternoon was to assemble in front of the TV on which the BBC would run a dignified Sunday afternoon quiz show called "Twenty Questions." The contestants were the usual British salad for such enterprises, containing a couple of academics, someone known to be waggish, and a socialite in relatively decent moral standing. At the beginning of each round a voice, audible to all but the participants, would give the answer. It was a deep voice, tranquil with the power of absolute knowledge, and it would intone, "The answer is *porridge*; the answer is *porridge*." I always thought the voice of God would sound like that; unruffled and awful as He asked me why I did not believe in Him unreservedly.

On Armistice Day in 1953 my father, in London on business, traveled down to Heatherdown to take me out. He arrived downstairs just as we heard the GMT signal on the radio and fell silent. Obliged to remember and revere the fallen in war, I would think of my Uncle Teeny who had died of malaria in

Italy in 1944. I had never known him but I would do my best to
imagine him fighting bravely; then, after about thirty seconds,
I would just concentrate on dead British soldiers generally and
say thank you. Along my pew, past Walduck who was fat and
who claimed his family name was Valdrake and had come over
with William and Mary, I could see out of the corner of my eye
MacLean, whose father had been killed in the war. Each year,
about fifty-five seconds after eleven, MacLean would start
crying. I think he felt he had to. There were about six boys
whose fathers had died in the war and usually they all cried,
chins tucked in and shoulders shaking a little. Though "blubbing" was normally despised, it was regarded as fine for Mac-
Lean and the others to cry on this particular occasion.

A few minutes later the service was over and I went downstairs to meet my father. He lost no time in hurrying me into an
ancient taxi waiting outside and we rattled off to Great Fosters,
a ghastly mock-Tudor establishment not far off, where we
would while away the rest of the day. Even before we got into
the taxi my father seemed to have a furtive, slightly hangdog
air. Other parents seemed to be glaring at him. I surmised with
a sinking heart that he had somehow attracted unwelcome attention — not perhaps as bad as the times he would barrack the
actors in London theaters ("Perfectly sound tradition; Elizabe-
thans did it all the time") but still alarming.

In the taxi he confessed all. He had arrived at about ten to
eleven and had joined the other parents in the headmaster's
study. "The conversation was a bit stilted and after a bit I
thought I would try to jolly things along by telling them a couple
of funny stories." My father was a very good storyteller, throwing himself into the anecdotes, which were often long. He used
florid motions of his hands to accentuate important turns in the
narrative. "After a bit," he continued, "I noticed that the other
people didn't seem to be following my story with any enthusiasm. When I got to the punch line they were all looking down
and no one laughed at all."

"Oh Daddy, you *didn't*!"

"I'm afraid so." So he had told jokes all the way through the
two-minute silence — a silence no other parent would break
even in order to ask him to shut up, and meanwhile MacLean

and the others were weeping upstairs. Most of the parents knew
by now that Cockburn's father, Claud, was some sort of a Red
and here were their darkest fears confirmed, with the scoundrel
polluting the memory of the dead with his foul banter.

The train ambled along and the conductor cried, "Next stop
Ascot!" The station looked relatively unchanged. On the far side
of the main London road was Ascot race course. Ascot race
week loomed large on the school calendar. Fathers, magnificently arrayed in morning coats and top hats, mothers with
amazing summer confections on their heads, would arrive to
take children for picnics of cold salmon and strawberries in the
enclosure. All morning long on the Saturday of the big weekend
we could see those great summer hats of the women as they
drove in open cars to the race course a couple of miles up the
road.

But now it was October, the track was bare and the enclosure
empty. My taxi driver said that he had heard that Heatherdown
was to be sold for real-estate development once the film crew
had gone. The driveway, fringed with fateful rhododendrons,
looked much the same and at last I entered the front door.
Heatherdown had actually been built as a school just before the
First World War, unlike many of the prep schools round about
which were simply converted Victorian country houses with
maids' rooms converted into diminutive dormitories. All such
schools were divided into the boys' zone of activity — classrooms, dormitories and the like — and the headmaster's private
quarters. The room of concern to us was the headmaster's
study, thickly carpeted, fragrant with tobacco and terror. It was
here that we were summoned for interrogation and punishment. In exact evocation of Freud's essay on *Haemlichkeit* —
"homeliness" with a sinister and uncanny core — the study was
both the closest echo of distant home and a parent's love but
also the Colosseum for the unleashed superego. My own father
never beat me. The closest he ever got to it was saying once that
had any other father endured such injury (I had let down the
tires of his bicycle to stop him from going into town one evening), this other father would have thrashed his son savagely.
But here, hundreds of miles from the security of my own fa-

ther's study, was this ersatz study, inhabited by the father-substitute who did indeed — on a few occasions — beat me with a clothes brush, once for repeatedly trying to conceal from Matron the fact that I had again wet my bed.

It was here too that the headmaster — a bouncy, bantam cock of a man called Charles Warner — interrogated me fiercely about the reason for my father's lateness in paying the hefty school bills. I knew the reason: not enough money. But this seemed a humiliating confession and I blubbed copiously as Warner plowed on remorselessly about the need for financial promptness. At least he didn't beat me for that, unlike Mr. Squeers in *Nicholas Nickleby*: " 'I have had disappointments to contend against,' said Squeers, looking very grim, 'Bolder's father was two pound ten short. Where is Bolder?' 'Here he is, please Sir,' rejoined twenty officious voices. Boys are very like men to be sure. 'Come here, Bolder,' said Squeers. An unhealthy-looking boy, with warts all over his hands, stepped from his place to the master's desk, and raised his eyes imploringly to Squeers's face; his own quite white from the rapid beating of his heart. . . ."

When I read accounts of the early explorers surrounded by natives who "seemed friendly" but who suddenly "attacked without warning," I know just how those natives felt and I sympathize with them. To this day I have only to hear the words "X wants to see you in his office" to be thrown into the state of hatred and fear with which I used to approach Warner's study, knock on his door and hear that falsely jocose voice cry, "Come in." Sometimes as I entered to my doom his wife, Patsy, used to scuttle out, giving me a cheery Hello, though she and I both knew the somber nature of the occasion.

This fear and hatred has colored my relationship with authority, both privately and officially vested, and I count it as one of the major consequences of my education, just as my father's Micawberish struggle, pursued with heroic tenacity to virtually the very moment he died — he dictated to my mother a column for the *Irish Times* almost with his last breath — to keep clear of financial disaster greatly conditioned my attitude to credit.

Early in life in Ireland I learned to appreciate the color of the envelopes containing the day's mail. White envelopes were good. Brown ones weren't and my father would leave them up on the mantelpiece unopened. Over the months they would gradually get demoted from this high station to his study and then to the bottom drawer of a desk in his study. We would all laugh heartily over the form letter to creditors my father threatened to send: "Dear Sir, I am in receipt of your fourth communication regarding my outstanding account. Let me explain how I pay my bills. I throw them all into a large basket. Each year I stir the basket with a stick, take out four bills and pay them. One more letter from you and you're out of the game."

The whole school seemed silent as I walked toward Warner's study. Presumably they were filming elsewhere. I pushed open the door of his study. It was bare. Two film electricians were sitting on milk crates, drinking out of beer bottles. They said that the company was having lunch in the canteen out back.

I wandered upstairs and found myself facing the door of the school chapel. It used to have a thick curtain in front of it, as if to separate spiritual affairs from the coarse business of an English prep school. The curtain was gone and the door was ajar. Here I had begun my career as a choirboy, nicely done up in a sort of long red tunic and white surplice. I had a reedy alto. As the years progressed I rose to become a bass in the choir in Glenalmond — my public school. Thus, from the age of nine to the age of eighteen, my schoolmates and I had about thirty minutes of prayer each morning and each night — about three hundred hours of public worship a year. On Sundays, at Glenalmond, we had at least an hour each of matins and evensong. During these prayer-choked years I acquired an extensive knowledge of Scripture, of the Book of Common Prayer and of *Hymns Ancient and Modern.* It is one of the reasons I favor compulsory prayer at schools. A childish soul not inoculated with compulsory prayer is a soul open to any religious infection. At the end of my compulsory religious observances I was a thoroughgoing atheist, with a sufficient knowledge of Scripture to combat the faithful.

There was a hymnal still in one of the pews and I leafed through it. "As pants the hart for cooling stream / When heated in the chase . . ." This had always been popular, owing to the fervor with which one could hit the D in "cooo-ling." "Eternal

Father strong to save . . ." wasn't bad either, with its mournful
call to the Almighty: "Oh hear us when we cry to thee / For
those in peril on the sea." But the big hit each term was undoubtedly "Onward, Christian Soldiers," with Sir Arthur Sullivan's pugnacious tune. "At the sound of triumph," we sang
vaingloriously, "Satan's host doth flee; / On then, Christian so-
o-oldiers, / On to victoreee!" The general religious line at
Heatherdown was that Victory was more or less assured for one,
unless very serious blunders let Satan squeeze in under the
door. We did not spend much time worrying about damnation,
except for after a serious bout of cursing God's name on a dare
to see what would happen. I had once got a tummy ache after
cursing God and believed in Him for at least a week. I went on
leafing through the hymnal. Here was a particularly chipper
one, "All things bright and beautiful," with its reassuring verse
— omitted from most American hymnals, as I later discovered:

> The rich man in his castle,
> The poor man at his gate,
> God made them high and lowly,
> He ordered their estate.

The class system was never far away. My father said that his
own radical beliefs had come as much from the words of the
Magnificat as from the works of Marx and Lenin. You could see
why. Even when chanted dolefully as a canticle the words carried a serious charge:

> He hath scattered the proud in the imagination of their hearts;
> He hath put down the mighty from their seat
> And hath exalted the humble and meek;
> He hath filled the hungry with good things
> And the rich he hath sent empty away.

At Heatherdown Christ was depicted as a limp-wristed pre-
Raphaelite with tepid social democratic convictions, urging a
better world but shunning any robust means to achieve it. Ha-
bituated to this version of Christ, I was startled at Glenalmond
when the Bishop of Dundee, preaching for an hour one Sunday
evening, reported on his own personal conversations with
Christ from which it had emerged that He had powerful revo-

lutionary views. "He meant what He said," the Bishop roared. "The furrrst sh-aall be last, and the last sha-all be furrst!" I was all for this in principle, though the town boys — who presumably would go to the front of the line while I dropped back — frightened me greatly.

I went downstairs and found Daisy and the others in the canteen, which had once been the carpentry shop. I had half-expected coarse film hands, rabid with cocaine and intent on debauching the girls temporarily at their mercy. To the contrary, they seemed a proper and restrained lot. To make up for lost school time a teacher had been imported and she would barely allow Daisy to talk to me before hurrying her away to her books. Daisy quickly steered me back to the main school building, along a corridor, and then pointed up. There I was in my farewell school photograph, looking rather like Daisy and exactly the same age as she was now. My eye wandered along the row: Piggott-Brown, who later founded a fashionable clothes store called Browns in South Moulton St.; Walduck, Cordy-Simpson, Miller-Mundy, Lycett-Green. I gazed along the corridor and saw another, slightly less familiar face; that of Sebastian Yorke, Daisy's mother's first husband, who had gone to Heatherdown some five years before me.

Daisy was full of gossip about the school. It had closed very suddenly. Boys going home for the summer holidays had fully expected to return. Mr. Edwards, who had taken over from Warner, had suddenly decided to sell up. A rescue bid mounted by another master and parents had only just failed. Now local real-estate interests were about to take over and had already announced the school's closure. Heatherdown would cease to exist — unless perhaps as a private nursing home. The photographs — the institutional record, as it were — would be thrown on the garbage heap.

It was the work of a moment to take my own photograph down, along with Sebastian's and one of the art dealer and historian Ian Dunlop, of whom I had no memory at Heatherdown but who was a friend of mine in New York. "Daisy to makeup," a voice shouted and she hurried away. I wandered along the corridor. A cupboard door was ajar and I peered in. The books were large and dusty and after a moment I realized with a shock that I was looking at the collective sporting memory of Heatherdown across half a century: the detailed record of every game of cricket played by Heatherdown's First Eleven between 1952 and 1978. The records of soccer and rugby went back to 1935.

I pulled out *The Unrivalled Cricket Scoring Book* covering the years 1952 to 1956. A note on the cover said that Heatherdown had played 52, won 22, lost 11 and drawn 19. I opened it and stared down at two pages detailing a game played between Heatherdown and Ludgrove on June 26, 1954. Ludgrove had won easily, by eight wickets. I remembered the game vividly. Ludgrove had a very fast bowler. Here he was in the book — Jefferson. He was vast and hurled the cricket ball down the pitch with horrifying speed. Our champions went out to bat and trailed back almost at once, out for 0, a "duck." Then our captain, Watson. Out for a duck too. I was last man in, and walked out slowly. There was a thunder of Jefferson's feet, a hard object swooped like a swallow down the pitch, hit my bat and spun away. "Run," screamed Lawson-Smith from the other end and I scampered to the other wicket and safety. Lawson-Smith was out next ball. Here it all was in the book, Cockburn 1 not out; Heatherdown all out for nineteen. "Lost by 8 wickets," Warner's notation across the page said gloomily.

The Queen's second son, Andrew, had gone to Heatherdown in the early 1970s and I turned to the score book covering 1971 to 1974 to see how he had done. The prince, flanked in the First Eleven by such revered names in British financial history as Hambro and Kleinwort, seems to have had his best game against Scaitcliffe on May 19, 1973, when he had bowled and got three wickets at a cost of fourteen runs. But in a needle game against Ludgrove on June 7 of the same year he was bowled by Agar for a duck and Ludgrove won by four runs. I dare say the memory haunts him to this day, and — should he ever assume the throne — will no doubt affect his overall performance. I found his brother, Prince Edward, battling for Heatherdown four years later. He doesn't seem to have done much better.

I turned to the book filled with soccer and rugby scores. Warner had started filling in the exercise book in 1935. His writing did not change in over thirty years. His last entry was for 1965 at which point he must have dropped dead, because another, more childish hand starts with the Michaelmas term of that year. I was good at rugby football, being left-footed and thus having an inbuilt advantage if I played in the position known as "hooker." Here was our great season — the Lent term of 1954 — when we lost only one game. Because I had this aptitude for being a hooker in the "scrum" I could be regarded as "good at games," which was a great help at school. At my next school it meant that every other week we got in a bus and went off to Edinburgh or Aberdeen to play. At the age of eighteen I stopped playing rugby, stopped hunting at home in Ireland and never took any exercise ever again. It is as though, having had cold baths and gone for early morning runs for nearly ten years, one has paid in advance the physical rent check for the next thirty years.

Daisy came back from makeup in the school uniform called for in the script. It slightly reminded me of the uniform worn by the girls at Heathfield, a well-known prep school for girls right next door. My aunt had gone there in the early part of the century and almost the only other fact I knew about it was that David Niven had been expelled from Heatherdown — or said he had — for climbing over the Heathfield wall to steal a cabbage out of its garden. It seemed an odd piece of flora for a person who relished the reputation of a lady's man to pride himself on having stolen. I suppose he thought that no one would believe him if he had claimed to have stolen a rose. Heatherdown had absolutely no contact with Heathfield all those years I was there. Our school was very definitely in the non-coed tradition, holding to the view that juxtaposition of the sexes would lead instantly to debauch. Aside from the Heathfield peril, women were successfully kept at bay. Heatherdown was not as purely masculine as Mount Athos. There were Patsy Warner and Matron, a steely creature who maintained an insensate interest in our bodily functions but who — perhaps for reasons of what Herbert Marcuse later called hyperrepressive desublimation (rare was the week in which she did not seize my private parts in a chill grip as part of some diagnostic test) — did not inflame our imaginations. There were the older sisters who came and were ogled on Visitors' Day, and that was about it.

Daisy reported that Gavin Millar had agreed that I could watch a scene being shot and that although my presence might make her feel awkward she did not really mind. I followed her up to the old school library, where the technicians were setting up the next scene.

I had read the script of *Secrets*. It was about bonding rituals among teenage girls, and a great many scenes consisted of Daisy and a couple of her schoolmates parodying Masonic rituals. The scene in preparation was simple enough. It involved the same girls making moderate nuisances of themselves during a Latin class. I waited, eyeing the film crew. As always with movies, the setup went on interminably, and my attention wandered to the shelves of the library. The books seemed to be mostly the same as in my day: G. A. Henty, W. E. Johns, Baroness Orczy, W. W. Jacobs, Sapper, Jules Verne, John Buchan, P. G. Wodehouse, and for more sophisticated tastes, Nevil Shute and A. J. Cronin.

So far as politics goes these authors were all stoutly counter-revolutionary, whether it was some lad in Henty trying to thwart the Indian Mutiny, a Buchan hero heading off a black nation-alist upsurge in *Prester John* or Bulldog Drummond and his "Black Gang" murdering Bolsheviks. Drummond could break a chap's neck like a twig and laugh while doing it. He dropped Henry Lakington into an acid bath, telling him as he did so that "the retribution is just." No author in our library had much time for the French Revolution or for Napoleon. Henty did not care for them and neither did C. S. Forester. The Scarlet Pimpernel devoted his entire professional life — if "professional" could be linked to so quintessential an amateur as Sir Percy, who yawned a lot and laughed down from under lazy eyelids — to the out-witting of the Committee of Public Safety and the stalwart rev-olutionary M. Chauvelin. And then there was Dickens too, with *The Tale of Two Cities* and the great sacrifice of Sidney Carton. In my case this ideological saturation bombing did not have much effect. One did a form of double-entry political bookkeep-ing — hoping for the victory of Sir Percy, Hornblower, Hannay or whoever, while simultaneously approving the deeds of St. Just, Danton, or Napoleon.

ALEXANDER COCKBURN 85

And of course the library permitted us to seek in literary guise
the woman we were denied in bodily form. In Henty and Verne,
women barely existed. Orczy tried harder. Sir Percy Blakeney
concealed beneath his foppish nonchalance the tenderest emotions toward the Lady Marguerite and would, after she had
swept away, lower his lips to the stone balustrade and stair
where her hand and foot had rested but a moment before. In
Sapper and Buchan women had literary utility as good little
troopers — like Matron, only younger. The moment of greatest
sexual tension in Buchan is when Hannay realizes from the
effeminate nature of furniture that Von Stumm is homosexual
("I was reminded of certain practices not unknown in the German General Staff") and, in a panic bordering on hysteria,
knocks him down.

Nevil Shute and H. E. Bates, powerfully represented in the
school library, permitted certain intimacies. There was a strong
scene in the latter's *The Purple Plain* in which the hero nearly
persuades the Burmese girl Anna to bathe naked with him. In
the end after many sufferings he gets into bed with her, with
the imprimatur of Mrs. McNab. I wandered along the shelves
and found the book — no doubt the same one I fingered excit-
edly thirty years before. Here it was: "Go in and lie down and
sleep with her. Nothing will be said in this house about that sort
of sleep together." *What* sort of sleep? I spent a lot of time
puzzling about this. Couples in those sorts of books used to
embrace, then there would be some tactful punctuation and
then, "Hours later they awoke." I used to think sex and sleep
were indivisible, just as everyone at my next school thought that
one's virginity would expire just as soon as one contrived to be
alone with a French girl. Words would be unnecessary, given
the torrid and impulsive morals of these women, though just to
be on the safe side we would complacently rehearse the words
Voulez-vous coucher avec moi. It was curious, in the late sixties, to
meet French adolescents rushing eagerly the other way, certain
that Swinging London would be the answer to their problems.

It's hard to know where these illusions about French morals
started. There was the French kiss and the French letter. Brothels were legal over there too. In Ireland there were no legal
brothels, no legal French letters and the rules of censorship

prevailing at that time did not permit French kissing in films. The great heads on the screen of Horgan's cinema would approach with lips puckered and then suddenly spring apart, lips relaxing after raptures excised by the scissors of the Catholic hierarchy. It was all very frustrating and I would retire to the adventures of my great hero, the shy, brilliant, and — to women — irresistibly attractive Horatio Hornblower. Who could forget the long-delayed embrace with Lady Barbara Leighton in *Beat to Quarters* or the spasm of passion with the Vicomtesse Marie de Graçay in *Flying Colors*? There were three copies of this book still on the Heatherdown shelves and soon I found the well-worn page: "It was madness to yield to the torrent of impulses let loose, but madness was somehow sweet. They were inside the room now, and the door was closed. There was sweet, healthy, satisfying flesh in his arms. There were no doubts, no uncertainties; no mystic speculation. Now blind instinct could take charge, all the bodily urges of months of celibacy. Her lips were ripe and rich and ready, the breasts which he crushed against him were hillocks of sweetness. . . . Just as another man might have given way to drink . . . so Hornblower numbed his own brain with lust and passion." C. S. Forester wasn't much given to this sort of thing, but he knew how to lay it on when he had to.

Sex was mostly literary at Heatherdown. Homosexuality, at least in my cohort, was unknown. My own psychosexual development was erratic. I liked to dress up in the holidays and would occasionally come down to dinner in long dress and carefully applied makeup. Years later David McEwen described to me the scene in some grim Scottish fortress when the son and heir of the house, then in his twenties, swept into dinner in long dress and white gloves. The aged butler muttered apologetically into the ear of the stricken father, "It's no' what I laid oot for him, my lorrrd."

Whatever unease my parents may have felt at such appearances would have, had they known of it, been balanced by the news of my engagement to Adrienne Hamilton. At the age of ten I proposed and was accepted in the course of a stay with Adrienne at Blarney Castle, owned at the time by her mother.

Next term at Heatherdown Adrienne's cousin Henry Combe made a laughing stock out of me by publicizing the fact that I was "in love" with Adrienne. This was thought to be very ridiculous. Our engagement was canceled. I never forgave her for the betrayal and the experience no doubt has powerfully colored my relations with women ever since. When next I met her, thirty years later in New York, she laughed prettily when I reminded her of her treachery. No matter. They laughed lightly at the Count of Monte Cristo too, when he reminded them of a long-forgotten fellow called Dantès.

I put down the Hornblower. By now the technicians had set up the scene. My daughter was sitting more or less exactly in the position that I was long ago when Warner had announced that all boys in the school — some fifty-five — were doing well, except for one. This one was slacking. "Cockburn," Warner was a great finger-crooker, and his finger now crooked horribly. "Come here, boy." He had a habit of getting one by the short hairs right behind the ear and pulling up sharply. "Some of us aren't working hard enough, are we?" Jerk. "No, Sir." "Some of us are going to work harder, aren't we?" Another savage jerk. "Yes, Sir." A final jerk and Cockburn, blubbing with pain and humiliation, stumbled back to his place.

Gavin Millar kindly gave me a script. "Miss Johnson" is teaching a Latin class and the girls are not behaving. Millar cries "Action" and the girls, Daisy included, start making furtive animal noises. Amid their snickers Miss Johnson tries doggedly to explain the structure and importance of the Latin grammatical construction known as the ablative absolute. Finally, peering irritably at one fractious girl, she says with heavy sarcasm, "Louise having been blessed with such talent, we don't have to bother to teach her," and goes on to outline the benefits of a classical education. "Ablative absolutes could be the key to your whole future. Think about it, Louise." Louise tries to look thoughtful and Millar says, "Cut."

Could it be that my classical education, commenced at Heatherdown, is at last going to be of some immediate, practical utility?

I raised my hand and saw, out of the corner of my eye, Daisy freeze with horror and embarrassment. It was clear to her that I was about to make a public ass of myself and, by extension, of her too.

"Gavin," I said quietly, "I don't suppose it matters, but your scriptwriter doesn't know Latin." I saw a tough-looking young woman bridle at this and realized that Noella Smith, script-writer, was in the room. I pressed on. "The clause 'Louise hav-ing been blessed with such talent' is really in apposition to 'her,' which in turn is the object of 'teach' — all of which makes it a participial accusative construction, not an ablative absolute. You could make it better by omitting the final 'her,' which would sequester the Louise clause as an ablative absolute."

Millar recognized superior fire power and "Miss Johnson" was instructed to drop the final "her." She kept forgetting and the scene was reshot five times. Millar pointed out the substantial sum my quibble had cost them. Daisy, having concluded that I had not made a major fool out of myself or her, hastened away to makeup and wardrobe, and the room emptied. Still ponder-ing ablative absolutes, I looked along the library shelves till I found *Latin Course for Schools, Part One*, by L. A. Wilding, first published in 1949.

"The study of a foreign language," wrote Mr. Wilding in his introduction, "is an exciting matter; it is like a key that will open many doors. . . . By a knowledge of Latin we are introduced to a great people, the Romans. The Romans led the world as men of action; they built good roads, made good laws, and organised what was in their time almost world-wide government and citi-zenship. At their best, too, they set the highest examples of honour, loyalty and self-sacrifice."

I leafed through the book. Exercise 65: " 'By means of justice and kindness Agricola wins over the natives of Britain.' Trans-late." This must be Tacitus. Tacitus, married to General Gnaeus Julius Agricola's daughter, wrote a toadying biography of his father-in-law. Wilding's textbook was strewn with what I could now see was heavy propaganda for the benefits of imperial con-quest, whether Roman or British. Exercise 171: "Render into Latin, 'It is just,' they say, 'to surrender our city to the Romans: such men know how to keep faith even in war. They have con-quered us, not by force, but by justice, and we and the Roman

people will hand down a good example to the human race.' "
Exercise 65: "Render into Latin: 'By means of justice and kindness Agricola wins over the natives of Britain. He then hastens
beyond Chester towards Scotland. He rouses his troops to battle
and to victory. At first Agricola wastes the land, then he displays
to the natives his moderation.' "

It is summer in 1952 and Mr. Toppin had us penned in, even
though the bell has gone for morning break. We are in Latin
class and Mr. Toppin is trying to give us a sense of occasion.
"This is the speech of Calgacus to his troops before the battle at
Graupian Hill in A.D. 84. Calgacus is the name Tacitus gives the
Scottish general. *Hodie pro patria adhuc libera . . .*' Cockburn?
'Today . . .' " "Today you will fight for a country still free
against the Romans. . . ." "Good. *Patriam vestram in dextris vestris
portatis*'?" "You carry your country in your right hand. . . ."

Wilding left it in no doubt, in his simplified and polite version
of Tacitus, that the Roman victory at Mons Graupius was a good
thing. Ten thousand Scots fell that day, the blood of kerns flowing in the heather near Inverness, not so far from where I was
born. The Romans slaughtered till their arms were tired. Night,
as Tacitus put it, was jubilant with triumph and plunder. The
Scots, scattering amid the grief of men and women, abandoned
their homes and set them on fire. The day after, bleak and wet,
disclosed more fully the lineaments of triumph: silence everywhere, lonely hills, houses smoldering to heaven.

Resolute to favor Roman imperialism over British nationalism
— Viking imperialism was a different matter — Wilding sup-
pressed the eloquence of Calgacus's appeal to his troops, as
conceived by Tacitus. Back in London the next day I looked it
up in the Loeb translation: "Here at the world's end, on its last
inch of liberty, we have lived unmolested to this day. . . ." Calgacus gestures down the hill to where the Romans — in actual
fact Provençal French, Spaniards and Italians — stand with
their German auxiliaries: "Harriers of the world, now that earth
fails their all-devastating hands — they probe even the sea: if
their enemy have wealth, they have greed; if he be poor, they
are ambitious; East nor West has glutted them; alone of mankind they behold with the same passion of concupiscence waste
and want alike. To plunder, butcher, steal, these things they

misname empire: they make a desolation and they call it peace."

Ubi solitudinem faciunt, pacem appellant. They make a desolation and they call it peace. The phrase has echoed down the ages as the tersest condemnation of Rome. Nothing of this in Wilding.

Those were the days in the early 1950s when the British Empire was falling rapidly apart. On Sundays boys at Heatherdown had to write a weekly letter home ("Dear Mummy and Daddy, I am very well. How are you . . .") and many of the envelopes at our school were addressed to army posts in Kenya, Malaya, Aden, Cyprus and other outposts of shriveling empire. At school I would hear grim tales of the Kenyan Mau Mau and then go home to hear my father consider such events in a very different way.

Both my father and I, forty years apart, studied classics. A significant portion of this study was spent considering the birth and practice of democracy in Athens in the fifth century B.C. It seemed to be the consensus of our teachers that between fifth-century Athens, the senate under the Roman Republic and nineteenth- and twentieth-century Westminster, nothing much of interest by way of political experiment had occurred, and that the virtues and glories of ancient Greece and modern Britain were essentially the same.

There was a problem, of course. One of the first words to be found in Wilding was *servus* meaning "slave." In our Greek primer the word *doulos* soon obtruded itself. Our schoolmasters could not conceal from us that Athenian "democracy" was practiced on the backs of hundreds and thousands of these *servi* or *douloi*. The fact of slavery was acknowledged, but with that acknowledgment the matter was closed. Thus the statement "Athenian democracy was a great and noble achievement" was accompanied by the footnote, "Athenian democracy was based on slavery." But the footnote remained a footnote and two people being given a ruling-class education in Britain at either end of the first half of the twentieth century were taught that democratic achievement and slavery were not mutually contradictory. This sort of instruction was helpful if one was to continue to run the British Empire with a clear conscience. (Twentieth-century British classics teachers were not the only people to remain somewhat silent on the matter of slavery in the ancient world. The great classical historian G.E.M. de Ste. Croix has written that he knows "of no general, outright condemnation of slavery inspired by a Christian outlook before the petition of the Mennonites in Germantown in Pennsylvania in 1668.")

I left the library and walked down to the old dining room, now changed by the set designers into a school laboratory. Daisy was hurrying through, on her way to another bout of tuition. At her London day school she had decided against Latin and in favor of German, despite some dutiful lectures from me on the merits, even if only from the vantage point of etymological comprehension, of a classical grounding. This was, for the second time in my life, my last day at school, though devoid of that immense spiritual and physical rapture connected to "ends of term" back in the fifties. In those days I would go up to London on the school train and there be met by my father who would take me off to a treat, usually lunch at some restaurant such as Rules, Simpsons, or Chez Victor. Once we went out with Gilbert Harding, a noted radio "personality" of the day. This "personality" was of the choleric Englishman, perpetually raging against poor service and so forth. We were never able to get through lunch because Harding, in order to keep this income-yielding "personality" at full stretch, would burst forth after about ten minutes with curses at management and waiters and we would have to leave. Then, later in the day, my father and I would board the boat train at Paddington in the company of about four thousand other Irish passengers. It was so crowded that once my father could not even get his hand into his upper pocket to get out a whiskey bottle and had to ask the man his other side to help him.

In these more sophisticated times Daisy and I discussed our Christmas rendezvous in New York after her term was over. I had hoped to persuade the set photographer to take a picture of her standing in front of the same rhododendron bush as I, when I had my farewell photograph taken. But by now the novelty of the old Heatherdown-boy-with-daughter-in-film was wearing off. I remembered how revisiting fathers, trying to find the initials they had carved in their school desks, had seemed vaguely ridiculous to us and decided not to outlast my welcome. The taxi took me off down the drive past the empty swimming pool, and I had carefully on my knee my old portrait, saved by my daughter from the wrecker's ball.

GERALD EARLY

The Passing of Jazz's Old Guard: Remembering Charles Mingus, Thelonious Monk, and Sonny Stitt

FROM THE KENYON REVIEW

Music is your experience, your thoughts, your wisdom. If you don't live it, it won't come out of your horn.
  — CHARLIE PARKER [1]

For, while the tale of how we suffer, and how we are delighted, and how we may triumph is never new, it always must be heard. There isn't any other tale to tell, it's the only light we've got in all this darkness.
  — JAMES BALDWIN, "Sonny's Blues" [2]

I SUPPOSE that jazz listening and prizefight watching are my two most passionate avocations, and this is largely so because the origins of my aesthetic urges are in the black working class. At times these avocations are a bit difficult to reconcile: boxers like to train in the early afternoon and jazz musicians like to jam late

---

[1] Charlie Parker, *Hear Me Talkin' to Ya: The Story of Jazz as Told by the Man Who Made It,* ed. Nat Shapiro and Nat Hentoff (New York: Dover Publications, 1966), p. 405.
[2] James Baldwin, *Going to Meet the Man* (New York: Dell paperback, 1976), p. 121.

at night. But I think they are, on the whole, more deeply related than one might suspect. They are such direct expressions, not of emotion, but rather of *emotive power,* and they are such risk-taking endeavors. The most vibrant memories I bear from my childhood are of my uncles crowded around a very small black-and-white television, drinking beer and watching the Gillette Friday Night Fights; my aunts would be in another room listening to old jazz records such as Lionel Hampton's "Flying Home" and Billie Holiday's "Don't Explain." The men would join them later to play Charlie Parker records and lots of rhythm and blues stuff. I liked those Friday nights as much as I have ever liked anything.

The person I associate most with these remembrances of Fridays past is my Uncle G., who has, for most of his life, struck me as a wonderfully wayward, perennially playful man. I learned a few years ago that he has cancer of the prostate gland. This struck me as being the rather absurd sort of insult that fate is very likely to add to a life that has seen its fair share of injury. He lost his eldest son in a street gang fight that took place nearly in front of his home. One of his daughters became pregnant while still in high school, and he has fought a very unsuccessful battle to keep himself and his ten children off the welfare roll, a pitched struggle where his embattled efforts have been to keep his dignity and eat at the same time, a trick as demanding for the working class as the childish game of patting your head and rubbing your stomach simultaneously.

I remember my Uncle G. on those Friday nights, fresh from being kicked out of the U.S. Army and the war effort in Korea — a slim, muscular man who loved to dance and laughed as raucously as any human being I have ever heard. And he loved to tell stories about his heroes, the jazzmen and the rhythm and blues cats of the underworld. It was he who told me about Count Basie's drummer, Jo Jones, throwing a cymbal at the feet of a fumbling Charlie Parker and shouting, "Get off the stand, motherfucker, you can't play." "Of course, after that, Bird went to the shed," Uncle G. continued, "and he learned how to blow that horn. He did what a man gotta do." I often wonder what it is that men must do and what happens to them when, as in the case of my uncle, the dilemmas of fatherhood and the social demands of manhood seem impossible not only to accommodate but even to bear painfully. When I learned that my uncle, who had been (and, I think, always wanted to be) a gloriously vigorous man with a cocky radiance of power, had cancer, I realized, with a certain formidable, bristling force, how precarious manhood of any sort is in this world: what a strangely perishing thing it is.

Part I: "I'm always making a comeback . . ."

Now they are nearly all gone — the old guard, the great black male presence which coalesced around bebop and post-bop: Booker Ervin, Lee Morgan, the latter-day Coleman Hawkins, Charlie Parker, Tadd Dameron, Clifford Brown, Bud Powell, Paul Chambers, the early-day John Coltrane, Charlie Christian, Wilbur Ware, and — most recently — Charles Mingus, Thelonious Monk, and Sonny Stitt. What a sense of loss to be a witness to the tail end, the burning out forever of that magnificent light of great music with its tough carnality and its depth of telling resonance that made not only storytellers but also heroes of its practitioners. They were the last heroes of jazz; never again will there be the likes of Dexter Gordon and Wardell Gray — hair slicked hard, big pants blowing in the wind, hats cocked to the side, pointed-toe shoes walking in rhyme and rhythm with the corner boys — batting on their tenor saxes in an endless version of "The Steeplechase." Never again will there be a watering hole like Minton's Playhouse where the experimentation in sound led to bebop and modern jazz. Although Monk once said that he "had no particular feeling that anything new was being built there," the stories are legion about how weird Monk, Parker, Dizzy Gillespie, Kenny Clarke, and others played to scare away the unhip. As Gillespie himself put it: " . . . Thelonious Monk and I began to work out some complex variations on chords and the like, and we used them at night at Minton's to scare away the no-talent guys."

Oh, those young black cats — all in their twenties, full of new ideas, and filled to the point of disgust with the virulent practice of racism as the social norm in World War II America — were

more than a little aware of what they were doing. As Amiri
Baraka (LeRoi Jones) wrote:

> Bop also carried with it a distinct element of social protest, not only
> in the sense that it was music that seemed antagonistically non-
> conformist, but also that the musicians who played it were loudly out-
> spoken about who they thought they were. "If you don't like it, don't
> listen," was the attitude. . . . These musicians seemed no longer to
> want to be thought of merely as "performers" in the Old Cotton Club
> — yellow hiney sense, but as musicians.[3]

Nowadays, young black musicians are as thoroughly trained
as a formal education can make one, and they pontificate, as
Yale-educated pianist Anthony Davis does, upon the death of
traditional improvisation. As Mercer Ellington put it: "Things
ain't what they used to be." But I do not wish to imply that the
golden era of jazz occurred before I was born, that now we are
experiencing merely the measured, misdirected march of a period of decline and decadence in a once noble art form. I firmly
believe that extensive formal education has created a core of
musicians who are generally better players than the old guys.
Younger musicians such as Wynton Marsalis, Arthur Blythe,
and Jay Hoggard are playing music which is as fine as any that
preceded it, and many of the younger men pay more than casual homage to their elders. Yet it must not be forgotten that
what makes the old bebop cats so vital in understanding post–
World War II Afro-American and American culture is not only
that they made wonderful music under less than ideal conditions but also that they bore witness to the terrors and anxieties
of the young black male coming of psychological age in America. Bebop was a mass performance of a male identity crisis.

But let us start here: to paraphrase James Baldwin, unless a
black artist lives as long as Eubie Blake, in which instance he
becomes a "cherished institution," then his death is bound to be
untimely and tragic. We have no trouble understanding this
when an artist dies quite young and accidentally as did Jimi
Hendrix or old-time rhythm and blues star, Johnny Ace, whose

---

[3] Amiri Baraka, *Black Music* (New York: William Morrow & Co., 1970), p. 23.

death in the early fifties caused many young black women, my mother included, to weep in the streets. We will even accept this when an artist dies quite unexpectedly in early middle age as did Rahsaan Roland Kirk. It is possibly a bit more difficult to see this point when an artist dies sick, broken, and at an advanced age, as did Coleman Hawkins and Ben Webster. But it must be understood that the latter is, in truth, the most untimely and rudely tragic of all. The black public performer never retires from the scene; his deterioration becomes the spectacle of a bitter public witness. The images of alcohol-ravaged Ben Webster unable to negotiate the steps to the bandstand and of a painfully ill Kenny Dorham being slowly poisoned by failing kidneys and unable to make even an easy run on his horn make me think that jazz musicians — particularly black jazz musicians because they, more than any other artists in our culture, symbolize the psychotic martyr and his attendant dubious honor in the backwater of the American imagination — that these men are destined or were destined to enact their fall as well as their rise. The tragedy of this role entails personifying that "sickness unto death" that has generally become a wretched but ineluctable cultural ritual for many black artists as they writhe in front of their audience. Much of jazz music till the seventies was performed by sick men.

Thelonious Monk, Charles Mingus, and Sonny Stitt were not particularly old at the time of their deaths. Indeed, both Mingus and Stitt were under sixty, and Monk was just a few years over that mark. Two of them were too sick to be able to perform publicly anymore and had, truly, spent their last few public years playing while quite ill. Stitt was still performing until his death but, although he was still able to play well, he had, in recent years, lost his stamina, a trademark of his greatness. I do not wish to imply that this sort of ghastly edge to the jazzer's public life is unique to blacks; the very different, strangely illuminating, slightly repulsive deaths of white alto saxophonists Paul Desmond and Art Pepper would deny such an implication. But I do think that the deaths of black jazz artists in general and of these three men of genius in particular are especially poignant and deeply meaningful. By this, I mean that the deaths of Monk, Mingus, and Stitt are in some spiritual and culturally relevant way tied to our complex fate, the magnificent curse of being a black American.

Each of these men lived well beyond the period of his greatest work. Each represented a different but major aspect of the jazz music that grew out of the forties: Mingus as the composer who learned from the best in jazz and classical music without resorting to "third stream" fusion; Monk as the composer who knew nothing but black music; and Stitt as the popular disseminator of the virtuosic technique of the language of bop.

It was nearly unbearable to hear about the decline of Mingus and Monk and the faltering of Stitt in their later years. And their deaths were untimely and tragic not only because they meant the closing of the book on a period of great music and the passing from earth of a type of masculine vitality not bound to resurge any time soon, but also, and most important, because these men died without having the luxury of ceasing to work. They saw their genius stretched out to the point of softness and serene decay; they were not able to die secure in what they had accomplished or in the recognition of that accomplishment. They will always be the old men who lost it. The black male performer is he who in youth conquered adverse circumstances, and he who in old age succumbed to them. There is a tacit admission, a downright undermining and unnerving confession of failure in the careers of most black jazz artists if they live long enough.

It occurs to me that with the deaths of Mingus, Monk, and Stitt in the last few years, I have an opportunity to talk about the passing of great black artists who had lived beyond the term of their greatness, a rare occasion for any writer.

I will talk about Mingus's autobiography, Thelonious Monk's innocence, and the color of Sonny Stitt's horn.

Part II: "But nobody ever tells me where I've been."

1. CHARLES MINGUS: A CALIFORNIA YANKEE STROLLING ON THE GANGES

"He went around with a lot of cheap white women. It was a disgusting book." So said Mari Evans, noted poet, literary critic, and musician, in referring to Charles Mingus's autobiography, *Beneath the Underdog.* It was said quite calmly, so calmly that one would hardly have suspected the depth of bitterness that threatened the chitchatty blandness of this dinner conversation like an undertow. The opinion was not taken lightly then, nor is it now. Evans is a sensible enough person not to be squeamish over the details in Mingus's book simply because they are graphically rehearsed. At the core of this complaint is the pathetic outrage that many black women feel when they discover that some black men prefer blondes. I call this sort of emotion pathetic not to denigrate the scope and intensity of the anguish but to say clearly that the men who generate this feeling simply are not worth such painfully wrought attention. In the end, all of us, black and white, are fairly shoddy or positively uninteresting as sexual beings.

The swirling dispute about Mingus and his relationship with white women did not die with his death. Shortly before his death he arranged to have Joni Mitchell do an album of his songs to which she would supply the lyrics. The album was released under the title of "Mingus," and while it was his most successful commercial venture, it was not, in the end, even his album. It was released under Joni Mitchell's name. Not everyone was pleased with the accolades the album received on the review pages of *Downbeat* magazine. Vi Redd, a black singer and saxophonist, wrote a letter to the editor which read in part:

> What is all this madness about non-singer Joni Mitchell? Who needs her wailing (which sounds like it's emanating from a maternity ward) to validate the artistry of the giant that Charles Mingus was?

In Ms. Redd's letter, the bitterness reaches an almost hysterical

pitch, and it is a bitterness which is unconsciously directed at
Mingus and not at Joni Mitchell at all. Like an injured adolescent, she angrily, outrageously asks how dare he allow a white
woman to be the instrument through which he should attempt
to reach a wider audience. But what black woman pop singer
would have been interested in recording an album of Mingus's
songs? Diana Ross? Dionne Warwick? Aretha Franklin? It is
quite likely that they would not have touched Mingus's material.
When I read Ms. Redd's letter in *Downbeat* a few years ago, I
recalled something my mother told me when I was a child. She
had seen blues singer Joe Williams perform at a cabaret the
night before and she was infuriated. She said she hated him and
would not see or listen to him again.

"He sang a song called 'I Don't Want No Monkey-faced
Woman,'" she said disdainfully. "And what women do you
think he was talking about? Colored women, that's who."

But Mari Evans's comment is, finally, not misplaced. It is Mingus himself who makes his sex life the dominant feature of his
autobiography, and it is he who gives the impression that he has
slept with every white woman from Maine to Texas.

"I think the book is meant to be a put-on," I replied to Ms.
Evans, leaning back in my chair and thinking to myself what a
great musician Mingus was. He had achieved something that
few other jazz musicians were capable of: he absorbed the les-
sons of Duke Ellington, America's greatest composer. Mingus
was a peerless bassist and he, in that regard, would rank alongside Jimmy Blanton, Slam Stewart, Scott Le Faro, Paul Chambers, Wilbur Ware, and Al Stinson. But Mingus's real importance as a jazz musician is in the realm of composition. He was
second only to Ellington as a composer. His great songs, "Good-
bye Old Pork Pie Hat," "Song with Orange," "Fables of Faubus,"
"Mingus Fingers," "Better Get It in Your Soul," and "Pithecan-
thropus Erectus," were all suffused with Ellington without
being derivative of the master. He was able to use avant-garde
elements in his works without sounding like someone making
random noise with kitchen utensils as so many of the young
black musicians of the late sixties did. John Coltrane, Ornette
Coleman, and Albert Ayler would have profited much from
recording some of Mingus's tunes. And, of course, some of the

best musicians in jazz played in various Mingus bands: Eric Dolphy, Ted Curson, Jimmy Knepper, Jaki Byard, John Handy, Jackie McLean, Max Roach, and Rahsaan Roland Kirk, whose stunt of playing three reed instruments at one time brings to mind such turn of the century black musicians as Wilbur C. Sweatman and Horace George. Ah, Mingus, I thought, your music makes up for whatever shortcomings you possessed. Indeed, your music is so glorious that I can be generous and excuse the sins of a thousand other men as well. Mingus, if I were God, your music would have made it possible for a thousand sinners to enjoy the celestial palace when they deserved to burn in hell.

Admittedly, *Beneath the Underdog* is a strange book, not the usual jazz musical memoir about travels on the road and the struggle for recognition. One is struck by the similarity between Mingus's book and Chester Himes's autobiography: neither talks very directly or extensively about the life of a practicing artist.

The one immediate distinction about Mingus in comparison to other jazz musicians of his era that the reader is made aware of is that he was not a dope addict. This is quite a noteworthy fact when one considers that so many musicians around him were. Mingus was as self-absorbed as any other autobiographer but, since Mingus was not addicted to drugs, one learns that he was largely obsessed with the nature of his sanity. He was more afraid of going crazy than of nearly anything else, which probably explains why he wrote such a self-consciously psychoanalytic book.

The book opens with Mingus talking about his three selves, a tongue-in-cheek way of saying that if he is a divided, irrational self, so is the concept of the Christian God. The true nature of his irrationality emerges when he shouts to his psychologist: "I am more of a man than any dirty white cocksucker! I *did* fuck twenty-three girls in one night, including the boss's wife!" For Mingus, sanity is tied to his idea of manhood, and manhood is tied to sex. The only way that Mingus can prove that he is better than a white man is through sex: one of two avenues of expression left open to him as a black man. Far from being unique, Mingus opens his book by making himself a psychological par-

adigm for every black man. The irrational nature of the black
man is largely the result of possessing too many dimensions, too
many selves to fit into the roles white America has proscribed
for him. His energy is, therefore, dammed up into very confin-
ing modes of expression. Mingus has three selves, yet there are
only two possible roles for him: a pimp or a jazz musician. The
artistic outlaw and the sexual outlaw become, for Mingus, equivalent roles: each provides entertainment for clients who can
pay. What Mingus is really railing against in his book is the fact
that the black male's heart, mind, and gonads are commodities
of exchange in an immoral marketplace. In a sense, sex has
become art for the black male in both his emotional needs and
expressive capacity for it. It is through sex that the black male
can have moments of being human. And art has become sex not
only in the very origin of the word *jazz* (to copulate) but also
because it is through this music that Mingus is able to attract
women. Jazz becomes the call of the sexual wilds; the nightclub
becomes the place where one can act out one's sexual fantasies.

At this point, Mingus's autobiography may sound a bit too
consciously clinical. Recalling Erik Erikson's definition for patienthood "as a sense of imposed suffering, of an intense need
for cure," the reader realizes that Mingus's book is the descriptive journey of his own patienthood from the book's opening
with a dialogue between Mingus and his psychologist to its culmination when Mingus succeeds in checking himself into the
psychiatric ward of Bellevue. That scene, as Mingus retells it, of
his attempt to be placed in Bellevue is hilarious in a dark and
horrible way, and it puts one in mind of other jazz musicians
who have been "treated" as criminals or diseased persons in
institutions: Charlie Parker, Billie Holiday, Tadd Dameron,
Bud Powell, Thelonious Monk, and Lester Young.

The four major black male characters in the book — Mingus's
father, Buddy Colette's father, Billy Bones the pimp, and Fats
Navarro, the tragic trumpeter known as "Fat Girl" because he
was overweight and had a high-pitched voice — all seem a bit
contrived as the father and older brother figures whom Mingus
seeks. The conflation of his white lover, Donna, and his black
wife, Lee-Marie, into the composite character he calls Donnalee
(after a Charlie Parker composition) seems a bit too much like

the fulfillment of a black male's sexual fantasy. All of this business with both the men and the women seems too symbolic of
Mingus's state of patienthood to be very useful as literary autobiography or as trenchant psychoanalysis. And Mingus is striving mightily for both. This little volume is fraught, burdened
really, with the self-conscious weight of its own significance.

But Mingus makes clear that his concern is not only with
patienthood but also with sainthood. Or perhaps, for Mingus,
patienthood and sainthood amount to the same thing. Freud
was always "struck by the resemblance between what are called
obsessive acts in neurotics and those religious observances by
means of which the faithful give expression to their piety." Mingus is something of a mystic, and the movement of the book
from the West (Mingus was raised in the Watts section of Los
Angeles) to the East (the book reaches another culmination with
Mingus's arrival in New York) is emblematic of his spiritual
concerns. Mingus says in various parts of the book:

> He was busy reading everything he could find in the library that went
> beyond his Christian Sunday School training — karma yoga, theoso-
> phy, reincarnation, Vedants — and sitting on park benches he often
> became so engrossed in finding God that he forgot about shining
> shoes. [Mingus often refers to himself in the third person throughout
> the book.][4]

> . . . I hope to God I can really love before it's too late . . . [5]

> Yes, and we got no directions or visions from the modern holy men
> who are growing in doubt of themselves.[6]

> Someday one of us put-down, outcast makers of jazz music should
> show those church-going clock punchers that people like Monk and
> Bird are dying for what they believe.[7]

Mingus's infantile search for religion and the core of spiritual
matters was not unusual for a black jazz musician, particularly a

[4] Charles Mingus, *Beneath the Underdog: His World as Composed by Mingus*, ed. Nel
King (New York: Knopf, 1971), p. 51.
[5] Ibid., p. 215.
[6] Ibid., p. 257.
[7] Ibid., p. 252.

jazz musician who was a young adult during the forties and fifties. Most looked toward the East for inspiration and many, as a result, became Muslim. Others, such as Mingus, free-lanced superficially with the terms of Hinduism and Buddhism. It is quite apparent why young black men of this era would be attracted to these religions: they were rebelling against their western (white) background; these religions gave a sense of history and ethnicity to a group of terribly deracinated men; finally, these young jazzers were able to achieve a sense of recognition — they suffered from a kind of double anonymity of being neglected by the white western world because they were black and being ignored by an essentially grasping, wealth-obsessed society because they were artists. This last became something like the burden of invisibility compounded by the ache of alienation. It is no wonder that these men were deeply neurotic. One wonders why many of them did not go stark raving mad.

Mingus died on January 5, 1979, in Mexico where he was being treated for amyotrophic lateral sclerosis (Lou Gehrig's disease). He was cremated and his ashes were scattered along the Ganges River in a Hindu ceremony. Presumably all of this was done on instructions Mingus left behind. So, all the spiritual seeking in the book is undoubtedly meant to be a sincere representation of the anxieties of the inner man. I suppose that it was fitting that in death he finally arrived at wholeness and holy annihilation in the East. But Mingus was no true believer in Freud's or Eric Hoffer's sense of the term. If anything, Mingus as holy man was simply another role he, as a black man, was expected to fill, just as he was expected to be a stud for white women. Uncle Tom, the dying, selfless, black male of Harriet Beecher Stowe, is the prototype for the religious black man in the West, no matter what religion he is attracted to. Mingus symbolizes this role through the relation of a conversation between Charlie Parker, the great alto saxophonist, and blind, white pianist Lennie Tristano. The contrast could not be more startling, nor more obvious: Tristano is an atheist, a composer and player of a very intricate, rather cold, technical sort of cool jazz; Bird, on the other hand, is a believer in God and mysticism, a composer and player of a very intricate but very warm, effusive music. Tristano is revealed to be, as most black people believe white people are, blind in more ways than one, overly civilized and overly cynical. Parker wins the debate by finally saying that God is "a bird without wings." In other words, God is a suffering, effusive, intelligent yet primitive black male. God is Charlie Parker, a Bird without wings. It is very consistent with Mingus's highly wrought sense of patienthood that he should believe in God and in the special holiness of the black male. After all, the suffering, both Mingus's and that of black men generally, must mean something in the end.

The perfect complementary text to Mingus's autobiography is his greatest album, "The Black Saint and the Sinner Lady," recorded on the Impulse label in January 1963. Mingus made many fine records, but on this one his compositional skills reach a culmination never really to be matched again. Everything in Mingus's book is here in miniature. In the title, we have the major religious, sexual, and racial imagery of the book. We discover that the music is meant to accompany dancers, so we are not listening to jazz as virtuosic music but as programmatic music, where its identity depends on the strength of the overall texture of composition and not on the strength of the solos by various players. It was as close as Mingus ever got to achieving the artistic, organizational anonymity of, say, the Julliard string quartet. And if the following passage from the autobiography is close enough to truth, then Mingus may have always been haunted by the platonic ideality of *players* simply and always in the act of *playing:*

> I've just been listening to Bartók quartets and wow! It's not the com-poser so much that prompted this writing as the musicians — the players, as Rheinschagen used to say. Their names were not an-nounced, just "The Julliard Quartet." That's the way it should be. They're good, good players and their names are unimportant . . . [8]

Mingus the composer, the arranger, and the orchestrator reigns supreme here. Finally, there are the liner notes. In them, Min-gus writes an extensive essay in which he talks about the music; indeed, there is a more concentrated and sustained discussion

[8] Ibid., p. 244.

of jazz here than in the entire autobiography. Mingus's essay is followed by a much shorter one by his psychologist, Edmund Pollock, who discusses the music in a psychoanalytic way. So, as in the book, Mingus insists that his white psychologist act as an alter ego. Mingus gives in miniature in this album the aesthetic mythology of his own patienthood. It is quite a terrifying record to experience. It is full of the fury and "put-on" that was the life of Mingus. No one believed more than Mingus in the psychoanalytic therapy of music which for him, of course, was equivalent to the psychoanalytic therapy of living. In one brilliant moment, finally and forever, Mingus enacted not simply the *dramatic* but the absolute *drama* of his psychological roles within a completely, almost immaculately, impersonal artistic realization. He did what all great artists must do: use his excesses instead of merely lumbering about with them with the self-conscious sanctity of someone dragging a cross.

2. THELONIOUS MONK: GOTHIC PROVINCIAL

When I heard on February 17, 1982, that Thelonious Monk, the great bebop pianist, had died of a stroke, I felt not only saddened but, oddly enough, relieved. It had seemed, for such a long time before his death (excluding the few years of artistic silence that preceded it), that Monk had become tiresome. How many times could one stand to hear him play "Straight, No Chaser," "Ruby, My Dear," or "Round Midnight"? For so many years, actually since the late forties when Monk recorded his first two albums for Blue Note, nothing really new emerged from the Monkian imagination. The fifties saw Monk refine and distill his art, perfecting his expression in an extraordinary canon of albums for Prestige and Riverside ranging from solo piano versions of Tin Pan Alley stuff to big band arrangements of his own compositions. The arrival of the sixties was the arrival of Monk: a cover story in the February 28, 1964, issue of *Time* magazine and a lucrative contract with Columbia Records. Then Monk proceeded to commit the terrifying mistake that has beset so many great artists, from Hemingway to George Cukor: he repeated himself; he tried to recapture the moment of his greatest triumphs and he failed. Some of the Columbia Records were quite good; most were merely competent; and many were, finally, boring, heartbreakingly so. The slow decline, the quaint staleness began to pervade his music, and his most aware fans realized that the "put-on" had finally and most devastatingly fooled the confidence man himself. Monk's music had been reduced from the controversy of uncompromised artistic engagement to the slouch of bedeviled laziness.

I suspect that Amiri Baraka (LeRoi Jones) knew that Monk would cease to be vital once he gained wide acceptance, and so Baraka wrote the essay called "Recent Monk" which appeared in *Downbeat* in 1963, an essay which said in one breath that success wouldn't spoil T. S. Monk, while saying in another breath, "say that it ain't so, Thelonious, that you sold out to the moguls on the hill."

But success did spoil Monk in a way that it spoils, destroys really, a fair number of black men in this country. The very persona that Monk encased himself in as the opaque, weird, high priest of the zombies in the forties, a persona so unacceptable to mainstream America then, became quite acceptable in the sixties. What initially made Monk just another outcast black jazzman eventually rendered him attractive and interesting, cute even, to, as Baraka put it, "a pretty good swath of that part of the American population called 'knowledgeable.' " Once Monk was accepted, he was trapped in the image of what made him an "interesting" black man to the white majority. This sort of thing happens very often to many performing black men: Richard Pryor and Muhammad Ali are two recent examples. When Monk was trapped in the image, he was no longer able to grow as an artist. Indeed, Monk, to the popular, simplifying mind, had even ceased to be a man; he had become an innocent primitive. Nat Hentoff, a usually very perceptive jazz critic, in an essay in his book, *The Jazz Life*, referred to Monk as a "child," and the *Time* article made it clear that Monk, after the death of his doting and overprotective mother, had simply transferred his allegiance and his need to be mothered to his doting and overprotective wife. Underneath all of this was the fairly hoary thesis that Monk was the product of black matriarchs and maybe even a white one, if one is to consider Monk's friendship with the Baroness Nica de Koenigswarter (for whom Monk wrote a lovely tune called "Pannonica").

If Monk had become, by the sixties, the noble innocent, then he was simply reenacting a sort of Nigger Jim–Queequeg role for the larger white public. It is quite in keeping that this black man-child, neurotic and mother-dominated, should have an exterior which white people found frightening. Perhaps it is because the appearance is so frightening that the figure has to be reduced: the Southern racist calls him a "boy," the Northern liberal, a "child." Nat Hentoff describes the incident which led to Monk's temporary stay in an insane asylum:

> In spring of 1959, he was booked for a week at Boston's Storyville. He had been up for some three days and nights without sleep. When he arrived, he came to the desk of the Copley Square Hotel, where Storyville was then located, with a glass of liquor in his hand after having flitted around the lobby rather disconcertedly, examining the walls. He was refused a room, and at first also declined to accompany his sidemen to the Hotel Bostonian where they were staying. At about ten o'clock, he finally went on stand. The room was nearly full of expectant but patient admirers. He played two numbers . . . and then sat motionless at the piano for what seemed like half an hour. His bewildered sidemen had left the stand after about eight minutes.
>
> Monk began wandering around the club, obviously disturbed at not having a hotel room. He finally registered at the Bostonian, didn't like the room, and left. He tried the Statler, was refused there, and took a cab to the airport with the idea of going home, collecting his wife, Nellie, and taking a room with her for the rest of the week. By that time of night planes were no longer running, and he was picked up by a state trooper to whom he would not or could not communicate. Monk later did reveal who he was, but it was too late, and he was transported to Grafton State Hospital near Worcester for observation.[9]

The passage seems to abstract the entire Monkian personality: the brooding, sullen demeanor, the dependency on his mothering wife, the inability to communicate through language. I feel deeply ambivalent about the entire episode. There is little

[9] Nat Hentoff, *The Jazz Life* (New York: Dial Press, 1961), pp. 190–91.

reason to doubt the accuracy of Hentoff's account; he was a very close friend of Monk and probably got this account from both Monk and his wife. To be sure, there is no denying the fact that Monk *was* emotionally disturbed, at least temporarily so.

I do not wish to sound like the overly sensitive minority person, but I believe that one cannot overemphasize the fact that Monk was committed to a mental institution mostly because he was a black man who refused to cooperate with authorities. Monk was surely not arrested because he acted like a child. To speak of the black male personality as being childlike — any black male's personality — is merely to describe euphemistically what white society perceives as the black male's psychopathology. Hentoff quotes jazz critic Paul Bacon as saying in reference to Monk that "to become an adult it's necessary to make a lot of concessions." There is a certain amount of truth in this assertion, but it fails to examine the complex depth of cultural resonance in precisely what it means to call a black man a child or the meaning of any black male's refusal to make "concessions." Surely, any half-thinking black male realizes it is only as an adult that the act of refusing to make concessions has any meaning beyond merely asserting the ego, in that such an act acquires a political aspect. Anyone who knows the history of the black male in America — the constant attempt by white society to reduce and restrict his impulses and personality, to make him submissive and tractable — anyone who knows how much black males hated this insultingly familiar diminution would realize that Monk, whatever his emotional disorders, was no child.

I would not even try to explain the whole of Monk's personality in racial terms, for he is much too complex a human being for that. But part of the manifestation of his psyche was largely an attempt to personify and symbolize, albeit subconsciously, the very *unknowable-ness* of the black male personality. Monk's actions as a public performer were a precise equivalent, a precise cognate for the function of slang or of the X in a Black Muslim's name. For so long had the black male been unrecognized — and I believe bebop symbolized this — that he chose, in response to years of invisibility, to be unrecognizable. In short, Monk is locked up not because he is a child but because he is a threatening, inscrutable black adult. The real ambiguity in role-playing here is the inability of many observers to understand that Monk's *willful* and somewhat deranged dependency is not synonymous with childishness. It is more closely akin to a distraughtly played game of deception.

It is in the great racial overtones of this story that one finds the true source, the touchstone, of Monk's personality: his gothic provincialism. One is reminded, when thinking of Monk, of those Poe heroes, so tortured yet so frightfully self-absorbed. That gothic provincialism had allowed Monk to survive and to operate in a white-dominated society.

Monk was born in the South but was raised in New York City and, indeed, lived there all his life. He spent his entire life in practically the same neighborhood, almost on the same block. (That sort of insulation is common with poor urban blacks. I remember working with some tough black kids for a social service agency and discovering that few of them knew how to get downtown. They had never been there!) He seemed to have little inclination to do anything but play the piano and compose, and he wrote many of his best pieces while he was still a very young man. His style of playing may have developed as an act of self-defense as much as for any other reason. He was very familiar with Art Tatum, whom he called "the greatest piano player I ever heard," and the recently deceased Earl Hines, and once hearing these men he realized that there was no need or even possibility of going the virtuoso route. One jazz critic called Monk's playing "fey" but, at times, it almost seems (to me) cowering in its effort to avoid being in any way "artistic."

When his music went unheard and unaccepted, Monk simply clammed up and waited. This was, in a sense, a very brave thing to do. It was, moreover, not only a sign of the depth of his determination but also of the intensity of his provincialism. While waiting, he showed little interest in doing anything else or in approaching anything differently. The cloistered environment of the black in the inner city made that kind of attitude possible. It is difficult to know whether this is lassitude or inner strength. The bourgeoisie have decided that if a poor boy succeeds, then it is inner strength; if he does not, then it is lassitude.

In Monk's case, we have a combination of both. Monk was surely a very great piano player in his way and a profoundly brilliant composer, but the music which was lauded by musicians and fans as being so rife with possibilities finally became quite narrow and restricting, just as Monk's gothic provincialism proved to be a source of tenacious inspiration and, eventually, the pathway to a kind of amazingly busy sloth. The problem lies in the fact that Monk never found a proper avenue for his musical expression. Many thought that Monk was a bluesman, pure and simple, and, to be sure, he was. Yet the essence of his music, where it was really tending, was toward the show tunes and songs of a W. C. Handy, a Will Marion Cook, and a Fats Waller. Most of Monk's music cries out for lyrics, and in another age his music would have been songs with lyrics sung from a stage. By the mid-sixties, Monk's days as a composer of new material and as a stylistic innovator on the piano were over. At this point, Cecil Taylor of the new school and Duke Ellington of the old school were much more bracing to listen to, both as pianists and composers. But the body of material that Monk wrote could have been mined in other ways. What if Monk had hired a lyricist to pen words to his songs? What if someone could have constructed a book around Monk's tunes and created a musical? It is an idea that might yet be realized but without Monk guiding and supervising such a project, it will be fairly much an empty exercise in commercializing the art of a heavyweight. But when I speak of making real songs from Monk's material, I do not mean to commercialize it but rather to extend further the aesthetic content, to *lyricize* formally a music already rich in lyricism.

It is often said that Monk was ahead of his time but he really was not. His music was a distillation and recapitulation of all the Afro-American *songwriters* before him. Only a man of considerable genius could have realized how much his cultural past was filled with the sounds of singing and could have exploited this realization with such unassuming deftness and quiet profundity.

3. SONNY STITT: THE BLUES HERO AS LONG-DISTANCE RUNNER

When Charlie "Yardbird" Parker singled out Edward "Sonny" Stitt as his saxophone successor, he did not present a compliment so much as chant a curse, an extremely successful curse. One wonders if Stitt spent his life trying to live up to Parker's pronouncement or trying to live it down. No matter: Stitt was, all his life, haunted by the ghost of Bird. Even Fate played the most horrible trick by seeing to it that Stitt's most memorable and artistically acclaimed album should be filled with Parker's compositions. "Stitt Plays Bird" was the best album Stitt ever made and all it did, at best, was make people think it was redundant or, at worst, make people put on their Bird sides to listen to the real thing.

Stitt was an incredibly gifted saxophonist who really did have a sound that was distinct from Parker's. Unfortunately, he sounded enough like an imitator of Parker to be forced to go through his career tagged as just that: one of Bird's better imitators. Stitt switched from being exclusively an alto saxophonist to being both a tenor and alto man, but nothing helped. When he played alto, he seemed to be playing Bird verbatim; and when he played tenor, he was merely doing Bird in a different voice.

Stitt, though, was able to do a few things that Bird was unable to achieve. First, Stitt was a survivor in an area of music that was notorious for its bloodthirsty propensity. Second, Stitt reached an entirely different audience from Bird's. Parker appealed to the white and black hipsters and intellectuals; Stitt, on the other hand, was a great draw for the ordinary, working-class folk whose favorite jazzmen did not have to be cultural rebels or the subject of articles in *Esquire*. The first fact is significant because it shows that Stitt never allowed his excesses or his frustrations to destroy him as a young man. The second fact reveals why Stitt was so important to jazz as Parker's alter ego: he demystified Bird's music; he made it accessible and freed it from the charismatic burden of its creator's shadow; he virtually made it over into rhythm and blues.

I remember Sonny Stitt as the skinny, nervous cat who was

billed with Gene Ammons in "the battle of the tenor saxes." He
and Ammons would always front an organ combo in a little
dingy nightclub filled to the rafters with slick papas with pro-
cessed hair and finger-poppin' mamas in tight dresses. You
rarely, if ever, saw any white people wander into these clubs;
they were always in the heart of some black community, sometimes in the same block as some notorious bucket of blood such
as the Clam Bar in South Philadelphia where my uncle once was
cut to pieces simply because he was a stranger. These were not
neighborhoods that took kindly to strangers.

The patrons of the club would thoroughly enjoy the tenor sax
battles, almost to the point of acting as if they were at some sort
of holy roller church service or a revival meeting. During Ammons's solos, people would yell, "Blow it, Mr. Man," or "Preach
it, Brother man," or "Brother Gene is saying a taste tonight."
During Stitt's solos, the chorus would be: "Make it talk, Sonny,
make it talk," or "Blow that shit, my man, and work it on out."
The music was extraordinarily loud; on a summer evening you
could stand outside the nightclub, as I did when I was a young-
ster, and hear everything quite clearly.

It was always difficult to tell who won the saxophone battles.
Stitt played more notes to a bar, but Ammons had a bigger,
bluesier tone. By playing with Ammons, Stitt had forsaken any
possibility of taking on Parker's highbrow audience. After all,
no one was going to mistake Ammons for anything but a gutsy
rhythm and blues man who played jazz in order to keep alive a
family tradition. But Stitt, I always thought, was a bit more than
this. It is a curious thing in jazz that a solo which goes beyond
90 seconds tends to become uninteresting and repetitive. Here
were two men, Stitt and Ammons, who played solos that seemed
to go on forever, solos that were so long that they seemed to be
parodies of jazz, reducing the music to simple rhythmic blocks
of cacophony. Yet in all this din, Stitt would sometimes play 90
seconds of extraordinarily well-conceived music. As I grew
older, I became convinced that Stitt was the better saxophonist.

I saw Stitt perform about ten years ago in the basement of a
church on the campus of the University of Pennsylvania. The
audience was small, made up mostly of young white college
students; the only drink to be had was organic apple juice. I

figured that in this kind of atmosphere Stitt was definitely out of his element. I remember three things most clearly about the performance.

First, Stitt was drunk or at least fairly loaded. He was not very steady on his feet, his eyes were terribly bloodshot, and his speech was thick and slurred. There were stories traveling like bad news through the audience about poor Hank Mobley, once a first-rate tenor man, and his drinking problem. Seeing Stitt stumbling around looking very old, very tired, and very much like a man who had been slowly and viciously used up made everyone feel uneasy. He stood on the bandstand for two minutes with his head down and a cigarette dangling from his lips. I thought for a moment that I was about to witness not merely a tragedy but a very messy affair of bad taste. Stitt finally put the horn in his mouth and began to play; he sounded better than anyone had a right to expect.

Second, Stitt held in his hand the most gleaming, golden Selmer saxophone I had ever seen. It was such an amazing counterpoint to the slightly shabby man — this cold, hard but brilliant piece of metal that scarcely seemed an instrument at all. It more deeply resembled a thing that could take flight, not an animated thing or a living thing, just the impersonal touched with a soaring grandeur.

Third, I remember one moment in the set as Stitt's triumph. He had played in a rather perfunctory manner, not bad but not outstanding. It was simply not his audience nor his element. He would never have that old-time audience again nor that old-time element. Clifford Jordan, a solid tenor sax man with Texas roots, sat in on a few numbers and seemed to lift Stitt out of his lethargy. Echoes of those old tenor battles with Ammons must have reverberated in Stitt's mind for a moment. They honked their way through Bird's "Constellation" like uncontrolled roller coasters careening toward a wall. Stitt then played a slow tempo version of "Skylark" while Jordan laid out. He returned to his lackadaisical self, giving a rather pedestrian reading of the song; then suddenly, during a two-minute cadenza, he played a solo which was simply the best played by a jazz saxophonist. It had not merely the fireworks of technique but it was faultlessly constructed. It was not merely as good as Bird, it was actually better.

For a brief moment, Stitt outdid the teacher; he was the king of the hill. After the cadenza, there was a brief silence before Stitt and his group launched back into the theme. In those few seconds, someone in the audience yelled, "Bird lives." Stitt started to play the theme but he abruptly stopped, peered at the audience a minute as if searching for someone, then said clearly into the microphone, "I don't play Bird." I suppose he meant to say that he didn't play *like* Bird. But that is really open. Perhaps he meant exactly what he said, just as when old black folk say, "The sun do move," they do not mean, "The sun does move." He never finished the theme of "Skylark." He simply walked off the stand. The unfinished set did not matter; he had played for a long time. Perhaps he found out that night he had played too long. As he walked off the stand, he looked quite sad, sadder than any man ought to look. I suppose Hemingway was right: "It is awfully easy to be hardboiled about everything in the daytime, but at night it is another thing."

KAI ERIKSON

Of Accidental Judgments and Casual Slaughters

FROM THE NATION

THE BOMBINGS of Hiroshima and Nagasaki, which took place forty years ago this month, are among the most thoroughly studied moments on human record. Together they constitute the only occasion in history when atomic weapons were dropped on living populations, and together they constitute the only occasion in history when a decision was made to employ them in that way.

I want to reflect here on the second of those points. The "decision to drop" — I will explain in a minute why quotation marks are useful here — is a fascinating historical episode. But it is also an exhibit of the most profound importance as we consider our prospects for the future. It is a case history well worth attending to. A compelling parable.

If one were to tell the story of that decision as historians normally do, the details arranged in an ordered narrative, one might begin in 1938 with the discovery of nuclear fission, or perhaps a year later with the delivery of Einstein's famous letter to President Roosevelt. No matter what its opening scene, though, the tale would then proceed along a string of events — a sequence of appointees named, committees formed, reports issued, orders signed, arguments won and lost, minds made up and changed — all of it coming to an end with a pair of tremendous blasts in the soft morning air over Japan.

The difficulty with that way of relating the story, as historians of the period all testify, is that the more closely one examines the record, the harder it is to make out where in the flow of events something that could reasonably be called a decision was reached at all. To be sure, a kind of consensus emerged from the sprawl of ideas and happenings that made up the climate of wartime Washington, but looking back, it is hard to distinguish those pivotal moments in the story when the crucial issues were identified, debated, reasoned through, resolved. The decision, to the extent that one can even speak of such a thing, was shaped and seasoned by a force very like inertia.

Let's say, then, that a wind began to blow, ever so gently at first, down the corridors along which power flows. And as it gradually gathered momentum during the course of the war, the people caught up in it began to assume, without ever checking up on it, that it had a logic and a motive, that it had been set in motion by sure hands acting on the basis of wise counsel.

Harry Truman, in particular, remembered it as a time of tough and lonely choices, and titled his memoir of that period *Year of Decisions.* But the bulk of those choices can in all fairness be said to have involved confirmation of projects already under way or implementation of decisions made at other levels of command. Brig. Gen. Leslie R. Groves, military head of the Manhattan Project, was close to the mark when he described Truman's decision as "one of noninterference — basically, a decision not to upset the existing plans." And J. Robert Oppenheimer spoke equally to the point when he observed some twenty years later: "The decision was implicit in the project. I don't know whether it could have been stopped."

In September of 1944, when it became more and more evident that a bomb would be produced in time for combat use, Franklin Roosevelt and Winston Churchill met at Hyde Park and initialed a brief *aide-mémoire*, noting, among other things, that the new weapon "might, perhaps, after mature consideration, be used against the Japanese." This document does not appear to have had any effect on the conduct of the war, and Truman knew nothing at all about it. But it would not have made a real difference in any case, for neither chief of state did much to initiate the "mature consideration" they spoke of so glancingly, and Truman, in turn, could only suppose that such matters had been considered already. "Truman did not inherit the question," writes Martin J. Sherwin, "he inherited the answer."

What would "mature consideration" have meant in such a setting as that anyway?

First of all, presumably, it would have meant seriously asking whether the weapon should be employed at all. But we have it on the authority of virtually all the principal players that no one in a position to do anything about it ever really considered alternatives to combat use. Henry L. Stimson, Secretary of War:

> At no time, from 1941 to 1945, did I ever hear it suggested by the President, or by any other responsible member of the government, that atomic energy should not be used in the war.

Harry Truman:

> I regarded the bomb as a military weapon and never had any doubt that it should be used.

General Groves:

> Certainly, there was no question in my mind, or, as far as I was ever aware, in the mind of either President Roosevelt or President Truman or any other responsible person, but that we were developing a weapon to be employed against the enemies of the United States.

Winston Churchill:

> There never was a moment's discussion as to whether the atomic bomb should be used or not.

And why should anyone be surprised? We were at war, after all, and with the most resolute of enemies, so the unanimity of that feeling is wholly understandable. But it was not, by any stretch of the imagination, a product of mature consideration.

"Combat use" meant a number of different things, however, and a second question began to be raised with some frequency in the final months of the war, all the more insistently after the defeat of Germany. Might a way be devised to demonstrate the awesome power of the bomb in a convincing enough fashion to induce the surrender of the Japanese without having to destroy huge numbers of civilians? Roosevelt may have been pondering something of the sort. In September of 1944, for example, three days after initialing the Hyde Park *aide-mémoire,* he asked Vannevar Bush, a trusted science adviser, whether the bomb "should actually be used against the Japanese or whether it should be used only as a threat." While that may have been little more than idle musing, a number of different schemes were explored within both the government and the scientific community in the months following.

One option involved a kind of *benign strike:* the dropping of a bomb on some built-up area, but only after advance notice had been issued so that residents could evacuate the area and leave an empty slate on which the bomb could write its terrifying signature. This plan was full of difficulties. A dud under those dramatic circumstances might do enormous damage to American credibility, and, moreover, to broadcast any warning was to risk the endeavor in other ways. Weak as the Japanese were by this time in the war, it was easy to imagine their finding a way to intercept an incoming airplane if they knew where and when it was expected, and officials in Washington were afraid that it would occur to the Japanese, as it had to them, that the venture would come to an abrupt end if American prisoners of war were brought into the target area.

The second option was a *tactical strike* against a purely military target — an arsenal, railroad yard, depot, factory, harbor — without advance notice. Early in the game, for example, someone had nominated the Japanese fleet concentration at Truk. The problem with this notion, however — and there is more than a passing irony here — was that no known military target had a wide enough compass to contain the whole of the destructive capacity of the weapon and so display its full range and power. The committee inquiring into likely targets wanted one "more than three miles in diameter," because anything smaller would be too inadequate a canvas for the picture it was supposed to hold.

The third option was to stage a kind of *dress rehearsal* by detonating a bomb in some remote corner of the world — a desert or empty island, say — to exhibit to international observers brought in for the purpose what the device could do. The idea had been proposed by a group of scientists in what has since been called the Franck Report, but it commanded no more than a moment's attention. It had the same problems as the benign strike: the risk of being embarrassed by a dud was more than most officials in a position to decide were willing to take, and there was a widespread feeling that any demonstration involving advance notice would give the enemy too much useful information.

The fourth option involved a kind of *warning shot*. The thought here was to drop a bomb without notice over a relatively uninhabited stretch of enemy land so that the Japanese high command might see at first hand what was in store for them if they failed to surrender soon. Edward Teller thought that an explosion at night high over Tokyo Bay would serve as a brilliant visual argument, and Adm. Lewis Strauss, soon to become a member (and later chair) of the Atomic Energy Commission, recommended a strike on a local forest, reasoning that the blast would "lay the trees out in windrows from the center of the explosion in all directions as though they were matchsticks," meanwhile igniting a fearsome firestorm at the epicenter. "It seemed to me," he added, "that a demonstration of this sort would prove to the Japanese that we could destroy any of their cities at will." The physicist Ernest O. Lawrence may have been speaking half in jest when he suggested that a bomb might be used to "blow the top off" Mount Fujiyama, but he was quite serious when he assured a friend early in the war: "The bomb will never be dropped on people. As soon as we get it, we'll use it only to dictate peace."

Now, hindsight is too easy a talent. But it seems evident on the face of it that the fourth of those options, the warning shot, was much to be preferred over the other three, and even more to be preferred over use on living targets. I do not want to argue the case here. I do want to ask, however, why that possibility was so easily dismissed.

The fact of the matter seems to have been that the notion of a demonstration was discussed on only a few occasions once the Manhattan Project neared completion, and most of those discussions were off the record. So a historian trying to reconstruct the drift of those conversations can only flatten an ear against the wall, as it were, and see if any sense can be made of the muffled voices next door. It seems very clear, for example, that the options involving advance notice were brought up so often and so early in official conversations that they came to *mean* demonstration in the minds of several important players. If a James Byrnes, say, soon to be named Secretary of State, were asked why one could not detonate a device in unoccupied territory, he might raise the problem posed by prisoners of war, and if the same question were asked of a James Bryant Conant, another science adviser, he might speak of the embarrassment that would follow a dud — thus, in both cases, joining ideas that had no logical relation to each other. Neither prisoners of war nor fear of failure, of course, posed any argument against a surprise demonstration.

There were two occasions, however, on which persons in a position to affect policy discussed the idea of a nonlethal demonstration. Those two conversations together consumed no more than a matter of minutes, so far as one can tell at this remove, and they, too, were off the record. But they seem to represent virtually the entire investment of the government of the United States in "mature consideration" of the subject.

The first discussion took place at a meeting of what was then called the Interim Committee, a striking gathering of military, scientific and government brass under the chairmanship of Secretary Stimson. This group, which included James Byrnes and Chief of Staff Gen. George C. Marshall, met on a number of occasions in May of 1945 to discuss policy issues raised by the new bomb, and Stimson recalled later that at one of their final meetings the members "carefully considered such alternatives as a detailed advance warning or a demonstration in some uninhabited area." But the minutes of the meeting, as well as the accounts of those present, suggest otherwise. The only exchange on the subject, in fact, took place during a luncheon break, and while we have no way of knowing what was actually said in that conversation, we do know what conclusion emerged from it. One participant, Arthur H. Compton, recalled later:

> Though the possibility of a demonstration that would not destroy human lives was attractive, no one could suggest a way in which it could be made so convincing that it would be likely to stop the war.

And the recording secretary of the meeting later recalled:

> Dr. Oppenheimer . . . said he doubted whether there could be devised any sufficiently startling demonstration that would convince the Japanese they ought to throw in the sponge.

Two weeks later, four physicists who served as advisers to the Interim Committee met in Los Alamos to consider once again the question of demonstration. They were Arthur Compton, Enrico Fermi, Ernest Lawrence and Robert Oppenheimer — as distinguished an assembly of scientific talent as could be imagined — and they concluded, after a discussion of which we have no record: "We can propose no technical demonstration likely to bring an end to the war; we see no acceptable alternative to direct military use." That, so far as anyone can tell, was the end of it.

We cannot be sure that a milder report would have made a difference, for the Manhattan Project was gathering momentum as it moved toward the more steeply pitched inclines of May and June, but we can be sure that the idea of a demonstration was at that point spent. The Los Alamos report ended with something of a disclaimer ("We have, however, no claim to special competence. . . ."), but its message was clear enough. When asked about that report nine years later in his security hearings, Oppenheimer said, with what might have been a somewhat defensive edge in his voice, "We did not think exploding one of those things as a firecracker over the desert was likely to be very impressive."

Perhaps not. But those fragments are telling for another reason. If you listen to them carefully for a moment or two, you realize that these are the voices of nuclear physicists trying to imagine how a strange and distant people will react to an atomic blast. These are the voices of nuclear physicists dealing with psychological and anthropological questions about Japanese culture, Japanese temperament, Japanese will to resist — topics, we must assume, about which they knew almost nothing. They did not know yet what the bomb could actually do, since its first test was not to take place for another month. But in principle, at least, Oppenheimer and Fermi reflecting on matters relating to the Japanese national character should have had about the same force as Ruth Benedict and Margaret Mead reflecting on matters relating to high-energy physics, the first difference being that Benedict and Mead would not have presumed to do so, and the second being that no one in authority would have listened to them if they had.

The first of the two morals I want to draw from the foregoing — this being a parable, after all — is that in moments of critical contemplation, it is often hard to know where the competencies of soldiers and scientists and all the rest of us begin and end. Many an accidental judgment can emerge from such confusions.

But what if the conclusions of the scientists had been correct? What if some kind of demonstration had been staged in a lightly occupied part of Japan and it *had* been greeted as a firecracker in the desert? What then?

Let me shift gears for a moment and discuss the subject in another way. It is standard wisdom for everyone in the United States old enough to remember the war, and for most of those to whom it is ancient history, that the bombings of Hiroshima and Nagasaki were the only alternative to an all-out invasion of the Japanese mainland involving hundreds of thousands and perhaps millions of casualties on both sides. Unless the Japanese came to understand the need to surrender quickly, we would have been drawn by an almost magnetic force toward those dreaded beaches. This has become an almost automatic pairing of ideas, an article of common lore. If you lament that so many civilians were incinerated or blown to bits in Hiroshima and Nagasaki, then somebody will remind you of the American lives thus saved. Truman was the person most frequently asked to account for the bombings, and his views were emphatic on the subject:

> It was a question of saving hundreds of thousands of American lives. I don't mind telling you that you don't feel normal when you have to plan hundreds of thousands of complete, final deaths of American boys who are alive and joking and having fun while you are doing your planning. You break your heart and your head trying to figure out a way to save one life. The name given to our invasion plan was "Olympic," but I saw nothing godly about the killing of all the people that would be necessary to make that invasion. I could not worry about what history would say about my personal morality. I made the only decision I ever knew how to make. I did what I thought was right.[1]

Veterans of the war, and particularly those who had reason to suppose that they would have been involved in an invasion, have drawn that same connection repeatedly, most recently Paul Fussell in the pages of *The New Republic*. Thank God for the bomb, the argument goes, it saved the lives of countless numbers of us. And so, in a sense, it may have.

But the destruction of Hiroshima and Nagasaki had nothing to do with it. It only makes sense to assume, even if few people were well enough positioned in early August to see the situation whole, that there simply was not going to be an invasion. Not ever.

For what sane power, with the atomic weapon securely in its

---

[1] Merle Miller notes, in *Plain Speaking: An Oral Biography of Harry S. Truman,* that Truman may have had moments of misgiving: "My only insight into Mr. Truman's feeling about the Bomb and its dropping, and it isn't much, came one day in his private library at the Truman Memorial Library. In one corner was every book ever published on the bomb, and at the end of one was Horatio's speech in the last scene of *Hamlet*." Truman had underlined these words:

> And let me speak to the yet unknowing world
> How these things came about. So shall you hear
> Of carnal, bloody, and unnatural acts,
> Of accidental judgments, casual slaughters
> Of deaths put on by cunning and forced cause,
> And, in this upshot, purposes mistook
> Fall'n on the inventors' heads.

arsenal, would hurl a million or more of its sturdiest young men on a heavily fortified mainland? To imagine anyone ordering an invasion when the means were at hand to blast Japan into a sea of gravel at virtually no cost in American lives is to imagine a madness beyond anything even the worst of war can induce. The invasion had not yet been called off, granted. But it surely would have been, and long before the November 1 deadline set for it.

The United States did not become a nuclear power on August 6, with the destruction of Hiroshima. It became a nuclear power on July 16, when the first test device was exploded in Alamogordo, New Mexico. Uncertainties remained, of course, many of them. But from that moment on, the United States knew how to produce a bomb, knew how to deliver it and knew it would work. Stimson said shortly after the war that the bombings of Hiroshima and Nagasaki "ended the ghastly specter of a clash of great land armies," but he could have said, with greater justice, that the ghastly specter ended at Alamogordo. Churchill came close to making exactly that point when he first learned of the New Mexico test:

> To quell the Japanese resistance man by man and conquer the country yard by yard might well require the loss of a million American lives and half that number of British. . . . Now all that nightmare picture had vanished.

It *had* vanished. The age of inch-by-inch crawling over enemy territory, the age of Guadalcanal and Iwo Jima and Okinawa, was just plain over.

The point is that once we had the bomb and were committed to its use, the terrible weight of invasion no longer hung over our heads. The Japanese were incapable of mounting any kind of offensive, as every observer has agreed, and it was our option when to close with the enemy and thus risk casualties. So we could have easily afforded to hold for a moment, to think it over, to introduce what Dwight Eisenhower called "that awful thing" to the world on the basis of something closer to mature consideration. We could have afforded to detonate a bomb over some less lethal target and then pause to see what happened.

And do it a second time, maybe a third. And if none of those demonstrations had made a difference, presumably we would have had to strike harder: Hiroshima and Nagasaki would still have been there a few weeks later for that purpose, silent and untouched — "unspoiled" was the term Gen. H. H. Arnold used — for whatever came next. Common lore also has it that there were not bombs enough for such niceties, but that seems not to have been the case. The United States was ready to deliver a third bomb toward the end of August, and Groves had already informed Marshall and Stimson that three or four more bombs would be available in September, a like number in October, at least five in November, and seven in December, with substantial increases to follow in early 1946. Even if we assume that Groves was being too hopeful about the productive machinery he had set in motion, as one expert close to the matter has suggested, a formidable number of bombs would have been available by the date originally set for invasion.

Which brings us back to the matter of momentum. The best way to tell the story of those days is to say that the "decision to drop" had become a force like gravity. It had taken life. The fact that it existed supplied its meaning, its reason for being. Elting E. Morison, Stimson's biographer, put it well:

> Any process started by men toward a special end tends, for reasons logical, biological, aesthetic or whatever they may be, to carry forward, if other things remain equal, to its climax. [This is] the inertia developed in a human system. . . . In a process where such a general tendency has been set to work it is difficult to separate the moment when men were still free to choose from the moment, if such there was, when they were no longer free to choose.

I have said very little about Nagasaki so far because it was not the subject of any thought at all. The orders of the bomber command were to attack Japan as soon as the bombs were ready. One was ready on August 9. Boom. When Groves was later asked why the attack on Nagasaki had come so soon after the attack on Hiroshima, leaving so little time for the Japanese to consider what had happened to them, he simply said: "Once you get your opponent reeling, you keep him reeling and never let him recover." And that is the point, really. There is no law of nature that compels a winning side to press its superiority, but it is hard to slow down, hard to relinquish an advantage, hard to rein the fury. The impulse to charge ahead, to strike at the throat, is so strong a habit of war that it almost ranks as a reflex, and if that thought does not frighten us when we consider our present nuclear predicament, nothing will. Many a casual slaughter can emerge from such moods.

If it is true, as I have suggested, that there were few military or logistic reasons for striking as sharply as we did and that the decision to drop moved in on the crest of an almost irreversible current, then it might be sensible to ask, on the fortieth anniversary of the event, what some of the drifts were that became a part of that larger current. An adequate accounting would have to consider a number of military, political and other matters far beyond the reach of this brief essay, the most important of them by far being the degree to which the huge shadow of the Soviet Union loomed over both official meetings and private thoughts. It is nearly impossible to read the remaining record without assuming that the wish to make a loud announcement to the Russians was a persuasive factor in the minds of many of the principal participants. There were other drifts as well, of course, and I would like to note a few of the sort that sometimes occur to social scientists.

For one thing, an extraordinary amount of money and material had been invested in the Manhattan Project — both of them in short supply in a wartime economy — and many observers thought that so large a public expense would be all the more willingly borne if it were followed by a striking display of what the money had been spent for.

And, too, extraordinary investments had been made in men and talent, both of them in short supply in a wartime economy. The oldest of the people involved in the Manhattan Project — soldiers, engineers and scientists — made sacrifices in the form of separated families, interrupted careers and a variety of other discomforts, and it makes a certain psychological sense that a decisive strike would serve as a kind of vindication for all the trouble. The youngest of them, though, had been held out of

combat, thus avoiding the fate of so many men of their generation, by accidents of professional training, personal skill and
sheer timing. The project was their theater of war, and it makes
even more psychological sense that some of them would want
the only shot they fired to be a truly resonant one.

The dropping of such a bomb, moreover, could serve as an
ending, something sharp and distinct in a world that had become ever more blurred. The Grand Alliance was breaking up,
and with it all hope for a secure postwar world. Roosevelt was
dead. The future was full of ambiguity. And, most important,
everybody was profoundly tired. In circumstances like that, a
resounding strike would serve to clarify things, to give them
form, to tidy them up a bit.

There are other matters one might point to, some of them
minor, some of them major, all of them strands in the larger
weave. There was a feeling, expressed by scientists and government officials alike, that the world needed a rude and decisive
shock to awaken it to the realities of the atomic age. There was
a feeling, hard to convey in words but easy to sense once one
has become immersed in some of the available material, that the
bomb had so much power and majesty, was so compelling a
force, that one was almost required to give it birth and a chance
to mature. There was a feeling, born of war, that for all its
ferocity the atomic bomb was nevertheless no more than a
minor increment on a scale of horror that already included the
firebombings of Tokyo and other Japanese cities. And there was
a feeling, also born of war, that living creatures on the other
side, even the children, had somehow lost title to the mercies
that normally accompany the fact of being human.

The kinds of points I have been making need to be stated
either very precisely or in some detail. I have not yet learned to
do the former; I do not have space enough here for the latter.
So let me just end with the observation that human decisions do
not always emerge from reflective counsels where facts are arrayed in order and logic is the prevailing currency of thought.
They emerge from complex fields of force, in which the vanities
of leaders and the moods of constituencies and the inertias of
bureaucracies play a critical part. That is as important a lesson

as one can learn from the events of 1945 — and as unnerving a one.

The bombings of Hiroshima and Nagasaki supply a rich case study for people who must live in times like ours. It is not important for us to apportion shares of responsibility to persons who played their parts so long ago, and I have not meant to do so here: these were unusually decent and compassionate people for the most part, operating with reflexes that had been tempered by war. We need to attend to such histories as this, however, because they provide the clearest illustrations we have of what human beings can do — this being the final moral to be drawn from our parable — when they find themselves in moments of crisis and literally have more destructive power at their disposal than they know what to do with. That is as good an argument for disarming as any that can be imagined.

ROBERT FITZGERALD

When the Cockroach Stood
by the Mickle Wood

FROM THE YALE REVIEW

ONE SUMMER DAY in 1923 I was taken with two small cousins by
trolley westward over the Queensborough Bridge. We were
making an excursion to a matinee at Roxy's. To our left as we
clanged across the great web of bridge I had my first full view
of Manhattan, the buildings in their dreamy altitudes piling up
down the island around the tallest of all, the Woolworth tower.
A heat haze enriched light and shadow on the distant masses.
Here and there small plumes of vapor appeared. As the vista
slowly shifted, I felt the wonder expected of me as a visiting
twelve-year-old from the Midwest. The city already belonged to
myth, standing like Asgard beyond the East River water, more
of the sky than of the earth. I felt, even so, some formless
question stirring at the edge of my mind as to what sense of life
that skyline honored or expressed. There was as yet nothing
like it in the world.

Going downtown we had glimpses, from an open bus-top, of
refined opulence behind plate glass. The very name of Tiffany's
had an expensive sheen or nap: a name of chased silver. Not
long before, I had been shown an article that my Uncle John
had written for his newspaper on the centenary of Fifth Avenue. It concluded: "Amid the ages of the empires, Fifth Avenue
is one hundred years young." The cadence thrilled me, and I
thought of the words now as the bus bowled along between
crowded sidewalks and shops. Uncle John was a first cousin of

my mother and had married my father's only sister. My two
small cousins were his children. The first fencing foils I had
ever seen, as a very small boy, were his — crossed on the wall of
the ivory-white apartment in Albany where he and my aunt first
lived. An old photograph of a Georgetown crew showed him
poised at bow oar with his curly head and high-hearted grin.
Some defect of eyesight had kept him out of Annapolis, to his
lifelong regret, but in his late thirties, when at five or six I first
knew him, he had the erect bearing and gaiety of a sea dog,
with his oarsman's shoulders still. In those days, a moment after
first meeting Uncle John, my younger brother and I would each
in turn find himself high in the air, then handed around over
shoulders and between legs and up again, breathless but secure.
We wondered if he could lick Douglas Fairbanks, and rather
thought he could.

Uncle John's father and mother, Uncle Charlie and Aunt
Elizabeth, lived in comfort in their quiet up-and-down townhouse on Willett Street in Albany. Uncle Charlie had curly white
hair and moustaches and attended without great effort to a
business in coal and ice. Aunt Elizabeth, with her kind gray eyes
magnified by her pince-nez, sat serenely over her knitting or
needlework as she commented on daily matters in her cool, well-
bred voice. She went in for beautiful grays — gray cashmeres
and gray shetlands, gray shawls and throws. Her son had her
vigilant eyes, but his were prepared to be merry. After the Albany Boys Academy and Georgetown, he had risen fast in newspaper work in Albany and then in New York, winning the
confidence of Mr. Munsey who had made him bureau chief for
the New York *Herald* in London at the time of the Peace Conference. He and my Aunt Marie had lived for several years in
places with literary names — Hampstead Heath, Kew Gardens,
Golders Green — sending their Midwestern nephew at Christ-
mastime Jaeger knitwear and gilded resplendent Christmas
numbers of the *Tatler* and the *Illustrated London News*. Professional photographs in soft focus showed their small beautiful
children in blond halos before tulip beds, and when they returned to America they brought with them an English nanny,
Olive Winch. It was Nanny Winch who had charge of us on
trolley and bus that day in 1923.

Closer to home, in Forest Hills, lay the daily and deep pleasures of the summer. My aunt and uncle had found and rented for a year a neat spacious house and garden, and in July and August they had a room for a nephew under the eaves. Half-timbering on the Long Island Railroad station and small shops nearby gave Forest Hills an English village air, and people spoke of going to shop "in the village." But even if there had been anything really snobbish about this it would have seemed all right to me, for among those well-off suburban homes and lawns a true aristocracy had its seat. For three or four weeks it showed its power on the curtained-off practice courts and in the small ivy-covered stucco stadium of the West Side Tennis Club, host to the best players on earth. I attended with passion the Davis Cup matches, the Wightman Cup matches, and the National Championships, often with my eight-year-old cousin, Jack. At ease on our cushions, waiting for a match in the sunlight, we looked down from our moderate height at the courts of shaven grass, where court attendants in olive green uniforms and little round-brimmed cotton hats perambulated the base lines and service and side lines at a brisk even pace, letting their marker carts gush ribbons of wet lime. Godlike young men or women in snowy whites came sauntering out with armloads of rackets — Olympian wealth, it seemed to me, since I had but one. Then there were the warm-ups, the pock . . . pock of superb ground shots, and the dauntless rallies. The striped marquee at the open end of the stadium held distinguished players with club members and guests, the elect in blazers enjoying the shade, but one day Helen Wills in pigtails, with her mother, climbed up the stadium tiers and sat near us to get a better view of a match. A day or two later she was going to beat Mrs. Mallory for the championship. Now, not wearing her white eyeshade, the divinely strapping girl with her Greek profile munched away at an apple while my heart thumped and I tried not to stare.

Perhaps the best amenity of all was the appearance of a tea cart for the English Wightman Cup ladies in the long interval after the second set. There by the umpire's stand they sat, and still sit, all in white tunics and roomy white skirts, nodding to their warm cups or pouring another, while the spectator tastes the mustard in his stadium hot dog, the fresh stadium flags curl in the breeze, the stadium shadow steadily grows toward the center court. England and the English who invented lawn tennis were represented to me thus, after the soft Jaeger winter things of other years, and after the postwar English magazines with page after page of notices offering for sale country houses with billiard rooms and gun rooms — for sale, now that so many of the billiard players and huntsmen were no more.

And Miss Winch was their daily representative, fair and firm about good order and good manners, dressed properly by day in her nanny uniform and cap and presiding over tea with quartered jelly sandwiches in the nursery every afternoon. She had a visible overbite and a lovely blush and would be remembered for her long pale buttoning fingers with rather flat nails, well trimmed and scrubbed. One morning she gave me special cause to remember her. Immediately on waking I had to be sick, and was, leaning from the bedside as one leans from a ship's rail. At home in Illinois, after the death of my small brother four years before, I had been an only child whose least illnesses were always matters of great concern — thermometers, cool washcloths, calls to the doctor, worried faces. What was my astonishment, therefore, when Nurse Winch, entering to clean up the mess, gave me quite a scolding. In not trying to reach the bathroom I had behaved like a baby, and jolly thoughtless, too. Taken aback and rueful as I was, I recognized instruction when I heard it.

Though in fact very near the city, we seemed well out of it in that peaceful place of summer light, garden light, and games on grass. I taught my cousin baseball, as he taught me cricket. On rainy days I read *Puck of Pook's Hill,* or I lay on the floor in the library leafing through exhibition catalogues in which absorbing nudes were here and there to be found. In my bedroom eyrie I spent several nights of exhausting terror with Poe's tales in a macabre illustrated edition. Aunt Marie joked and hugged me and combed my hair, recalling that I had been her first baby, born to Anne my mother whom she had loved and who died long ago, and to my father her favorite brother, now for some years bedridden in Springfield where the electric fan hummed this way and that in sweltering August. She could sit down at her baby grand and play cascading *arpeggi* that reminded you of her girlhood studies in conservatories in Brussels and Berlin. I had seen a portrait photograph of the young beauty she had been, with her long throat and a wealth of white ostrich feather clasped to her head. She told me of her stock reply when anyone remarked on her surprising biceps: that she had got them washing diapers. I loved her humor, as I loved her powder puffs and scent bottles and ivory brush and comb on an ivory tray. Late one afternoon when we young ones were to dine apart because the elders were having a dinner party, she sent me to the village for a pint of cream. When I came back she had changed, seemed vague about the cream, seemed half-asleep, slow-spoken and redolent, and for the first time I knew that this quick-witted lovely woman, like her father and at least two of her brothers, could be so transformed. I scented, too, in my confusion, something secret and sweet and abandoned, a turn toward oblivion. But so far as I could see, though out of it, the evening party passed off well, and nothing so strange happened again that summer.

1

All is not well forever with prosperities and abilities and loving families, flowers and music and books. What the years do to almost everything they proceeded to do to that Long Island household, slowly but not very surreptitiously. While I was going to school and suffering my father's death and going on to college, good times became overblown and withered into hard times in the world. The change came home to me in a single shock when I returned to Illinois in the summer of 1932 and my Uncle Ed, whom I had never seen otherwise than dignified and spruce, came down the steps to embrace me, tieless and unshaven, his voice breaking. Before long I was to see distress in the East as well. Uncle John had taken a fearful beating in a crash on Queens Boulevard and spent a winter laid up with fractures and wounds that left him grayer and frailer and feeling, as he told me under his breath, like a hollow shell. He had moved his family to a house on the Sound where the winter damp, with cartons of Piedmont cigarettes, brought hard coughing on his injured chest. Then he was no longer a star reporter but a writer of press releases for devil-may-care aviation people, Mineola and Roosevelt Field people, with whom late nights in speakeasies were too often required. My aunt with her long yellow hair in braids would lie abed reading until all hours, waiting for the last train. The unpaid bills grew longer. The Depression and The Jitters grew worse.

Crossing the sunny courtyard of my college House one day in late May of 1933, I fell in with a swarthy Irish history tutor named Doolin who had no humor and always said quickly what he thought. "You should have had a *magna*," he announced abruptly. "What are you going to do? You should settle down to work." This last, at any rate, was true and would remain true throughout life. As to what I was going to do, I told Doolin truthfully that I didn't know, but I didn't tell him what I had in the back of my mind. In the course of the year, proof had been offered me that there would be no money for tuition at law school or for the study of philosophy in Paris, my earlier and later aspirations, and in short that I would have to make a living without undue delay. My Uncle John then suggested that I try working for a New York newspaper; one editor, a friend, he said with brave loyalty, would be sure to have a place for me. A few days after my exchange with Doolin, I confided this to a Mallarméan and professor of Greek whom I invited to lunch in my dining hall. This man, Milman Parry, had a thin bony face, a fine moustache and goatee, and black eyes, very bright. He studied me and my prospects for a moment over his coffee, then put the cup down and smiled vividly. "You go to your destruction," he said with relish and smiled on.

Parry liked the theater and had been a devotee in Paris of Sacha Guitry and Yvonne Printemps. He had coached me in a play of Sophocles performed by students in Greek. I took his remark as theatrical in a mock-tragic mode, but every now and again for years his voice would become audible to me, saying those words. They acquired great ironic pitch, because in two years he himself was gone from the earth, killed by a pistol jolted when the safety was off. Parry may have been right about my fate, but I would always prefer to believe that it was a near thing. In any case, my plans at the time were soon made: I who had never had a job of any kind and knew nothing but a little philosophy and Greek would jobhunt in the big city that had beglamored my boyhood. First I would look for work on my own in the summer and only as a last resort would I fall back on my uncle, who had indeed many friends in hard times or any. I revisited my remaining family in Illinois, then came East as I had often enough before, on the Pennsylvania Railroad in a lower berth on a Pullman sleeper.

The routine of railroading at that time broke this journey midway. Late at night at Altoona, between shuntings and couplings in the big yards, there would be long waiting and stillness in the dark. You might hear a muffled footstep or two as someone passed in the carpeted aisle. Finally the train would be under way again minus the diner and with a new locomotive, settling into a lulling rhythm, smooth and swift, clickety-click, clickety-click. That might be the last thing you remembered before you felt the porter's hand on your foot, mussing and shaking through sheet and blanket. The dense curtain on the aisle side of the berth rustled back in place, and he was gone. Pinching the center clamp of the window blind, you could push it up for early light on smoky New Jersey factory sidings or vistas of wastelands and reeds shaken by the wind. From the net hammock slung across the window you unfolded underwear and trousers and with contortions got into them. With luck you might reach the men's room in time to get a nickel-finished washbowl and join the other occupants, men in BVD shirts, lathering and shaving in silence, teetering a little when the train swayed.

When you came out in early morning into the main concourse, you looked up to crossbeams of sunlight, parallelograms great in span, under a vaulted loftiness of pale buff stone. No one thought or cared how lavish were these heights and volumes of air. The architects had never heard that form follows function, but they had designed this terminal on that principle: its function was to serve public convenience with majesty, not at all unlike the imperial Roman baths which had been its model. Across from the train side a flight of very broad shallow steps led toward Seventh Avenue by way of a shop-lined arcade, itself wide as an avenue, and just beyond the top landing on the left you could turn and enter the Savarin lunch room for breakfast. Here were fixed stools at long low counters and everything, again, luxuriously spacious and full of light. Black men in white jackets, as in a Pullman diner but here with all the elbow room in the world, moved about to bring the first customers orange juice, coffee, cereals, flapjacks, bacon and eggs, sausages, toast. The newcomer might be faint of heart and woozy with loss of sleep, but the city provided grandeur and refection on his arrival.

If the city was your destination, you would leave the main concourse at the taxi end, coming out in a cavernous ramp amid an ever-moving file of yellow cabs that concentrated in that chamber the engine roar and brake noise and blue exhaust fumes of the street. Arriving this time, I wanted no taxi but after breakfast went below to the Long Island station. My uncle and aunt were again to take me in. From my base, my bed in their house, I began making daily forays into Manhattan, wearing my old cotton seersucker, going through the newspaper want ads on the blowy, gritty Long Island train. Then I trudged the streets between dingy offices where I talked to discouraged men. Mr. Roosevelt's first administration had not yet relieved his countrymen of fear, nor were any that I interviewed reassured by me. A hundred times that summer I failed to get a job. When September came, I agreed that Uncle John might drop a word. What came of this was an appointment on a Monday to see Stanley Walker, city editor of the *Herald Tribune*.

From a plain entrance like a freight entrance on 40th Street, an elevator took me up to a bare vestibule kept by a one-eyed old lady beadily dressed, seated at a table with a few chairs nearby. She sent me through an open doorway into the city room, which took in most of one whole floor, furnished to my left and ahead with desks and typewriters in strong light, some of it daylight from tall windows on 41st Street. Typewriter noise came from here and there, not so loud as the perforating racket from a bank of teletype machines. Men in shirtsleeves and eyeshades drifted about. Office boys made haste. At the center of this scene at facing desks reigned the day city editor and his assistant, each having before him his phone, pencils, baskets, and spike.

Walker received me mumbling shyly, shirt collar unbuttoned, sleeves rolled up, for it was a warm day, and he used his handkerchief once or twice on his brow. After joking and sweating for a few minutes he asked me to come back same time, same day, next week. I did, and all went as before. Well into October he put me off from week to week, waiting for something to happen, I could never make out precisely what — waiting for me to vanish, the chances are. Then one day he introduced me to Wilcox, the managing editor, a leathery slow-moving presence in the background, and they hired me to do city reporting at eighteen a week. Walker took me over to meet a reporter who sat reading a paper at a desk nearby, a pale young man in a new light-gray suit who wore rimless glasses and looked like a bright student. He was lame, and limped a little when he rose to shake hands. Tom Sugrue. He had joined the paper after Fordham and had been reporting more than a year. My desk and typewriter would be next to his. He showed me how to handle a swatch of copy paper and how much, a third, to leave blank on the first one. After a while, using his cane, he took me down to dinner at Bleeck's, the local saloon on 40th Street. A dry martini, the first I had ever seen, appeared before him like a jewel.

2

Mr. Strunsky, who owned most of Washington Square South, brownstones with top-floor studio skylights, wore an old brown overcoat a little ragged at the buttonholes, buttoned to the top, and a worn brown felt hat, beneath which his eyes were ingenious and kind. He told me I should read Pushkin and showed me the furnished room I could afford: a semi-underground room down a few steps at the corner of Sullivan and Third Streets. It had a bathroom to the left as you entered and a fireplace in the wall to the right. A barred window high in the left wall — the Sullivan Street side — and another on Third Street, both heavily curtained; a double bed covered in what had been a wine-colored spread; a table, a threadbare easy chair, a straight chair, and a standing lamp. Eight dollars a week. I moved in early in November. On the mantelpiece I placed a small silver fish, pliable with overlapping scales, that I had picked up in some Boston antique shop, and a bottle of Cointreau that someone had given me. Across the entryway was a similar apartment occupied by a young Japanese, to whom old Strunsky introduced me. I rarely saw him but owed to him the knowledge that tightly rolled newspapers would do, though briefly, as logs in the fireplace. Overhead in this place by day and night sounded the approaching racket of the Elevated, grating to round the Sixth Avenue corner some blocks away.

Now I had the city before me as a grid of bitter streets to be pillaged of sights and words daily in the name of news. Assignments were given out around two o'clock at the city editor's desk and entered on his assignment sheet. Off you would go by subway downtown or uptown or to another borough to ask questions and register scenes. You got the names, addresses, ages, and quotes by soft pencil on a wad of copy paper. Back at your desk you tried to read what you had written and to beat out before dinner the few paragraphs desired of your first or first two stories. If you needed background you got a packet of clippings out of the morgue. You might then with luck be assigned to a banquet. Organizations hoping for publicity for their speakers or themselves provided at banquets a press table with places for the morning dailies, the City News Service, and sometimes for specialized publications like *Variety* and *Women's Wear Daily*. The city desk passed these assignments out with careful equity to new and thin-bellied reporters to assure them each week of at least one good dinner with a cigar. A figure met fairly often on daily or evening rounds was the mayor. Small, round, genial, swarthy, with a black forelock and a piping voice, this perspiring bundle of force might turn up at any gathering anywhere in the city, ready to speak at the drop of a hat.

If La Guardia knew the town through the soles of his feet, the two Texans who ruled the city desk carried it all in their heads. On the day side Walker only at first seemed frail and boyish, his tousled head too big for his childlike stem of neck, his little chin tucked in. He mumbled around his cigar and never raised his voice, but before long you saw how on top of everything he was, quick and easy, hawk-eyed, yellow-eyed. Across from him sat the day assistant, John McLendon, burly and black-haired, the only editor who wore glasses, enlarging

his indignant brown eyes. Around dinner time their successor
came on. Engelking, Walker's counterpart, twice his height,
pale, bald, big-boned, always in shirtsleeves and the gunsling-
er's unbuttoned vest, always chewing a cigar, frowning under
his green eyeshade, loomed and brooded over the desk. Nobody
called him by his first names — or knew them: Lessing Lanham;
older men called him Engel. His assistant was a lanky, alert
young man named Joe Herzberg. To watch these men handle
copy was to see an unconscious display of style. Engelking's L's
marking indentation were inserted with small flourishes; with
elegance he used the fork of two long fingers to deposit edited
stories in the basket.

On the one hand the phantasmagoria of the great city, on the
other this offhand professionalism at making a newspaper, gave
me, six days a week and nine or ten hours a day, all I could cope
with. Apart from the cigars, the atmosphere of that city room
smacked not at all of *The Front Page*. There were no rowdy
scenes. On the job, at least, nobody was ever drunk. A competi-
tive spirit, never mentioned, in fact ran high. On each of my
two or three daily assignments I would meet an opposition number from the *Times* for whom that single story would be the
day's work. The *Times,* a block away, had twice the money and
twice the staff, leaving agility to the *Herald Tribune*. One asset
was a certain infusion of the New York wits. Walker counted as
one and would soon publish a salty book on the nightclub era.
Lucius Beebe did a column and could be seen at times in all his
sang-froid and custom-made shirtsleeves. Very young men, Joe
Alsop and St. Clair McKelway, to name two, were writing for
the paper with fluency and élan. Out of his cubby and into the
city room from time to time plodded Franklin P. Adams,
homely and swarthy and savory, he too in shirtsleeves, eyeshade, and cigar, engaging in filling his column, The Conning
Tower, with his own or contributed prose and verse. Agreeable
reading, it almost always was, and soon after I went to work it
contained to my blissful amusement the wildest of all Kipling
parodies, by Don Marquis:

The cockroach stood by the mickle wood in the astral flush
    of dawn,

And he sniffed the air from the hidden lair where the Khyber
    swordfish spawn,
And the bulge and belch of the glutton Welsh as they smelted their
    warlock cheese
Surge to and fro where the grinding flo wrenched at the headland's
    knees.

Then there was a sonnet by Merrill Moore that memorably
ended:

> Knowledge of nature gives exemption to
> No one, his father, and to no one's son.
> No one is probably the only one
> Who lives any longer than most mortals do.

At first I secretly felt that the term "copy" for all written
compositions implied a slap at art. If so, the slap fell gently at
the *Herald Tribune.* Practically everyone in the shop either wrote
well or hoped to, up to a point. The older and seasoned hands,
such as Allen Raymond, who covered the Scottsboro trial, and
Joe Driscoll, who covered the trial of Bruno Hauptman, rapidly
turned out clear, accurate narrative and were praised for this.
Bob Peck, dean of the rewrite desk, converted simple data into
human-interest stories with a light hand that reporters admired.
Nobody despised well-noted detail and well-turned paragraphs.
One night, as I toiled over a piece on a Greek Orthodox ceremony, Herzberg came over to counsel cutting it short and startled me a little by using the term of art: "I think it's beautiful
now and I don't want it overwritten."
    If I had been smarter or more ambitious I might have studied
the city, as I had a perfect chance to do, to get a grasp of it by
sectors and departments and put my daily missions into some
larger frame. As it was, I saw each for itself in its peculiar light,
and if the light seemed pictorial to my imagination I would have
gone on describing it all night if I could. "Let's see you charm
me," said Engelking one evening from his great height over my
desk, consenting to further paragraphs about something or
other of no importance. I did not charm him, at any rate not
enough to get that piece in the paper. The truth was that I had
more taste in writing than skill at it. And it often took me too

long, detaching one thing from another in my gummy mind
and deciding what to put down in what order. They were
patient with me, all the same, never sharp or caustic. No
doubt they had Alsop in mind; he had rewarded patience after
taking the better part of a year to get the knack. After I had
been for some months on the 2:00 P.M. shift, they tried me
for some months on the day rewrite desk alongside the city desk
from ten to six. This job meant doing brief pieces for boxes
and writing obituaries, for which one went to a booth and
called the bereaved. It also meant taking news stories by phone
from stringers outside the city, one of whom awed me by his
impeccable dictation of an impeccable narrative about an army
pilot's bad time trying to fly the mail out of Newark in heavy
weather.

When I knocked off on winter evenings or late at night, I
took the shuttle from Times Square to Grand Central and the
East Side subway downtown to Eighth Street, then I walked
west to Washington Square. On freezing nights as I passed
Wanamaker's I would see in the deep ground-floor window
embrasures the shapes of many derelict men sleeping under
newspapers. They must have had the benefit of some heat from
inside the building. I could thank God for a warm room and a
bath. I had many excellent meals, too, in the Automat on 42nd
Street, where the beans baked with molasses came in small ap-
petizing earthenware jars. I even bought two books, *The Gentleman from San Francisco*, by Ivan Bunin, and *A Nest of Simple Folk*,
by Sean O'Faolain. On the tenth of January I was able to attend
the opening performance of the Ballet Russe de Monte Carlo,
seeing Tamara Toumanova and David Lichine in *Petrouchka*, an
access of life in movement and music that would lift up hearts
to the end of time. Few hearts were more than middling high
that winter.

Reported in the paper in those months were these events
among many: Governor Wilbur Cross of Connecticut approved
plans for the $15,000,000 Merritt Parkway, to run from Port
Chester, New York, to Hartford, Connecticut; one hundred and
seventeen professors were dismissed from the University of
Berlin; Navy beat Notre Dame on Borries's touchdown in the

third period; Governor Henry Horner of Illinois spoke at the dedication of a reconstructed New Salem; Henry Pennypacker, from whom in 1929 I had received a handwritten affirmative note, died after years as Harvard's Dean of Admissions; the Prix Goncourt went to *La Condition humaine;* the repeal of Prohibition went into effect, and the paper printed page after page of notices for licensed liquor stores; Judge John Munro Wolsey ruled in favor of *Ulysses,* and Morris Ernst called it another repeal — of squeamishness in literature.

In February, extreme cold, as low as fourteen below, came to the city. As it happened, I owned no overcoat but got along with a voluminous black Burberry, worn with a soft black hat and a Left Bank air. This garment now failed me. Nauseated and fevered on waking one morning, I went shuddering across the Square to the Fifth Avenue Chemists at the Eighth Street corner and called McLendon to say I had the flu and would not be in. All I could do then was to stay in bed, and I did so for three days, fully aware of not being missed on the newspaper or anywhere else. When the fever finally broke, I made it again, like thistledown, across the Square to the softly sparkling dining room of the Grosvenor Hotel, where a white-jacketed waiter served me hot milk and buttered toast, one on the other, sugared, steaming lightly, yellow and white, pure and delectable, alimentation's very soul.

3

Sam Brewer had been at the University of Paris the year before and had been taken on the paper at about the same time as I had, a tall, soft-spoken, cheerful boy whose instincts and destiny were those of a newspaperman. He was reading Jules Romains's *roman à fleuve* and lent me some of the volumes. We dined at Bleeck's a few times, watching Walker and the established reporters playing the famous match game, but the Automat better suited our position in life. On evenings when we got off early we would sometimes, for lack of anything better to do, spend an hour in Minsky's Burlesque House on 42nd Street, listening to the bawdy buffoonery of comedians and watching the routines of the strippers, Gypsy Rose Lee pacing back and forth like a lady as she coquettishly plucked off her clothes, or pug-faced Georgia Southern, a striding strumpet, tossing her red hair in a tom-tom beat of bumps and grinds.

The only girl I had in the world, if indeed I had any, was holding down a job in St. Louis. No girls appeared in the city room, where there was only one woman reporter, steely-gray Emma Bugbee, who attended to society news. Too hard-pressed most of the time to think of that missing half of humanity, I could suddenly become aware of it after work and head for the Rosebud taxi-dance parlor on 42nd Street. Here a few dollars would buy tickets for brief dancing with the essentially naked though silk-sheathed figure of your choice, often a quite pretty and well-spoken girl. A number that winter were from Fall River, their jobs gone, no doubt, when the mills shut down. Dancing could be a preliminary with at least some of them, but I could afford no more and only made free now and then, as with one girl's memorable nipples that seemed the Rosebud incarnate. Olive-skinned and sturdy, she took no particular notice. Late in the winter I met through friends in the city two good-looking girls who were nicer, or at least not in need of employment. One, with honey hair, I took to a performance of *Tristan* at the Metropolitan and permanently miffed by dozing off beside her. The other I took to *Four Saints in Three Acts* and impulsively kissed at parting. She had left her compact in my pocket. The next day I was called on the telephone in the city room and had to arrange to return this, aroused but with sinking heart at what I divined to be my destiny.

"To Carthage then I came/Burning . . ." Apart from having fallen in love several times and communed with the girls in question in retired places — rather boldly, I thought in my ignorance — I had scarcely burned like the saint in the poem, before or after coming to Carthage. In Paris at eighteen I had made fun of my school roommate for wanting to try a cherished address someone had given him to a house in the Rue Blondel. What figures we would have cut! My companion had cursed me heartily and justly, but he had refrained. Now as the American city extended its snares I wouldn't have known how to fall into them if I had wanted to. But I had one startling experience of burning, not my own.

One night in mild weather at the end of winter I woke up at three or so in the morning to a scratching noise at my door. I thought it must be a dog, then heard in the dead silence of that hour a low voice that made my hair stand up, for it pled to be let in, not as one suffering from cold and exposure but as a wooer. It seemed a young man's educated voice but I had certainly never heard it before. "Oh, don't be afraid," it pled. "Oh, don't be afraid," it sobbed. Vain appeal. I was very much afraid, afraid of the mystery of that extremity directed at myself, and afraid to do or say anything whatever. Homosexual advances had been made to me to my embarrassment in my teens: one by a feverish nudging youth in a movie theater, one by a graying small-town aesthete and satyr; but nothing had prepared me for this last-ditch supplication in the small hours. Whoever he was, in the end he gave up and went away.

Nightmares, then, were to be met in the city by night, and souls driven to verges. Of the traditional underworld of vice and crime I learned little on assignment beyond what a few police sergeants had to say to incidental questioning by phone. My desk in the city room was directly behind that of the police reporter, Lem Jones, who looked like a brawny plowboy, but what he had to say he usually said at length and loudly on his typewriter, and I saw nothing of him in other hours. Once, though, he loped in, flinging his jacket off, jerking at his tie, and as he sat down to bang away he expressed himself vocally for a change: "Jesus Christ I never saw anything like it in my life" followed by a few explosive details. What had broken was a story of perversion in the prison on Welfare Island, of prisoners with wigs and paint making themselves women for other prisoners. There was a nightmare, sure enough.

Other odd moments in the life of the city room would remain with me all my days: red-headed Jack Gould with his pale face and sardonic eyes grinning and murmuring out of the side of his mouth, "Look at Walker . . ." as the city editor paced balefully up and down behind a writer far behind in delivering necessary copy; Homer Bigart, stiffly busy, briefly amused, set-

ting his honest face with its thin moustache against the badinage
of reporters bent on wasting their time and his — his that would
turn out as the years passed to be that of a first-rate professional; Ben Robertson, an ever cool and melodious Alabaman,
speaking in his soft voice of the "Mr. Flood" stories that Joseph
Mitchell of the *World Telegram* had begun to publish in *The New
Yorker,* "Ah think Joe Mitchell's a genius . . ."

After my period of breaking in on the day rewrite desk, I
went back on the 2:00 P.M. shift in the spring. Wilcox now gave
me a raise to twenty-five a week. So enriched, I thought I could
move up in the world, or at least out of Strunsky's basement.
Half a block away on Sullivan Street two tenements had been
remodeled into a small stucco apartment house with the amenity
of a courtyard in which a puny fountain played. My room and
bath on the top floor, up four flights, cost me thirty-five a
month. Since an open kitchenette occupied one wall, I could
save money by making my own breakfasts. I knew how to scram-
ble eggs. At Macy's I bought on terms a studio couch, sheets,
blankets, an unpainted chest of drawers, an unpainted table and
chair, a desk lamp, a pot, a pan, a skillet, and a percolator, with
a few cups and dishes and some tableware. My two windows
gave on the courtyard, and under one I placed my table in the
light from a lot of sky. Off to the right through many washing
lines I could look down on a section of the Elevated. I bought
two candlesticks and candles and set them on the table with my
Oxford text of the *Odyssey* beneath, making a kind of lectern or
altar in imitation of Aschenbach, toward whom in fact I felt
irreverent. Ritually, when I could, I read a few lines of Homer
by candlelight. I bought another book, Huxley's edition of Lawrence's letters. That would hold me.

It was not what the upper class is supposed to call a good
neighborhood. In the tenements nearby were discontented
women, highly audible as windows were left open in the spring
weather: viragos, who went in for prolonged bouts of screeching
over their washing lines. Short of screeching back, nothing
could be done about this. Then another threat to sleep in the
morning hours came through the flimsy wall near which I lay
— a far pleasanter but still rousing noise. At eight o'clock regularly someone began plucking at a stringed instrument, practic-

ROBERT FITZGERALD 147

ing, over and over, the tune of "Greensleeves." After a week of this, I got into bathrobe and slippers and knocked. A thin and dark young woman, saucer-eyed and voluble, sympathized at once and told me all about herself. Her father was Ernst Bloch, conductor of the Berlin Philharmonic. Her name was Suzanne. She had only one ovary. Her instrument was a lute. An upright piano stood against her wall. What a godsend! Assured of access to the piano by my new and admirable friend, I brought over my settings of Elizabethan lute songs.

As the weather turned warmer, a new and insidious distraction turned up. Across the courtyard lived a woman who wore nothing at all while she did her housework, briskly dusting her window sills. When her husband came home, she took him on in what seemed a naked fencing match. Aware that I had no business being aware of these people at all, I would try on my day off to sit and work at my table before the window, by turns denying and conceding my attention to the windows across the way. I told my friends that I had a couple of nudists for neighbors, a way of dismissing the matter lightly, but in truth I felt seduced and annoyed. Once more, something by my lights and previous learning unthinkable presented itself in the city.

That spring I covered among other things the model sailboat regatta in Central Park. I did a story on a foolhardy boy with an unpromising little sloop setting out on a round-the-world cruise. He sent me a letter from the Canal Zone, then disappeared forever. I wrote up a Civilian Conservation Corps camp across the Hudson under command of a regular army major, a tall and extremely trim West Pointer, proud of the road his battalion of salvaged city boys had begun to build through the woods. There were days of great interest, like that one, and days on which I felt I did well as a reporter. I never shirked anything and I did a day's labor. There had also been, from the beginning, stale and weary days when the city room seemed alien and I had to call on fortitude to take me to work. Now in May came the assignment that brought things to a head for me on the paper: that of covering a demonstration at the National Academy of Sciences. Someone had had the bright idea of recording a symphony from various points in the orchestra so that strings, woodwinds, brasses, and percussion, for example, would each stand

out as an entity. What I heard in the course of this experiment
struck me as something other than music, and less. Back at the
city desk I told Engleking it was worth three paragraphs, which
I then produced. In the next day's *Times* Bill Lawrence, the
science writer, made the front page with a signed two-column
story on this event, correctly perceived as the beginning of all
that it began.

No one could miss this revelation of at least two traits that
unfitted me for reporting as a profession. I was incurious about
twentieth-century gadgets and almost pathologically unim-
pressed by them, and I had no real interest in the newspaperman's dream of a byline on the front page. The emulation that
kept my friends on their toes, the longing for a scoop and the
chance to bat it out, take after take, did not really move me at
all. Although no one told me, I knew I had muffed that assignment and before long knew that conclusions had been drawn,
when one day Walker confided to me that he heard there was a
good job opening at J. Walter Thompson. Scorning J. Walter
Thompson, I elected to stick at reporting, but the next thing I
knew Walker amiably put me under the wing of the business
editor, who needed an assistant, and I moved to a desk next to
his in his corner.

This was not quite like being sent to Siberia. It was even a
modest position of trust, because when the business editor took
his two-week vacation in August I had the duty of filling his
three columns daily and sweated faithfully over the job. But I
had come to a standstill of a kind. The business editor, Harvey
Runner, had been a newspaperman all his life, first on a number
of small-town papers and then in the city; he knew no other life.
Square-toed, narrow-shouldered, pale, Palooka-like, he always
spoke a little as though his mouth were full, winning from
Walker, so I had heard but I am sure he had not, the *commedia
dell'arte* title, Flanneltongue. He lived alone in a flat somewhere
and was a kind and decent man. "Business" meant the retail
business. Norman Stabler, who edited the financial section and
news of corporations and markets, never meddled with Runner's three columns, which appeared daily under their separate
heading. His beat, which I now began to share, took him daily

to the New York headquarters of various trade associations, notably the National Retail Dry Goods Association, for scuttle-butt from their press agents as well as news stories ready to release. Press releases, in any case, cut down and touched up, gave us a good proportion of our space. With him I got further instruction on the making of the newspaper, helping to write headlines to fit or going along to the press room, where correc-tions could be made directly on the Linotype machines.

Two or three poems that I had done the year before appeared in *Poetry* that year. In the city room one day on the way to the water cooler I met Jack Gould and felt myself being looked over. "Say," he said, "did you have some stuff in *Poetry*? My sister says it's pretty good." As he did not disassociate himself from his sister, I took this as more friendly than not. It was one more reminder, though, of the distance between my daily occupation and the matters that I thought about when I could. Not that the business corner focused the mind on a negligible side of life. The uneasiness I had felt as a boy about the Manhattan skyline, for example, could now be formulated: while the steeples of America seen in country towns or inland cities invoked heaven and aspired to it, the skyscrapers did not; they chiefly aspired to multiply office floors upward so that a small plot of ground, of island rock, would hold a huge working force. So much for their ostentation and power. In the light of art and imagination my daily routine had become grubbier. At the same time the practice of art and imagination seemed more and more fre-quently recalled to mind. My friend Jim Agee over at *Fortune* with his transcending passion would not let them drop. Other friends turned up, gifted writing men who had weathered the year in poverty elsewhere: Bill Maxwell from the West Indies, Sherry Mangan from Mexico. I could and did sometimes visit Suzy in the flat next door and try things like "The Peaceful Western Wind" on her piano while she came in with her lute. When a professional friend, a gnomelike Dolmetsch, came over from England, Suzy did me the honor of having me in. A man I had known in college took me along to hear his friend Ralph Kirkpatrick beautifully play the Goldberg Variations on some-one's grand piano. In September a sculptress, a moon-faced

serious young woman, moved into the empty flat on my floor
with her smock, her armatures, her wet clay under rags, so that
now I had someone practicing an art on each side of me, hem-
ming me in. Moreover I now fell in love, as I had thought I
would, with the girl whom I had taken to *Four Saints in Three
Acts* — a girl with a haunting flair for acting and dancing and
writing as well.

Then there were the Stocktons. Herbert, big and gray and
blind-looking but hearty, practiced law in a firm downtown,
Miriam brought people who interested her together in their
softly lit house on 76th Street. Over the mantel young Miriam
with a ribbon round her lovely throat looked out with sibylline
brown eyes as Sargent had seen her. He had not seen her in her
rowboat with her Bostonian friend, Fanny, crossing the water
to drop in on the monks at Mount Athos, a figure I preferred
in fancy to Mr. Sargent's. The Stocktons had supported the
Laboratory Theater in the twenties and were modest patrons of
several arts. On every New Year's Eve they gave a party for
classmates of their only son, Peter, whom they had lost to his
own hand in Santa Fe. At this party, this year, I had met them.
After that from time to time they invited me for an evening or,
having a spare ticket, to a concert by the Dessof Choirs or the
Philharmonic. They would have liked me to believe, as they did,
in Rudolf Steiner.

In those days what I believed in and conceived, in spite of
everything, to be my calling was the making of poems. And I
had one under way, a movement that my ear had given me,
perhaps under the spell of all the music — one that demanded
a certain length. I had never composed anything remotely of
that length. It was possibly the most important thing in the
world. I had at most one day a week on which to envision it and
hear it, to let it happen or make it happen. I wasn't getting
anywhere, much, on this poem. And with one thing and another, as summer turned to fall, I began to feel pinned down.
My Long Island uncle and aunt had taken their family to California where Uncle John had a new and better job. "Hang on,"
he wrote to me. "Hang on a little longer." But I had on my
hands, so to speak, the destruction prophesied by Milman
Parry. Doubly defeated, I had failed as a reporter and I had

failed my gift. And I could see no way out. Lying in bed that fall, in solitude at dead of night, I let myself go several times in a prisoner's paroxysm, resting on head and heels with my body buckled up rigidly as a bent bow. There in the darkness, contorted rather as in the old days in a Pullman berth but this time in anguish, I strove with my muscles against my fate.

WILLIAM GASS

China Still Lifes

FROM HOUSE & GARDEN

IF YOU ARE a visitor in Beijing, a bus will take you to the Great Wall where the people clambering about on it will likely outnumber the stones. However, not everyone in China is standing inside the circle of the buses, breathing his last, or pushing his way up that ancient barrier's many steps and steel slopes, although it may seem so; nor is the Great Wall this incredible country's only dragon-shaped defender, because a billion people require the comfort of at least a million walls: walls concealing houses, safeguarding factories, lending themselves to banks and office buildings, hotels and new construction, defining villages, compounds, parks, and squares, protecting pagodas, temples, shrines, and palaces; and along the top of many of these walls a snakelike creature made of slate and tile and stucco seems to crawl, its odd equine head bearing a dog's teeth, with thin wire flames, like antennae, breathing from its nose. For all their apparent ferocity, the intentions of these monsters are pacific, as are the quiet courses of fired clay they serpentine upon. The city streets themselves appear to pass between walls and beneath trees as if they were enclosed, and the shops open out into them as open doors pour into halls.

In Beijing, alongside even the immediate edge of an avenue, rank after rank of potted flowers have been brought to attention — thousands of salvias, for instance, clearly a favorite — as if a pot had to be put out for every cyclist who might possibly pass. These are protected by low wire loops or sometimes by an iron fence of impeccable design when it is not displaying panda-

covered kitsch. Success is hit or miss. For the cyclists, too, colli-
sions are not infrequent. I saw a small truck run over a wheel
and a leg as though they were bumps in the road. The wheel
bent like soft tin and the cyclist's mouth went "O!" Cyclists *are*
the street as water is the river, and you can walk across in safety
only if your movements are slow and deliberate and resemble a
stone's. The bikes sail down the dark streets at night and show
no lights, though the buses like to flare theirs. The Chinese say
they do it for safety's sake, but each burst is blinding. In their
own much narrower lanes, which in intersections they cannot
keep to, trucks and buses honk and growl; you will hear occasionally a hawker's cry; otherwise the city is silent except for the
continuous ching-a-ching of the bicycle bells. Serenity is always
startling. You take close hold of yourself as if your spirit were
about to float away, and you say: "Perhaps it's true, and I have
a soul after all, other than the one emitted by the exhaust pipe
of the motorcar."

Near the long red line of blooming plants, as if to root them
for as many seasons as the trees shall persevere, there is a grand
row or two of weeping birch or sycamore, then a handsome
wide walk — crowded of course — and finally the rich red or
yellow plastered wall of a public garden or royal house, the
whitewashed wall of a simple shop, or often, in the poorer quarters, one of loosely stacked brick in both alternating and parallel
courses, in chevrons, on edge, at length, sometimes like a pattern book they lie so side by side in every posture, frequently
free of mortar too, the builder expressing his mastery of eco-
nomics, gravity, and tradition in the humblest stretch of work.
These are walls against which the spangled shadows of the trees
fall like a celebration, and through which the light runs like
driven rain.

In China, to understand some of its most appealing aspects,
Necessity should be the first stop for the mind. The comparative
freedom of the streets from cars, the sidewalks from dogs,
drunks, and vandals, the gutters from trash: these are a few of
the slim benefits of poverty and a socialist state. The brooms of
the sweepers pass beneath the feet of shoppers as if the shoppers' shoes were simply leaves. Pets compete for a desperately
outstretched food supply, and are therefore only surreptitiously

kept. And if an improving economy fills these beautiful streets
with automobiles, it will be a calamity. But Necessity is never to
be admired; it is, at best, only the stepmother of invention; and
in China, as elsewhere, it is the cause (or rather, the excuse) for
hurried, cheap, high-rise buildings, which appear to repeat
every greedy callous Western gesture.

One should not sentimentalize (at least not overly much)
about the rich street-and-alley culture of the slums, yet the cities
of China are made of streets made of people — walking, biking,
working, hanging out. In the paths between buildings there is a
world of narrow outdoor rooms; along the walks of wider
streets, goods are set out for display and sale; in the open doorways workers enjoy the air and light and sun while they repair
shoes, sew, shave a round of wood for chopsticks, clean chickens, and wash pans. The edges of the street are lined with bar-
rows, the center is filled with pedestrians, and out over everyone, from both sides, waves the household wash, hung from
bamboo poles propped out of second-story windows and held
firmly by a slammed sash. Hong Kong is a world away, but the
poles still bristle from the windows of the high rises there: a
bit of wash can flutter away in the wind like a kite ten floors
from the street; the sanitation is superior; water rises magically
in hidden pipes; there is more than the personal forty square
feet of living space which is Shanghai's average; and you can no
longer see your neighbor, smell his fires — a situation which
many planners and politicians approve. As a visitor, a Westerner, a tourist, unburdened by the local "necessities," I say,
"Let the rich rot in their concrete trees like unpicked fruit, and
leave the earth to the people."

For the curious passing eye, of course, these open doors and
drawn shades, these tiny passageways and little courtyards, including every inadvertent jiggle in the course of the street, afford, literally, a sudden "insight." Chinese gardens, with their
doorless doors, round as the eye says the world is, their Gibson
girl and keyhole shaped gates, their doors framed like paintings
or sometimes like windows, as well as every other kind of inter-
mission in a wall that they delight in — punched, screened,
glazed, shuttered, beaded, barred — have established the motif
of the maze, that arena for interacting forms which seems end-

less in its arbitrary variety yet one which does not entirely conceal its underlying plans, as zigzag bridges, covered paths, and pools of multiplying water make a small space large, and negligently wandering walls and their surprising openings constantly offer charmingly contorted eye lines, while contributing, along with the swooping roofs and undulating levels of the ground, to the ambiguity of every dimension, especially those of out and in, whose mixture is also the experience provided by the city streets.

The big cities now have vast blank squares like Tian Anmen in Beijing — they are people pastures, really — fit mainly for mass meetings, hysteria, and hypnotism, while the new wide and always wounding central avenues are suitable for totalitarian parades and military reviews; although it was no different in the old days, since some of the courtyards in the Imperial Palace can hold a hundred thousand heads together in a state of nodding dunder. This is one reason why it is comforting to find these streets, yards, and squares, filled with running children, strollers, and bicycles, because they are such splendid examples of free movement — of being "under one's own power." Walking, running, swimming, skating, cycling, support the moral realm, as sailing does, inasmuch as each seeks to understand and enjoy energies already present and often self-made, whereas the horse, train, rocket, car, and plane require and encourage the skills of domination on the one hand, and passivity on the other. The pedicab, alas, is coming back. And one sees people still pulling heavy loads like beasts. In such cases, the load is truly Lord and Master. But the present regime has lifted many a beastly burden from many a human back. I like to imagine that the warm blue autumn skies I enjoyed during most of my stay in China were the radiant reflection of the faces of the people.

That word, and the familiar image I have called back again into service — "a stream of people" — would not seem farfetched or even hackneyed if you were to look down into Guangzhou's Renmin Road (or "street of the people") where a glut of pedestrians slowly moves, not impatiently, though shoulder to shoulder, but reflectively, as a crowd leaves after a splendid concert. It is not New Year's; it is not an occasion of any kind; it is simply midmorning, and the people twine through the streets, living as closely as fibers in cloth. In this crowded world the wall is like one of those inner skins that keeps organs from intervening in the actions of others; they corner chaos like an unruly dog and command its obedience. I saw in a park a pair of lovers fondling one another while lying perilously in the thick fork of a tree. Couples go to such places to quarrel, too, or work out their incompatibilities with one another's relatives, to play with the baby by themselves, or simply to have an unobstructed view of their spouse's face. It is that difficult to be alone.

Nor normally is the eye left empty. The tourist will have to look high and low for the fierce stone lion behind the stiff grins and adopted postures of the Chinese, one hundred of whom are having their pictures taken in the lap of a seated Buddha, on the back of a bronze ox, in front of a garden of rock, beside a still and helpless pool: by whatever seems majestical, ancient, and handy. The photographers thrust the camera toward the ground until it hangs from their arms like the seat of a swing. Taking aim from below their knees, they stare down at the viewfinder as though peering into a well. Whatever their reasons (perhaps, like me, they are waiting for a clear shot), they take their time, so poses are held like bouquets.

That is, they try to stand as still as the burnished brass bowl or stone lamp or painted door they are leaning against. But their lips quiver and their eyes shift and the heart beats high up in their chests. Bystanders fidget and giggle. Movement, not fixity, neither of photograph or statue, is the essence of life. It is an ancient tenet. These walls that I have made the symbolic center of this piece might be thought to be in opposition to mutability and alteration, but in China this is not so. The Great Wall rolls over the mountain ridges like a coaster.

And within the walls, the walls walk; not slowly, according to some customary means of reckoning, but swiftly, each step of brick marking a year as sand does seconds sliding the sides of its glass; and it is perhaps this paradox we understand least when we try to understand China: how calm, how still, and how steadfastly sustaining change in China is; how quickly, like the expression on a face, even bronze can alter; how smartly the same state can come about like a sailboat in the wind; yet the bronze endures and maintains its vigil; the ship, the water, and the wind remain themselves while disappearing into their actions; so that now, as this great nation opens itself to the West and selects some Western ways to welcome, in nearly every chest, as though it shaped a soft cage for the soul, the revolution still holds its breath, while the breath itself goes in and out of its jar as anciently and as rhythmically, almost, as moods move through a man, and men move from one place to another like vagabonds.

The Great Wall rolls over its ridges, I dared to say, yet the Great Wall stands. The Great Wall draws only tourists now who sometimes steal its stones, not invaders or brigands. Still the Great Wall stands for the past. So it is the past that rolls over the hills here; it is the past which stands, the past which lures the tourist; and the past, when it speaks, speaks obsessively of the present.

In China, the long dispute between tradition and revolution, rest and motion, action and contemplation, openness and secrecy, commitment and withdrawal, politics and art, the individual and the mass, the family and the state, the convoluted and the simple continues with voices raised and much at stake. That's why, perhaps, amid the crush and the closeness, the delighted yet frantic building and trading and making, I was struck by slower times and more wall-like movements.

On a busy Shanghai street, I am brought face to face, not with faces for a change, but with a weather-beaten wooden box, a bowl, a simple pile of goods, all stacked so as to still life, and my sleeping sensuality is shaken awake as it might be by an appealing nakedness.

Or perhaps I notice two women in the act of hanging out a bright banner of wash, arrested for a moment by a thought; or I see on the sidewalk by my feet a display of fruit or school of glistening silver fish or a spread of dried mulberries in the center of which a butterfly has lit and now folds its black-and-white wings.

Or it is a set of tools resting against a garden wall in such a way their energies seem harmonized inside them; another time it is a group of whitewash pots, jugs of wine, or sacks of grain, or an alley empty of everything but chickens, or a stretch of silent street with freshly washed honey pots, their lids ajar to breathe, sunning themselves in the doorways. Chairs draped with bedding may be taking the air; a brush has been thrust between a drainpipe and its building to dry, an ooze of color down the wall like a drip of egg. Shadows of trees, wires, wash, the tassels of lanterns: these further animate even the busiest lanes. I fancy I see in them operatic masks, kites, the ghosts of released balloons. Or you discover your own shadow cast across a golden sheet of drying rice, and you realize that you are still at home in Missouri and that this is your shade, loose in the midst of China's life.

The sill may rot, the bowl fall, but nothing is more ageless and enduring than the simple act of sitting — simply being here or there. The alleys of every city are creased by ledges, crannies, corners, cracks where a rag is wedged, a pot of paint rests, or a basket hangs, a broom leans, a basin waits; and where a plant, placed out of the way like a locked bike, is not a plant now, but will resume its native movements later.

Down a whitewashed little lane in Suzhou, you may find white bread and flour for sale on a white box beneath a white sheet stretched out like an awning, and casting a shadow so pale it seems white as well. Through an open window with blowing white curtains you will be handed your change in the soiled palm of a white glove.

In the same lane is a teahouse where a Vermeer may be found: benches, table, tray, row of glasses, teapot just so, wall right there — all composed and rendered by the master. On top of the teahouse stove, the tools of the cook's trade lie in a sensuous confusion akin to bedclothes. Even the steam holds its shape and station like a spoon. In front of a few chairs, on a small stage, a lectern for the storyteller has been placed. There is one chair on either side of it, both draped with cloths. I make up an artificial audience, sitting there, looking at the wooden figures where the old tales are spoken, and I am truly overcome by the richness of this world: its care for the small things; this tidiness that transcends need and becomes art; the presence of the past in even the most impoverished places and simplest things, for the act of recitation, too, is as importantly immortal as the lean of a spade or a pot's rest.

China seems today in glorious and healthy tumult, but the visitor, charmed by the plenitude or patient genius of the people, the vast landscape and exotic monuments, should not neglect the corners of quiet — the resting bamboo boats or idle ladders, the humblest honey pot or plastic purse or rouged wall — for these things and spaces are everywhere as well, and they are easily as ancient, fully as lively in their own interior way, and certainly as honestly and openly sensual as any rice-ripe, yellow, autumn landscape or langorous stretch of back or thigh.

So it is not by one of the many Buddhas one may see in China that I am reminded of Rilke's poem about that figure,

> As if he listened. Silence: depth . . .
> And we hold back our breath.

nor is it while I am bemused by the admittedly similar grandeur of the burnished bronze bowl that stands, in company with a carefully regulated tree, in front of a bit of royal wall in the Imperial Palace Garden,

> Oh, he is fat. Do we suppose
> he'll see us? He has need of that?

but during another kind of encounter entirely, in a commonplace Shanghai street, with a bunch of baskets hung above a stone sink. There is a lame straw fan nearby, and on the sink a blushing cup from which a watercolor brush has been allowed to stick. What hidden field of force has drawn these objects into their conjunction? A wooden bowl leans at the sink's feet, its rosy basin open to the sun. Beside the sink sits a teapot, while behind it rises a pipe where a washrag, dark still from its own dampness, dangles as though done for. There is also a brazier by the sink's side like a sullen brother, a handled pot perched uneasily on its head where a shiny tin lid similarly slides. On top of the sink, again, an enameled saucer waits on a drainboard of worn wood. It contains another jutting brush — a nice touch. It is by these plain things that the lines about the Buddha were returned to my mind, for I was looking at the altar of a way of life. The simple items of this precise and impertinent collection had been arranged by circumstances so complex, historical, and social, so vagarious and yet determined, that I felt obliged to believe an entire culture — a whole people — had composed it. Vermeer indeed, or some solemn Buddha, could only hold a candle, as though they were another witness, to this peaceful and ardent gathering of things.

> For that which lures us to his feet
> has circled in him now a million years.
> He has forgotten all we must endure,
> encloses all we would escape.

STEPHEN JAY GOULD

Nasty Little Facts

FROM NATURAL HISTORY

As a DEVOTEE of Grade B detective films, from Charlie Chan (in all his incarnations) to the *Thin Man*, I have, perforce, spent an undue amount of time passively engaged in conversations about fingerprints. Since these discussions are interminable, one might suspect that they have also been eternal in the annals of criminology.

In fact, Scotland Yard officially introduced fingerprints as a tool for identifying criminals in 1901 (replacing the older Bertillon system, based on complex series of body measurements and the accompanying assumption, not always vindicated, that no two people will be alike in so many ways). The chief architect and promoter of the new system was Francis Galton, England's most eccentric scientific genius.

In his autobiography, Galton tells a story of Herbert Spencer's visit to his fingerprint lab. Galton took Spencer's prints and "spoke of the failure to discover the origin of these patterns, and how the fingers of unborn children had been dissected to ascertain their earliest stages." Spencer, quick to offer certain opinions about almost anything, told Galton that he had been working the wrong way round.

> Spencer remarked . . . that I ought to consider the purpose the ridges had to fulfil, and to work backwards. Here, he said, it was obvious that the delicate mouths of the sudorific glands required the protection given to them by the ridges on either side of them, and therefrom he elaborated a consistent and ingenious hypothesis at

great length. I replied that his arguments were beautiful and deserved to be true, but it happened that the mouths of the ducts did
not run in the valleys between the crests, but along the crests of the
ridges themselves.

Galton then ends his anecdote by giving the original source
for one of the top ten among scientific quotes. Spencer, dining
with T. H. Huxley one night at the Athenaeum, stated that he
had once written a tragedy. Huxley replied that he knew all
about it. Spencer rebutted Huxley, arguing that he had never
mentioned it to anyone. But Huxley insisted that he knew anyway and identified Spencer's debacle — "a beautiful theory,
killed by a nasty, ugly little fact."

Some theories may be subject to such instant, brutal, and
unambiguous rejection. I stated last month, for example, that
no left-coiling periwinkle had ever been found among millions
of snails examined. If I happen to find one during my walk on
Nopsca Beach tomorrow morning, a century of well-nurtured
negative evidence will collapse in an instant.

This Huxleyan vision of clean refutation buttresses one of
our worst stereotypes about science. We tend to view science as
a truth-seeking machine, driven by two forces that winnow
error: the new discovery and the crucial experiment — prime
generators of those nasty, ugly little facts. Science does, of
course, seek truth; it even succeeds reasonably often, so far as
we can tell. But science, like all of life, is filled with rich and
complex ambiguity. The path to truth is rarely straight, marked
by a gate of entry that sorts applicants by such relatively simple
criteria as age and height. (When I was a kid, you could get into
Yankee Stadium for half price if your head didn't reach a line
prominently drawn on the entrance gate about four and a half
feet above the ground. You could scrunch down, but they
checked. One nasty, ugly day, I started to pay full price, and
that was that.)

Little facts rarely undo big theories all by themselves — the
myth of David and Goliath notwithstanding. They can refute
little, highly specific theories, like my conjecture about lefty periwinkles, but they rarely slay grand and comprehensive views of
nature. No single, pristine fact taught us that the earth revolves

STEPHEN JAY GOULD   163

around the sun or that evolution produced the similarities among organisms. Overarching theories are much bigger than single facts, just as the army of Grenada really didn't have much chance against the combined forces of the United States (though you'd think from the consequent appeals to patriotism that some gigantic and improbable victory had been won).

Instead, little facts are assimilated into large theories. They may reside there uncomfortably, bothering the honorable proponents. Large numbers of little facts may eventually combine with other social and intellectual forces to topple a grand theory. The history of ideas is a play of complex human passions interacting with an external reality only slightly less intricate. We debase the richness of both nature and our own minds if we view the great pageant of our intellectual history as a compendium of new information leading from primal superstition to final exactitude. We know that the sun is hub to our little corner of the universe, and that ties of genealogy connect all living things on our planet, because these theories assemble and explain so much otherwise disparate and unrelated information — not because Galileo trained his telescope on the moons of Jupiter or because Darwin took a ride on a Galápagos tortoise.

This essay tells the story of a pristine, unexpected little fact that should have mattered, but didn't particularly. It was widely reported, discussed, and personally studied by the greatest naturalists of Europe, and then assimilated into each of several contradictory systems. Fifty years later, in 1865, a second discovery resolved the paradox generated by the first fact — and should have won, by Huxley's principle, a big and important victory for Darwin and evolution. It was welcomed, to be sure, but largely ignored. One foot soldier could not decide a battle waged on so many fronts.

Trigonia is a distinctive clam, thick shelled and triangular in shape. It flourished with dinosaurs during the Mesozoic era and then became extinct in the same debacle that wiped out the ruling reptiles — one of the five greatest mass dyings in our geologic record. No trigonian had ever been found in the overlying Cenozoic strata — the entire age of mammals (about sixty million years, as we now know). *Trigonia* had therefore become a valued "guide fossil"; when you found one, you knew you had rocks of the earth's middle age. Everyone (who was anybody) understood this.

Then, the nasty, ugly little — and quite undeniable — fact. In 1802, P. Péron, a French naturalist, found the shell of a living trigonian washed up on the beaches of southern Australia. Twenty-five years later, and following several failures, J. Quoy and J. Gaimard, naturalists aboard the *Astrolabe*, finally found a live trigonian. They had dredged for several days with definite purpose, but without success. Becalmed one night in Bass Strait and with little else to do, they tried again and brought up their single prize, a molluscan life soon snuffed and preserved in the (perhaps welcome) medium of the collector's trade — a bottle of alcohol. Quoy and Gaimard treasured their booty and wrote later:

> We were so anxious to bring back this shell with its animal that when we were, for three days, stranded on the reefs of Tonga-Tabu, it was the only object that we took from our collection. Doesn't this recall the ardent shell collector who, during seven years' war, carried constantly in his pocket an extraordinary *Phasianella*, which he had bought for twenty-five louis?

A simple story. A fact and a puzzle. *Trigonia* had not disappeared in the great Cretaceous debacle, for it was hanging tough in Australia. But no fossil trigonians had been found in all the strata in between — throughout the long and well-recorded history of the age of mammals (now called the Cenozoic era). Where were they? Had they ever existed? Could such a distinctive animal die and be reborn (or re-created) later? The "Cenozoic gap" became as puzzling and portentous as the one later associated with Mr. Nixon and Ms. Woods.

Trigonia occupies a specially interesting place in the history of biology because its unexpected fact and consequent puzzle arose and prevailed at such an important time — at the dawn and through the greatest conceptual transition ever experienced by the profession: from creationist to evolutionary views of life. It also (or rather therefore) attracted the attention and commentary of most leaders in nineteenth-century natural history. J. B.

Lamarck, most famous of pre-Darwinian evolutionists, formally described the first living trigonian. Darwin himself thought and commented about *Trigonia* for thirty years. Louis Agassiz, most able and cogent of Darwin's opponents, wrote the major technical monograph of his generation on the genus *Trigonia*.

The lesson of the living *Trigonia* can be distilled in a sentence: Everyone made the best of it, incorporating favorable aspects of this new fact into his system and either ignoring or explaining away the difficulties. *Trigonia* became an illustration for everyone, not a crucial test of rival theories. Evolutionists celebrated the differences in form and distribution between ancient and modern trigonians — and ignored the Cenozoic gap. Creationists highlighted the gap and made light of the differences.

Today, we remember Lamarck best as the author of a rejected evolutionary theory based on the inheritance of acquired characters (quite an unfair designation since so-called Lamarckian inheritance represents a minor part of Lamarck's own system — this, however, is another story, for another time). But his day-to-day work in post-revolutionary France involved the description of living and fossil invertebrates in his role as curator at the *Muséum d'Histoire Naturelle* in Paris. He therefore received Péron's precious shell for formal description, and he named it *Trigonia margaritacea* in 1804 (*margarita* is a Latin pearl, and the interior of a trigonian shell shines with a beautiful pearly luster). But since 1804 lay squarely between Lamarck's initial (1802) and definitive (1809) statement of his evolutionary theory, he also used his short paper on *Trigonia* to sharpen and defend his developing transmutationist views.

Most fossil trigonians are ornamented with concentric ridges at their anterior ends (enclosing the mouth and digestive apparatus) and radial ribs on the rear flank. A single strong rib usually separates these two areas. But all modern trigonians cover their shells entirely with radial ribs (although the embryonic shell still bears traces of the ancestral concentrics). Lamarck seized upon these differences to claim that changing environments had pressed their influence upon the shell. The shell had then altered in response and the animal within passed the favorable change to future generations by "Lamarckian" inheritance.

They have undergone changes under the influence of circumstances that act upon them and that have themselves changed; so that fossil remains . . . of the greatest antiquity may display several differences from animals of the same type living now but nevertheless derived from them.

(But Lamarck had only demonstrated that the fossils looked different from the moderns. Any theory could account for this basic datum in the absence of further information — evolution by use and disuse, by natural selection, or even re-creation by God for that matter.)

Lamarck then proceeded to extract more from modern trigonians to buttress other pet themes. He was, for example, a partisan at the wrong end of a great debate resolved a decade later to his disadvantage by Cuvier — does extinction occur in nature? Human rapacity, Lamarck believed, might exterminate some conspicuous beasts, but the ways of nature do not include termination without descent (Lamarck, as a transmutationist, obviously accepted the pseudoextinction that occurs when one form evolves into another). Lamarck gave the old arguments against extinction a novel twist by embedding his justification within his newfangled evolutionary views. How can extinction occur if all organisms respond creatively to changing environments and pass their favorable responses to future generations in the form of altered inheritance?

Yet Lamarck's conviction was sorely challenged by burgeoning data in his own field of marine invertebrate paleontology. So many kinds of fossils are confined to rocks of early periods. Where are their descendants today? Lamarck offered the only plausible argument in a world with few remaining terrae incognitae — they live still in the unexplored depths of the sea. Since Lamarck reveals his own discomfort with such an ad hoc solution in the form of a defense too often and too zealously repeated — recall Shakespeare's "the lady doth protest too much, methinks" — we may take as genuine his delight in *Trigonia* as a real case for a generalization devoutly to be wished: "Small species, especially those that dwell in the depths of the sea, have the means to escape man; truly among these we do not find any that are really extinct." Lamarck then ends his paper by pre-

dicting that a large suite of creatures apparently extinct will
soon be found at oceanic depths. We are still waiting.

Since Lamarck's argument centers upon an explanation for
why creatures still living yield no evidence of their continued
vitality, we should not be surprised that the Cenozoic gap inspired no commentary at all. We must assume that trigonians
spent the entire Cenozoic safe in the bosom of Neptune, full
fathom five hundred or more, and unrecorded in a fossil ar-
chive of shallow-water sediments.

Charles Darwin, leading evolutionist of the next generation,
selected yet another aspect of living trigonians — their geographic distribution — to bolster a different theme dear to his
view of life. Darwin's creationist opponents, as we shall see,
rendered the history of life as a series of static faunas and floras
separated by episodes of sudden extirpation and renewal. To
confute this catastrophist credo, and to advance his own distinctive and uncompromisingly gradualist view of nature, Darwin
argued that the extinction of a group should be as smooth and
extended as its origin. A group should peter out, dwindle
slowly, decrease steadily in numbers and geographic range —
not die in full vigor during an environmental crisis. What better
evidence than a family once spread throughout the world in
stunning diversity but now confined to one small region and
one single species. In his private essay of 1844, precursor to the
Origin of Species (1859), Darwin wrote: "We have reason to believe that . . . the numbers of the species decrease till finally the
group becomes extinct — the *Trigonia* was extinct much sooner
in Europe, but now lives in the seas of Australia."

(We now regard this claim for extinction of large groups as
gradual dwindling in the face of competition from more successful forms — the central theme of chapter 10 in the *Origin of
Species* — as among the least successful of Darwin's major arguments. Darwin may have feared that mass extinction supported
the creationist view of debacle followed by divine reconstitution.
But mass extinction may also clear the way for subsequent, vigorous periods of *evolution*. Again, as so often, Darwin's commitment to gradualism restricted his options for legitimate
evolutionary hypotheses.)

Darwin followed Lamarck in dismissing the Cenozoic gap as

an artifact of our imperfect fossil record (I can, indeed, imagine no other option for an evolutionist committed to genealogical connection). But Darwin was explicit where Lamarck had been silent. Darwin also tried to accentuate the positive by arguing that the rarity of such long gaps strongly implied their artificial status. He wrote in the *Origin of Species:*

> A group does not reappear after it has once disappeared; or its existence, as long as it lasts, is continuous. I am aware that there are some apparent exceptions to this rule, but the exceptions are surprisingly few, so few that . . . the rule strictly accords with my theory.

Creationists, meanwhile, looked at *Trigonia* from the other side. They treasured the Cenozoic gap and found nearly everything else puzzling. The major creationist thinkers tended to agree that life's history had been episodic — a series of stages separated by sudden, worldwide paroxysms that removed the old and set a stage for the new. But they divided into two camps on the issue of progress. Did each new episode improve upon the last; was God, in other words, learning by doing? Or had life maintained a fairly consistent complexity throughout its episodic history? Progressionists and nonprogressionists found different messages in *Trigonia*.

James Parkinson, England's leading progressionist (though he switched allegiances later on), chose *Trigonia* as a premier example in his *Organic Remains of a Former World* (1811). He read the Cenozoic gap literally, extracting from it the congenial message that life's history features a series of creations not connected by ties of genealogy and physical continuity.

But *Trigonia* also presented a special problem for Parkinson. He argued that each successive episode of creation had been marked "with increasing excellence in its objects," thus matching in all ways but one the Mosaic progression from chaos to Adam as described in Genesis. "So close indeed is this agreement, that the Mosaic account is thereby confirmed in every respect except as to the age of the world" (a problem then resolved by an allegorical interpretation of God's six creative "days"). Now a *Trigonia,* as some folks say about roses, is a *Tri-*

gonia (subtleties evident to the professional eye aside). Why should a modern shell with radial ribs alone be better than a fossil representative with radials and concentrics? Why are the modern versions superior, as Parkinson's theory of progressive creation required? Parkinson was evidently troubled. In the summary statement to his three-volume work, he devoted more space to *Trigonia* than to any other genus. He clutched at the one available straw, but clearly without conviction. At least the modern trigonians are different. *"Raffiniert ist der Herrgott"* (Subtle is the Lord), as Einstein said later. We don't know why, but different must be better:

> This shell, although really of this genus, is of a different species from any shell, which has been found in a fossil state. So that none of the species of shells of this genus, which are known in a fossil state, have, in fact, been found in any stratum above the hard chalk [the Cretaceous, or last period of dinosaurs], or in our present seas.

Louis Agassiz, most able of all creationists, followed Parkinson's personal route in reverse. He began as an advocate of progress in each successive creation and ended by defending the earliest of God's creatures as fully up to snuff (largely because he despised Darwinism with such passion and felt that any admission of progress would bolster the evolutionary cause). For him, therefore, the apparent lack of improvement in modern trigonians posed no problem, while the Cenozoic gap brought nothing but pleasure and confirmation. In the major pre-Darwinian work on these clams, his *Mémoire sur les trigonies* (1840), Agassiz argued explicitly that a Cenozoic gap, if conclusively affirmed, would effectively disprove evolution (quite a cogent claim, by the way):

> The absence of *Trigonia* in Tertiary [Cenozoic] strata is a very important fact for discussions of the origin and relationships of species of different epochs; for if it could one day be shown that *Trigonia* never existed throughout the entire duration of Tertiary time, it would no longer be possible to maintain the principle that species of a genus living in successive geological epochs are derived from each other.

But Agassiz well understood the discomforting uncertainty of negative evidence. Find one nasty, ugly little Cenozoic trigonian tomorrow, and the entire argument collapses. So Agassiz decided to cover his rear and disclaim: No Cenozoic trigonian is dandy; but future discovery of a Cenozoic trigonian would prove nothing. God may, after all, ordain temporal continuity among a group of related, created forms.

Although his passage is an exercise in special pleading, it also contains one of the most succinct and eloquent defenses ever written for the Platonic version of creationism.

> Although I now invoke this fact [the Cenozoic gap] to support my conviction that the different species of a genus are not variants of a single type . . . the discovery of a Tertiary trigonian would still not demonstrate, to my eyes, that the relationship among species of a genus is one of direct descent and successive transformation of original types. . . . I certainly do not deny that natural relationships exist among different species of a genus; on the contrary, I am convinced that species are related to each other by bonds of a higher nature than those of simple direct procreation, bonds that may be compared to the order of a system of ideas whose elements, developed at different times, form in their union an organic whole — although the elements of each time period also appear, within their limits, to be finished products.

In summary, as Darwin's revolution dawned in 1859, the supposedly pure and simple little fact of modern trigonians stood neither as arbiter nor slayer of theories but as touted support for all major conflicting and contradictory views of life — for evolution by Lamarckian and Darwinian agencies, and for creationism in both progressionist and directionless versions. How can something so important be so undecisive? Unless Huxley's heroic vision of raw empiricism triumphant rarely describes the history of ideas or even the progress of science. Percepts do not create and drive concepts; but concepts are not intractable and immune to perceptual nudges either. Thought and observation form a wonderfully complex web of interpenetration and mutual influence — and the interaction often seems to get us somewhere useful.

The *Trigonia* story has a natural ending that should be conventional and happy, but isn't quite. The resolution is not hard to guess, since Darwin's vision has prevailed. The elusive Cenozoic trigonian was found in Australian rocks — at just the right time, in 1865, when nascent evolutionism needed all the help it could get.

H. M. Jenkins, a minor figure in British geology, explicitly defended Darwin in describing the first Cenozoic trigonians. He interpreted the happy closure of the Cenozoic gap as a clear vindication of Darwin's characteristic attitude toward the fossil record and as direct support for evolution. Darwin viewed the fossil record as riddled with imperfections — "a history of the world imperfectly kept . . . of this history we possess the last volume alone. . . . Of this volume, only here and there a short chapter has been preserved; and of each page, only here and there a few lines" *(Origin of Species,* 1859). Gaps, as the old saying goes, represent absence of evidence, not evidence of absence. Jenkins wrote, linking the newly discovered Cenozoic trigonian to this fundamental Darwinian prediction:

> Every paleontologist believes that, when a genus of animals is represented by species occurring in strata of widely different ages, it must have been perpetuated by some one or more species during the whole of the intervening period. . . . The only rational meaning that has ever been attached to this presumed general law . . . is that the perpetuation of the genus . . . has been due to "descent with modification." *Trigonia subundulata* [the formal name for the Cenozoic trigonian] is one of the links hitherto wanting; first, in explanation of the existence of the genus *Trigonia* in the Australian seas of the present day; and secondly, as showing that the great gap which before existed in its life-history was . . . simply a consequence of the imperfection of our knowledge of the geological record.

Finally, a personal confession in closing. This essay has been an exercise in self-indulgence and expiation. I put together the trigonian story at the very beginning of my professional career (when I was just barely big enough to pay full price at the stadium). I published a rather poor account in a technical journal in 1968 (frankly, it stunk).

I got part of the story right. I did recognize that everyone managed to slot the living trigonian into his system and that simple, single facts did not (at least in this case) undo general theories. But I got the end all wrong because the traditional, Huxleyan view still beguiled me. I told the happy ending because I read Jenkins's quote and took it at face value — as an evolutionary prediction fulfilled and an empirical vindication provided. I forgot (or hadn't yet learned) a cardinal rule of scholarly detection: Don't only weigh what you have; ask why you don't see what you ought to find. Negative evidence is important — especially when the record is sufficiently complete to indicate that an absence may be genuine.

I now read the Cenozoic discovery quite differently, because I have confronted what should have happened but didn't. If Darwin's vindication required a set of new, clean, pristine, unexpected facts, then why didn't the Cenozoic trigonian inspire a wave of rejoicing? Darwin had predicted it; Agassiz had invested much hope in its nonexistence.

Sure, Jenkins said the right things in his article; I quoted them and regarded my task as complete. But the key to the story lies elsewhere — in the nonevents. Jenkins wrote a two and a half page note in a minor journal. No one else seemed to notice. Darwin never commented, though the *Origin of Species* still had several editions to run. *Trigonia* did not become a textbook example of evolution triumphant. Most curiously, Jenkins did not find the Cenozoic trigonian. It was unearthed by Frederick McCoy, an eminent leader of Australian science, the founder and head of the Museum of Natural History and Geology in Melbourne. He must have known what he had and what it meant. But he didn't even bother to publish his description. I should have taken my clue from the opening lines of Jenkins's paper, but I passed them by:

> The very interesting discovery of a species of *Trigonia* in the Tertiary deposits of Australia has in England remained entirely in the background, and I have been several times surprised at finding students of Tertiary paleontology, generally *au courant* with the progress of their special branch of science, unacquainted with the circumstance. Its importance, in a theoretical point of view, is beyond all question, hence the deep interest always exhibited by those to whom I have spoken on the subject.

I had, in short, succumbed to the view I was questioning. I had recognized that the original discovery of the living trigonian upended no theory, but I had let the Cenozoic fossil act as a Huxleyan nasty fact because Jenkins had so presented it. But when we consider what the Cenozoic trigonian did *not* provoke, we obtain a more general and consistent account of the entire affair. The living trigonian changed no theory, because it could fit (however uncomfortably) with all major views of life. The Cenozoic trigonian did not prove evolution either, because Agassiz's position of retreat was defensible (however embarrassing) and because evolution was too big a revolution to rely critically on any one datum. *Trigonia* didn't hurt, but a multitude of fish were frying, and one extra clam, however clean and pretty, didn't bring the meal to perfection (I shall anticipate a suitable recipe next month, Mr. Sokolov).

Sherlock Holmes once solved a case because the dog didn't bark, but would have sounded off had it been a dog. Nonevents matter, not only the new and nasty facts. Which reminds me: I must have looked at a thousand periwinkles this morning. Still no lefties. Maybe someday.

ANNE HOLLANDER

Dressed to Thrill

FROM THE NEW REPUBLIC

WHEN QUENTIN BELL applied Veblen's principles of Conspicuous Consumption and Conspicuous Waste to fashion, he added another — Conspicuous Outrage. This one now clearly leads the other two. In this decade we want the latest trends in appearance to strain our sense of the suitable and give us a real jolt. The old social systems that generated a need for conspicuous display have modified enough to dull the chic of straight extravagance: the chic of shock has continuous vitality. Dramatically perverse sexual signals are always powerful elements in the modern fashionable vocabulary; and the most sensational component among present trends is something referred to as androgyny. Many modish women's clothes imitate what Robert Taylor wore in 1940 publicity stills, and Michael Jackson's startling feminine beauty challenges public responses from every store window, as well as in many living replicas.

The mode in appearance mirrors collective fantasy, not fundamental aims and beliefs. We are not all really longing for two sexes in a single body, and the true hermaphrodite still counts as a monster. We are not seeing a complete and free interchange of physical characteristics across the sexual divide. There are no silky false moustaches or dashing fake goatees finely crafted of imported sable for the discriminating woman, or luxuriant jaw-length sideburns of the softest bristle sold with moisturizing glue and a designer applicator. Although the new ideal feminine torso has strong square shoulders, flat hips, and no belly at all, the corresponding ideal male body is certainly not displaying the beauties of a soft round stomach, flaring hips, full thighs, and delicately sloping shoulders. On the new woman's ideally athletic shape, breasts may be large or not — a flat chest is not required; and below the belt in back, the buttocks may sharply protrude. But no space remains in front to house a safely cushioned uterus and ovaries, or even well-upholstered labia: under the lower half of the new, high-cut minimal swimsuits, there is room only for a clitoris. Meanwhile the thrilling style of male beauty embodied by Michael Jackson runs chiefly to unprecedented surface adornment — cosmetics and sequins, jewels and elaborate hair, all the old privileges once granted to women, to give them every erotic advantage in the sex wars of the past.

The point about all this is clearly not androgyny at all, but the idea of detachable pleasure. Each sex is not trying to take up the fundamental qualities of the other sex, but rather of the other sexuality — the erotic dimension, which can transcend biology and its attendant social assumptions and institutions. Eroticism is being shown to float free of sexual function. Virility is displayed as a capacity for feeling and generating excitement, not for felling trees or enemies and generating children. Femininity has abandoned the old gestures of passivity to take on main force: ravishing female models now stare purposefully into the viewer's eyes instead of flashing provocative glances or gazing remotely away. Erotic attractiveness appears ready to exert its strength in unforeseeable and formerly forbidden ways and places. Recognition is now being given to sexual desire for objects of all kinds once considered unsuitable — some of them inanimate, judging from the seductiveness of most advertising photography.

Homosexual desire is now an acknowledged aspect of common life, deserving of truthful representation in popular culture, not just in coterie vehicles of expression. The aging parents of youthful characters in movie and television dramas are no longer rendered as mentally stuffy and physically withered, but as stunningly attractive sexual beings — legitimate and nonridiculous rivals for the lustful attentions of the young. The curved flanks of travel irons and food processors in Bloomingdale's catalogue make as strong an appeal to erotic desire as the satiny behinds and moist lips of the makeup and underwear models. So do the unfolding petals of lettuces and the rosy flesh of cut tomatoes on TV food commercials. In this general eroticization of the material world, visual culture is openly acknowledging that lust is by nature wayward.

To register as attractive under current assumptions, a female body may now show its affinities not only with delicious objects but with attractive male bodies, without having to relinquish any feminine erotic resources. Male beauty may be enhanced by feminine usages that increase rather than diminish its masculine effect. Men and women may both wear clothes loosely fashioned by designers like Gianni Versace or Issey Miyake to render all bodies attractive whatever their structure, like the drapery of antiquity. In such clothes, sexuality is expressed obliquely in a fluid fabric envelope that follows bodily movement and also forms a graceful counterpoint to the nonchalant postures of modern repose. The aim of such dress is to emphasize the sexiness of a rather generalized sensuality, not of male or female characteristics; and our present sense of personal appearance, like our sense of all material display, shows that we are more interested in generalized sensuality than in anything else. In our multiform culture, it seems to serve as an equalizer.

In fashion, however, pervasive eroticism is still frequently being represented as the perpetual overthrow of all the restrictive categories left over from the last century, a sort of ongoing revolution. We are still pretending to congratulate ourselves on what a long way we have come. The lush men and strong girls now on view in the media may be continuing a long-range trend that began between the World Wars; but there have been significant interruptions and an important shift of tone. Then, too, men had smooth faces, thick, wavy hair and full, pouting lips, and women often wore pants, had shingled hair, and athletic torsos. But the important point in those days was to be as anti-Victorian as possible. The rigid and bearded Victorian male was being eased out of his tight carapace and distancing whiskers; the whole ladylike panoply was being simplified so that the actual woman became apparent to the eye and touch. Much of our present female mannishness and feminized manhood is a nostalgic reference to the effects fashionable for men and women in those pioneering days, rather than a new revolutionary expression of the same authentic kind.

There is obviously more to it all now than there was between the wars. We have already gone through some fake Victorian revivals, both unself-conscious in the 1950s and self-conscious in the sixties and seventies, and lately our sense of all style has become slightly corrupt. Apart from the sexiness of sex, we have discovered the stylishness of style and the fashionableness of fashion. Evolving conventions of dress and sudden revolts from them have both become stylistically forced; there have been heavy quotation marks around almost all conspicuous modes of clothing in the last fifteen or twenty years, as there were not in more hopeful days. Life is now recognized to have a grotesque and inflated media dimension by which ordinary experience is measured, and all fashion has taken to looking over its own shoulder. Our contemporary revolutionary modes are mostly theatrical costumes, since we have now learned to assume that appearances are detachable and interchangeable and only have provisional meanings.

Many of the more extreme new sartorial phenomena display such uncooked incoherence that they fail to represent any main trend in twentieth-century taste except a certain perverse taste for garbage — which is similarly fragmented and inexpressive, even though it can always be sifted and categorized. We have become obsessed with picking over the past instead of plowing it under, where it can do some good. Perversity has moreover been fostered in fashion by its relentless presentation as a form of ongoing public entertainment. The need for constant impact naturally causes originality to get confused with the capacity to cause a sensation; and sensations can always be created, just as in all show business, by the crudest of allusions.

In the twenties, the revolutionary new fashions were much more important but much less brutally intrusive. Photos from the twenties, thirties, and even the very early forties, show the young Tyrone Power and Robert Taylor smiling with scintillating confidence, caressed by soft focus and glittering highlights, and wearing the full-cut, casual topcoats with the collar up that we see in today's ads for women, then as now opened to show the fully-draped trousers, loose sweaters, and long, broad jackets of that time. Then it was an alluringly modern and feminized version of male beauty, freshly suggesting pleasure without violence or loss of decorum, a high level of civilization without any forbidding and tyrannical stiffness or antiquated formality. At the same time, women's fashions were stressing an articulated female shape that sought to be perceived as clearly as the male. Both were the first modern styles to take up the flavor of general physical ease, in timely and pertinent defiance of the social restrictions and symbolic sexual distinctions made by dress in the preceding time. Now, however, those same easy men's clothes are being worn by women; and the honest old figure of freedom seems to be dressed up in the spirit of pastiche. We did come a long way for a while, but then we stopped and went on the stage.

Strong and separate sexual definition in the old Victorian manner tried to forbid the generally erotic and foster the romantic. Against such a background even slightly blurring the definition automatically did the opposite; and so when Victorian women dared adopt any partial assortment of male dress they were always extremely disturbing. They called attention to those aspects of female sexuality that develop in sharp contrast to both female biology and romantic rhetoric. Consequently, when female fashion underwent its great changes early in this century, such aspects were deliberately and vehemently emphasized by a new mobility and quasi-masculine leanness. Women with no plump extensions at all but with obvious and movable legs suddenly made their appearance, occasionally even in trousers. They indicated a mettlesome eagerness for action, even unencumbered amorous action, and great lack of interest in sitting still receiving homage or rocking the cradle. Meanwhile when men adopted the casual suits of modern leisure, they began to suggest a certain new readiness to sit and talk, to listen and laugh at themselves, to dally and tarry rather than couple briskly and straightway depart for work or battle. Men and women visibly desired to rewrite the rules about how the two sexes should express their interest in sex; and the liberated modern ideal was crystallized.

But a sexual ideal of maturity and enlightened savoir faire

also informed that period of our imaginative history. In the
fantasy of the thirties, manifested in the films of Claudette Col-
bert, for example, or Gable and Lombard, adult men and
women ideally pursued pleasure without sacrificing reason,
humor, or courtesy — even in those dramas devoted to the ridiculous. The sexes were still regarded as fundamentally different kinds of being, although the style of their sexuality was
reconceived. The aim of amorous life was still to take on the
challenging dialectic of the sexes, which alone could yield the
fullest kind of sexual pleasure. Erotic feeling was inseparable
from dramatic situation.

By those same thirties, modern adult clothing was also a fully
developed stylistic achievement. It duly continued to refine,
until it finally became unbearably mannered in the first half of
the sixties. The famous ensuing sartorial revolution, though
perfectly authentic, was also the first to occur in front of the
camera — always in the mirror, as it were. And somehow the
subsequent two decades have seen a great fragmentation both
of fashion and of sexuality.

Extreme imagery, much of it androgynous like Boy George's
looks, or the many punk styles and all the raunchier fashion
photos, has become quite commonplace; but it has also become
progressively remote from most common practice. It offers appearances that we may label "fashion," but that we really know
to be media inventions created especially to stun, provoke, and
dismay us. At the same time, some very conventional outrageous
effects have been revived in the realm of accessible fashion,
where there is always room for them. Ordinary outrageousness
and perverse daring in dress are the signs of licensed play,
never the signal of serious action. They are licitly engaged in by
the basically powerless, including clowns and children and other
innocuous performers, who are always allowed to make extreme
emotional claims that may stir up strong personal responses but
have no serious public importance. Women's fashion constantly
made use of outrage in this way during the centuries of female
powerlessness, and selective borrowing from men was one of its
most effective motifs.

After the sixties and before the present menswear mode, the
masculine components in women's fashions still made girls look

either excitingly shocking or touchingly pathetic. The various neat tuxedos made famous by Yves St. Laurent, for example, were intended to give a woman the look of a depraved youth, a sort of tempting Dorian Gray. The *Annie Hall* clothes swamped the woman in oversized male garments, so that she looked at first like a small child being funny in adult gear, and then like a fragile girl wrapped in a strong man's coat, a combined emblem of bruised innocence and clownishness. These are both familiar "outrageous" devices culled particularly from the theatrical past.

Long before modern fashion took it up, the conventionally outrageous theme of an attractive feminine woman in breeches proved an invariably stimulating refinement in the long history of racy popular art, both for the stage and in print. The most important erotic aim of this theme was never to make a woman actually seem to be a man — looking butch has never been generally attractive — but to make a girl assume the unsettling beauty that dwells in the sexual uncertainty of an adolescent boy. It is an obvious clever move for modern fashionable women to combine the old show-businesslike excitement of the suggestive trousered female with the cultivated self-possession of early twentieth-century menswear — itself already a feminized male style. It suits, especially in the present disintegrated erotic climate that has rendered the purer forms of outrageousness somewhat passé.

Such uses of men's clothes have nothing to do with an impulse toward androgyny. They instead invoke all the old tension between the sexes; and complete drag, whichever sex wears it, also insists on sexual polarity. Most drag for men veers toward the exaggerated accoutrements of the standard siren; and on the current screen, *Tootsie* and *Yentl* are both demonstrating how different and how divided the sexes are.

While the extreme phenomena are getting all the attention, however, we are acting out quite another forbidden fantasy in our ordinary lives. The really androgynous realm in personal appearance is that of active sports clothing. The unprecedented appeal of running gear and gym clothes and all the other garb associated with strenuous physical effort seems to be offering an alternative in sexual expression. Beyond the simple pleasures of physical fitness, and the right-minded satisfactions of banishing class difference that were first expressed in the blue-jeans revolution of the sixties, this version of pastoral suggests a new erotic appeal in the perceived androgyny of childhood. The short shorts and other ingenuous bright play clothes in primary colors that now clothe bodies of all sizes and sexes are giving a startling kindergarten cast to everybody's public looks, especially in summer.

The real excitement of androgynous appearance is again revealed as associated only with extreme youth — apparently the more extreme the better. The natural androgyny of old age has acquired no appeal. The tendency of male and female bodies to resemble each other in late maturity is still conventionally ridiculous and deplorable; sportswear on old women looks crisp and convenient, not sexually attractive. But the fresh, unfinished androgyny of the nursery is evidently a newly expanded arena for sexual fantasy.

In the unisex look of the ordinary clothing that has become increasingly common in the past two decades, there has been a submerged but unmistakable element of child-worship. This note has been struck at a great distance from the slick and expensive ambiguities of high fashion that include couture children's clothes aping the vagaries of current adult chic. It resonates instead in the everyday sexual ambiguity of rough duck or corduroy pants, flannel shirts, T-shirts, sweaters, and sneakers. Any subway car or supermarket is full of people dressed this way. The guises for this fantasy have extended past play clothes to children's underwear, the little knitted shirts and briefs that everyone wears at the age of five. One ubiquitous ad for these even showed a shirtee sliding up to expose an adult breast, to emphasize the sexiness of the fashion; but the breast has been prudently canceled in publicly displayed versions.

Our erotic obsession with children has overt and easily deplored expressions in the media, where steamy twelve-year-old fashion models star in ads and twelve-year-old prostitutes figure in dramas and news stories. The high-fashion modes for children also have the flavor of forced eroticism. Child abuse and kiddy porn are now publicly discussed concerns, ventilated in the righteous spirit of reform; and yet unconscious custom reflects the same preoccupation with the sexual condition of childhood. The androgynous sportswear that was formerly the acceptable everyday dress only of children is now everyone's leisure clothing; its new currency must have more than one meaning.

On the surface, of course, it invokes the straight appeal of the physical life, the rural life, and perhaps even especially the taxing life of the dedicated athlete, which used to include sexual abstinence along with the chance of glory. The world may wish to look as if it were constantly in training to win, or equipped to explore; but there is another condition it is also less obviously longing for — freedom from the strain of fully adult sexuality. These styles of clothing signal a retreat into the unfinished, undefined sexuality of childhood that we are now finding so erotic, and that carries no difficult social or personal responsibilities.

From 1925 to 1965, four-year-old girls and boys could tumble in the sandbox in identical cotton overalls or knitted suits, innocently aping the clothes of skiers, railroadmen, or miners, while their mom wore a dress, hat, and stockings, and their dad a suit, hat, and tie — the modern dress of sexual maturity, also worn by Gable, Lombard, and all the young and glittering Hollywood company. Now the whole family wears sweat suits and overalls and goes bareheaded. Such gear is also designed to encourage the game of dressing up like all the non-amorous and ultraphysical heroes of modern folklore — forest rangers and cowboys, spacemen and frogmen, pilots and motorcyclists, migrant workers and terrorists — that is constantly urged on children. The great masquerade party of the late sixties ostensibly came to an end; but it had irreversibly given to ordinary grownups the right to wear fancy costumes for fun that was formerly a child's privilege. The traditional dress of the separate adult sexes is reserved for public appearances, and in general it is now socially correct to express impatience with it. "Informal" is the only proper style in middle-class social life; and for private leisure, when impulse governs choices, kids' clothes are the leading one. Apparently the erotic androgynous child is the new forbidden creature of unconscious fantasy, not

only the infantile fashion model or rock star but the ordinary
kid, who has exciting sexual potential hidden under its unsexed
dress-up play clothes.

Fashions of the remote past dealt straightforwardly with the
sexuality of children by dressing them just like ordinary adults,
suitably different according to sex. But in Romantic times, children were perceived to exist in a special condition much purer
and closer to beneficent nature than their elders, requiring
clothes that kept them visibly separate from the complex cor-
ruptions of adult society, including full-scale erotic awareness.
The habit of putting children in fancy dress began then, too,
especially boys. They were dressed as wee, chubby, and harmless soldiers and sailors, or Turks and Romans, to emphasize
their innocence by contrast. Children's clothes still differed according to sex — girls had sweet little chemises and sashes instead of fancy costumes — but their overriding common flavor
was one of artlessness.

Later on the Victorians overdid it, and loaded their children
with clothing, but it was still two-sexed and distinctively designed for them. Finally the enlightened twentieth century invented the use of mock sportswear for the wiggly little bodies of
both boys and girls. Nevertheless, the costumes now suitable for
children on display still tend toward the Victorian, with a good
deal of nostalgic velvet and lace. In line with Romantic views of
women, some feminine styles also used to feature infantine suggestions drawn from little girls' costumes: the last was the tiny
baby dress worn with big shoes and big hair in the later sixties,
just before the eruption of the women's movement. But only
since then has a whole generation of adults felt like dressing up
in mock rough gear, like androgynous children at play, to form
a race of apparently presexual but unmistakably erotic beings.

Once again, very pointedly, the clothes for the role are male.
Our modern sense of artlessness seems to prefer the masculine
brand; and when we dress our little boys and girls alike to
blur their sexuality — or ourselves in imitation of them — that
means we dress the girls like the boys, in the manifold costumes
celebrating nonsexual physical prowess. At leisure, both men
and women prefer to suggest versions of Adam alone in Eden

before he knew he had a sex, innocently wearing his primal sweat suit made only of native worth and honor.

The Romantic sense of the child as naturally privileged and instinctively good like Adam seems to stay with us. But we have lately added the belief in a child's potential depravity, which may go unpaid for and unpunished just because of all children's categorical innocence. Perhaps this society abuses its children, and also aggressively dresses them in lipstick and sequins, for the same reason it imitates them — from a helpless envy of what they get away with. The everyday androgynous costume is the suit of diminished erotic responsibility and exemption from adult sexual risk. What it clothes is the child's license to make demands and receive gratification with no risk of dishonor — to be erotic, but to pose as unsexual and therefore unaccountable.

Even more forbidden and outrageous than the sexual child is its near relation, the erotic angel. While the ordinary world is routinely dressing itself and its kids in unisex jeans, it is simultaneously conjuring up mercurial apparitions who offer an enchanting counterpoint to life's mundane transactions. In the rock star form, they embody the opposing fantasy face of the troublesome domestic child or adolescent: the angelic visitor who needs to obey no earthly rules. Funny little E.T. was only one version. The type includes all those supremely compelling creatures who may shine while they stomp and whirl and scream and hum and never suffer the slightest humiliation.

A child, however ideologized, is always real and problematic, but an angel has a fine mythic remoteness however palpable he seems. The opposing kind of androgyny invests him: he exists not before but beyond human sexual life, and he comes as a powerful messenger from spheres where there is no taking or giving in marriage, but where extreme kinds of joy are said to be infinite. Our rock-video beings cultivate the unhuman look of ultimate synthesis: they aim to transcend sexual conflict by becoming fearsome angels, universally stimulating creatures fit for real existence only out of this world. Like all angels, they profoundly excite; but they don't excite desire, even though they do make the air crackle with promise and menace. Their job is to bring the message and then leave, having somehow transformed the world. Michael Jackson reportedly leads a life both angelic and artificially childlike, and he makes his appearances in epiphanic style. David Bowie still appears to be the man who fell to earth, not someone born here. Grace Jones also seems to come from altogether elsewhere. Such idols only function in the sphere of unattainability. While they flourish they remain sojourners, leading lives of vivid otherness in what seems a sexual no man's land.

Angels were in fact once firmly male and uncompromisingly austere. The disturbing sensuality they acquired in the art of later centuries, like that of the luscious angel in Leonardo's *Virgin of the Rocks*, always reads as a feminization — and from this one must conclude that adding feminine elements to the male is what produces androgyny's most intense effects. Almost all our androgynous stars are in fact males in feminized trim; their muscular and crop-haired female counterparts, such as Annie Lennox, are less numerous and have a more limited appeal. The meaning in all our androgyny, both modish and ordinary, still seems to be the same: the male is the primary sex, straightforward, simple, and active. He can be improved and embellished, however, and have and give a better time if he allows himself to be modified by the complexities of female influence.

The process does not work the other way. Elegant women in fashionable menswear expound the same thought, not its opposite: traditional jackets and trousers are austerely beautiful, but they are patently enhanced by high heels, flowing scarves, cosmetics, and earrings. Lisa Lyon, the body builder, has been photographed by Robert Mapplethorpe to show that her excessively developed muscles do not make her mannish but instead have been feminized to go with, not against, her flowered hats and lipstick. Ordinary women wearing men's active gear while wheeling strollers on the street or carrying bags across the parking lot are subduing and adapting harsh male dress to flexible female life and giving it some new scope. Common androgynous costume is always some kind of suit or jumpsuit, or pants, shirt and jacket, not some kind of dress, bodice and skirt, or gown. A hat may go with it, or perhaps a hood or scarf, but not a coif or veil. A few real female skirts (not kilts or Greek evzone skirts) are now being very occasionally and sensationally tried out by some highly visible men — daring designers, media performers and their imitators, fashion models and theirs — but all kinds of pants are being worn by all kinds of women all the time. We can read the message: the male is the first sex, now at last prepared to consider the other one anew, with much fanfare. It is still a case of female sexuality enlightening the straight male world — still the arrival of Eve and all her subsequent business in and beyond the garden — that is being celebrated. The "androgynous" mode for both sexes suggests that the female has come on the scene to educate the male about the imaginative pleasures of sex, signified chiefly by the pleasures of adornment. About its difficulties, summed up by that glaringly absent round belly, she is naturally keeping quiet.

Meanwhile the more glittering versions of modish androgyny continue to reflect what we adore in fantasy. Many of us seem to feel that the most erotic condition of all could not be that of any man or woman, or of any child, or of a human being with two sexes, but that of a very young and effeminate male angel — a new version of art history's lascivious *putto*. Such a being may give and take a guiltless delight, wield limitless sexual power without sexual politics, feel all the pleasures of sex with none of the personal risks, can never grow up, never get wise, and never be old. It is a futureless vision, undoubtedly appropriate to a nuclear age; but if any of us manages to survive, the soft round belly will surely again have its day.

In the meantime, as we approach the end of the century and the millennium, the impulse toward a certain fusion in the habits of the sexes may have a more hopeful meaning. After a hundred years of underground struggle, trousers are no longer male dress sometimes worn by women. They have been successfully feminized so as to become authentic costume for both sexes, and to regain the authoritative bisexual status the gown once had in the early Middle Ages. This development is clearly not a quick trend but a true change, generations in the making. Male skirts have yet to prove themselves; but men have in fact succeeded in making long-term capital out of the short-lived and now forgotten Peacock Revolution of the late sixties. Whole new ranges of rich color, interesting pattern, texture, and unusual cut have become generally acceptable in male dress since then, and so has a variety of jewelry. The sort of fashionable experiment once associated only with women has become a standard male option. Some new agreement between the sexes may actually be forming, signaled by all these persistent visual projections; but just what that accord will turn out to be it is not safe to predict, nor whether it will continue to civilize us further or only perplex us more.

GEORGE F. KENNAN

Morality and Foreign Policy

FROM FOREIGN AFFAIRS

IN A SMALL VOLUME of lectures published nearly thirty-five years ago,[1] I had the temerity to suggest that the American statesmen of the turn of the twentieth century were unduly legalistic and moralistic in their judgment of the actions of other governments. This seemed to be an approach that carried them away from the sterner requirements of political realism and caused their statements and actions, however impressive to the domestic political audience, to lose effectiveness in the international arena.

These observations were doubtless brought forward too cryptically and thus invited a wide variety of interpretations, not excluding the thesis that I had advocated an amoral, or even immoral, foreign policy for this country. There have since been demands, particularly from the younger generation, that I should make clearer my views on the relationship of moral considerations to American foreign policy. The challenge is a fair one and deserves a response.

1

Certain distinctions should be made before one wanders further into this thicket of problems.

First of all, the conduct of diplomacy is the responsibility of governments. For purely practical reasons, this is unavoidable

[1] *American Diplomacy 1900–1950* (Chicago: University of Chicago Press, 1951).

and inalterable. This responsibility is not diminished by the fact that government, in formulating foreign policy, may choose to be influenced by private opinion. What we are talking about, therefore, when we attempt to relate moral considerations to foreign policy, is the behavior of governments, not of individuals or entire peoples.

Second, let us recognize that the functions, commitments and moral obligations of governments are not the same as those of the individual. Government is an agent, not a principal. Its primary obligation is to the *interests* of the national society it represents, not to the moral impulses that individual elements of that society may experience. No more than the attorney vis-à-vis the client, nor the doctor vis-à-vis the patient, can government attempt to insert itself into the consciences of those whose interests it represents.

Let me explain. The interests of the national society for which government has to concern itself are basically those of its military security, the integrity of its political life and the well-being of its people. These needs have no moral quality. They arise from the very existence of the national state in question and from the status of national sovereignty it enjoys. They are the unavoidable necessities of a national existence and therefore not subject to classification as either "good" or "bad." They may be questioned from a detached philosophic point of view. But the government of the sovereign state cannot make such judgments. When it accepts the responsibilities of governing, implicit in that acceptance is the assumption that it is right that the state should be sovereign, that the integrity of its political life should be assured, that its people should enjoy the blessings of military security, material prosperity and a reasonable opportunity for, as the Declaration of Independence put it, the pursuit of happiness. For these assumptions the government needs no moral justification, nor need it accept any moral reproach for acting on the basis of them.

This assertion assumes, however, that the concept of national security taken as the basis for governmental concern is one reasonably, not extravagantly, conceived. In an age of nuclear striking power, national security can never be more than relative; and to the extent that it can be assured at all, it must find its sanction in the intentions of rival powers as well as in their capabilities. A concept of national security that ignores this reality and, above all, one that fails to concede the same legitimacy to the security needs of others that it claims for its own, lays itself open to the same moral reproach from which, in normal circumstances, it would be immune.

Whoever looks thoughtfully at the present situation of the United States in particular will have to agree that to assure these blessings to the American people is a task of such dimensions that the government attempting to meet it successfully will have very little, if any, energy and attention left to devote to other undertakings, including those suggested by the moral impulses of these or those of its citizens.

Finally, let us note that there are no internationally accepted standards of morality to which the U.S. government could appeal if it wished to act in the name of moral principles. It is true that there are certain words and phrases sufficiently high-sounding the world over so that most governments, when asked to declare themselves for or against, will cheerfully subscribe to them, considering that such is their vagueness that the mere act of subscribing to them carries with it no danger of having one's freedom of action significantly impaired. To this category of pronouncements belong such documents as the Kellogg-Briand Pact, the Atlantic Charter, the Yalta Declaration on Liberated Europe, and the prologues of innumerable other international agreements.

Ever since Secretary of State John Hay staged a political coup in 1899 by summoning the supposedly wicked European powers to sign up to the lofty principles of his Open Door notes (principles which neither they nor we had any awkward intention of observing), American statesmen have had a fondness for hurling just such semantic challenges at their foreign counterparts, thereby placing themselves in a graceful posture before domestic American opinion and reaping whatever political fruits are to be derived from the somewhat grudging and embarrassed responses these challenges evoke.

To say these things, I know, is to invite the question: how about the Helsinki accords of 1975? These, of course, were numerous and varied. There is no disposition here to question the value of many of them as refinements of the norms of international intercourse. But there were some, particularly those related to human rights, which it is hard to relegate to any category other than that of the high-minded but innocuous professions just referred to. These accords were declaratory in nature, not contractual. The very general terms in which they were drawn up, involving the use of words and phrases that had different meanings for different people, deprived them of the character of specific obligations to which signatory governments could usefully be held. The Western statesmen who pressed for Soviet adherence to these pronouncements must have been aware that some of them could not be implemented on the Soviet side, within the meanings we would normally attach to their workings, without fundamental changes in the Soviet system of power — changes we had no reason to expect would, or could, be introduced by the men then in power. Whether it is morally commendable to induce others to sign up to declarations, however high-minded in resonance, which one knows will not and cannot be implemented, is a reasonable question. The Western negotiators, in any case, had no reason to plead naïveté as their excuse for doing so.

When we talk about the application of moral standards to foreign policy, therefore, we are not talking about compliance with some clear and generally accepted international code of behavior. If the policies and actions of the U.S. government are to be made to conform to moral standards, those standards are going to have to be America's own, founded on traditional American principles of justice and propriety. When others fail to conform to those principles, and when their failure to conform has an adverse effect on American *interests*, as distinct from political tastes, we have every right to complain and, if necessary, to take retaliatory action. What we cannot do is to assume that our moral standards are theirs as well, and to appeal to those standards as the source of our grievances.

2

So much for basic principles. Let us now consider some categories of action that the U.S. government is frequently asked to
take, and sometimes does take, in the name of moral principle.

These actions fall into two broad general categories: those
that relate to the behavior of other governments that we find
morally unacceptable, and those that relate to the behavior of
our own government. Let us take them in that order.

There have been many instances, particularly in recent years,
when the U.S. government has taken umbrage at the behavior
of other governments on grounds that at least implied moral
criteria for judgment, and in some of these instances the verbal
protests have been reinforced by more tangible means of pressure. These various interventions have marched, so to speak,
under a number of banners: democracy, human rights, majority
rule, fidelity to treaties, fidelity to the U.N. Charter, and so on.
Their targets have sometimes been the external policies and
actions of the offending states, more often the internal practices. The interventions have served, in the eyes of their American inspirers, as demonstrations not only of the moral
deficiencies of others but of the positive morality of ourselves;
for it was seen as our moral duty to detect these lapses on the
part of others, to denounce them before the world, and to assure — as far as we could with measures short of military action
— that they were corrected.

Those who have inspired or initiated efforts of this nature
would certainly have claimed to be acting in the name of moral
principle, and in many instances they would no doubt have been
sincere in doing so. But whether the results of this inspiration,
like those of so many other good intentions, would justify this
claim is questionable from a number of standpoints.

Let us take first those of our interventions that relate to internal practices of the offending governments. Let us reflect for a
moment on how these interventions appear in the eyes of the
governments in question and of many outsiders.

The situations that arouse our discontent are ones existing, as
a rule, far from our own shores. Few of us can profess to be
perfect judges of their rights and their wrongs. These are, for

the governments in question, matters of internal affairs. It is customary for governments to resent interference by outside powers in affairs of this nature, and if our diplomatic history is any indication, we ourselves are not above resenting and resisting it when we find ourselves its object.

Interventions of this nature can be formally defensible only if the practices against which they are directed are seriously injurious to our interests, rather than just our sensibilities. There will, of course, be those readers who will argue that the encouragement and promotion of democracy elsewhere is always in the interests of the security, political integrity and prosperity of the United States. If this can be demonstrated in a given instance, well and good. But it is not invariably the case. Democracy is a loose term. Many varieties of folly and injustice contrive to masquerade under this designation. The mere fact that a country acquires the trappings of self-government does not automatically mean that the interests of the United States are thereby furthered. There are forms of plebiscitary "democracy" that may well prove less favorable to American interests than a wise and benevolent authoritarianism. There can be tyrannies of a majority as well as tyrannies of a minority, with the one hardly less odious than the other. Hitler came into power (albeit under highly unusual circumstances) with an electoral mandate, and there is scarcely a dictatorship of this age that would not claim the legitimacy of mass support.

There are parts of the world where the main requirement of American security is not an unnatural imitation of the American model but sheer stability, and this last is not always assured by a government of what appears to be popular acclaim. In approaching this question, Americans must overcome their tendency toward generalization and learn to examine each case on its own merits. The best measure of these merits is not the attractiveness of certain general semantic symbols but the effect of the given situation on the tangible and demonstrable interests of the United States.

Furthermore, while we are quick to allege that this or that practice in a foreign country is bad and deserves correction, seldom if ever do we seem to occupy ourselves seriously or realistically with the conceivable alternatives. It seems seldom to occur to us that even if a given situation is bad, the alternatives to it might be worse — even though history provides plenty of examples of just this phenomenon. In the eyes of many Americans it is enough for us to indicate the changes that ought, as we see it, to be made. We assume, of course, that the consequences will be benign and happy ones. But this is not always assured. It is, in any case, not we who are going to have to live with those consequences: it is the offending government and its people. We are demanding, in effect, a species of veto power over those of their practices that we dislike, while denying responsibility for whatever may flow from the acceptance of our demands.

Finally, we might note that our government, in raising such demands, is frequently responding not to its own moral impulses or to any wide general movements of American opinion but rather to pressures generated by politically influential minority elements among us that have some special interest — ethnic, racial, religious, ideological or several of these together — in the foreign situation in question. Sometimes it is the sympathies of these minorities that are most prominently aroused, sometimes their antipathies. But in view of this diversity of motive, the U.S. government, in responding to such pressures and making itself their spokesman, seldom acts consistently. Practices or policies that arouse our official displeasure in one country are cheerfully condoned or ignored in another. What is bad in the behavior of our opponents is good, or at least acceptable, in the case of our friends. What is unobjectionable to us at one period of our history is seen as offensive in another.

This is unfortunate, for a lack of consistency implies a lack of principle in the eyes of much of the world; whereas morality, if not principled, is not really morality. Foreigners, observing these anomalies, may be forgiven for suspecting that what passes as the product of moral inspiration in the rhetoric of our government is more likely to be a fair reflection of the mosaic of residual ethnic loyalties and passions that make themselves felt in the rough and tumble of our political life.

Similar things could be said when it is not the internal practices of the offending government but its actions on the international scene that are at issue. There is, here, the same reluctance to occupy oneself with the conceivable alternatives to the procedures one complains about or with the consequences likely to flow from the acceptance of one's demands. And there is frequently the same lack of consistency in the reaction. The Soviet action in Afghanistan, for example, is condemned, resented and responded to by sanctions. One recalls little of such reaction in the case of the somewhat similar, and apparently no less drastic, action taken by China in Tibet some years ago. The question inevitably arises: is it principle that determines our reaction? Or are there other motives?

Where measures taken by foreign governments affect adversely American interests rather than just American moral sensibilities, protests and retaliation are obviously in order; but then they should be carried forward frankly for what they are, and not allowed to masquerade under the mantle of moral principle.

There will be a tendency, I know, on the part of some readers to see in these observations an apology for the various situations, both domestic and international, against which we have protested and acted in the past. They are not meant to have any such connotations. These words are being written — for whatever this is worth — by one who regards the action in Afghanistan as a grievous and reprehensible mistake of Soviet policy, a mistake that could and should certainly have been avoided. Certain of the procedures of the South African police have been no less odious to me than to many others.

What is being said here does not relate to the reactions of individual Americans, of private organizations in this country, or of the media, to the situations in question. All these may think and say what they like. It relates to the reactions of the U.S. government, as a government among governments, and to the motivation cited for those reactions. Democracy, as Americans understand it, is not necessarily the future of all mankind, nor is it the duty of the U.S. government to assure that it becomes that. Despite frequent assertions to the contrary, not everyone in this world is responsible, after all, for the actions of everyone else, everywhere. Without the power to compel change, there is no responsibility for its absence. In the case of governments it is important for purely practical reasons that the lines of responsibility be kept straight, and that there be, in particular, a clear association of the power to act with the consequences of action or inaction.

3

If, then, the criticism and reproof of perceived moral lapses in the conduct of others are at best a dubious way of expressing our moral commitment, how about our own policies and actions? Here, at least, the connection between power and responsibility — between the sowing and the reaping — is integral. Can it be true that here, too, there is no room for the application of moral principle and that all must be left to the workings of expediency, national egoism and cynicism?

The answer, of course, is no, but the possibilities that exist are only too often ones that run against the grain of powerful tendencies and reflexes in our political establishment.

In a less than perfect world, where the ideal so obviously lies beyond human reach, it is natural that the avoidance of the worst should often be a more practical undertaking than the achievement of the best, and that some of the strongest imperatives of moral conduct should be ones of a negative rather than a positive nature. The strictures of the Ten Commandments are perhaps the best illustration of this state of affairs. This being the case, it is not surprising that some of the most significant possibilities for the observance of moral considerations in American foreign policy relate to the avoidance of actions that have a negative moral significance, rather than to those from which positive results are to be expected.

Many of these possibilities lie in the intuitive qualities of diplomacy — such things as the methodology, manners, style, restraint and elevation of diplomatic discourse — and they can be illustrated only on the basis of a multitude of minor practical examples, for which this article is not the place. There are, however, two negative considerations that deserve mention here.

The first of these relates to the avoidance of what might be called the histrionics of moralism at the expense of its substance.

By that is meant the projection of attitudes, poses and rhetoric that cause us to appear noble and altruistic in the mirror of our own vanity but lack substance when related to the realities of international life. It is a sad feature of the human predicament, in personal as in public life, that whenever one has the agreeable sensation of being impressively moral, one probably is not. What one does without self-consciousness or self-admiration, as a matter of duty or common decency, is apt to be closer to the real thing.

The second of these negative considerations pertains to something commonly called secret operations — a branch of governmental activity closely connected with, but not to be confused with, secret intelligence.

Earlier in this century the great secular despotisms headed by Hitler and Stalin introduced into the pattern of their interaction with other governments clandestine methods of operation that can only be described as ones of unbridled cynicism, audacity and brutality. These were expressed not only by a total lack of scruple on their own part but also by a boundless contempt for the countries against which these efforts were directed (and, one feels, a certain contempt for themselves as well). This was in essence not new, of course; the relations among the nation-states of earlier centuries abounded in examples of clandestine iniquities of every conceivable variety. But these were usually moderated in practice by a greater underlying sense of humanity and a greater respect for at least the outward decencies of national power. Seldom was their intent so cynically destructive, and never was their scale remotely so great, as some of the efforts we have witnessed in this century.

In recent years these undertakings have been supplemented, in their effects on the Western public, by a wholly different phenomenon arising in a wholly different quarter: namely, the unrestrained personal terrorism that has been employed by certain governments or political movements on the fringes of Europe as well as by radical-criminal elements within Western society itself. These phenomena have represented, at different times, serious challenges to the security of nearly all Western countries. It is not surprising, therefore, that among the reactions evoked has been a demand that fire should be fought with fire, that the countries threatened by efforts of this nature should respond with similar efforts.

No one will deny that resistance to these attacks requires secret intelligence of a superior quality and a severe ruthlessness of punishment wherever they fall afoul of the judicial systems of the countries against which they are directed. It is not intended here to comment in any way on the means by which they might or should be opposed by countries other than the United States. Nor is it intended to suggest that any of these activities that carry into this country should not be met by anything less than the full rigor of the law. On the contrary, one could wish the laws were even more rigorous in this respect. But when it comes to governmental operations — or disguised operations — beyond our borders, we Americans have a problem.

In the years immediately following the Second World War the practices of the Stalin regime in this respect were so far-reaching, and presented so great an apparent danger to a Western Europe still weakened by the vicissitudes of war, that our government felt itself justified in setting up facilities for clandestine defensive operations of its own; all available evidence suggests that it has since conducted a number of activities under this heading. As one of those who, at the time, favored the decision to set up such facilities, I regret today, in light of the experience of the intervening years, that the decision was taken. Operations of this nature are not in character for this country. They do not accord with its traditions or with its established procedures of government. The effort to conduct them involves dilemmas and situations of moral ambiguity in which the American statesman is deprived of principled guidance and loses a sense of what is fitting and what is not. Excessive secrecy, duplicity and clandestine skullduggery are simply not our dish — not only because we are incapable of keeping a secret anyway (our commercial media of communication see to that) but, more importantly, because such operations conflict with our own traditional standards and compromise our diplomacy in other areas.

One must not be dogmatic about such matters, of course.

Foreign policy is too intricate a topic to suffer any total taboos. There may be rare moments when a secret operation appears indispensable. A striking example of this was the action of the United States in apprehending the kidnapers of the *Achille Lauro*. But such operations should not be allowed to become a regular and routine feature of the governmental process, cast in the concrete of unquestioned habit and institutionalized bureaucracy. It is there that the dangers lie.

One may say that to deny ourselves this species of capability is to accept a serious limitation on our ability to contend with forces now directed against us. Perhaps; but if so, it is a limitation with which we shall have to live. The success of our diplomacy has always depended, and will continue to depend, on its inherent honesty and openness of purpose and on the forthrightness with which it is carried out. Deprive us of that and we are deprived of our strongest armor and our most effective weapon. If this is a limitation, it is one that reflects no discredit on us. We may accept it in good conscience, for in national as in personal affairs the acceptance of one's limitations is surely one of the first marks of a true morality.

4

So much, then, for the negative imperatives. When we turn to the positive ones there are, again, two that stand out.

The first of them is closely connected with what has just been observed about the acceptance of one's limitations. It relates to the duty of bringing one's commitments and undertakings into a reasonable relationship with one's real possibilities for acting upon the international environment. This is not by any means just a question of military strength, and particularly not of the purely destructive and ultimately self-destructive sort of strength to be found in the nuclear weapon. It is not entirely, or even mainly, a question of foreign policy. It is a duty that requires the shaping of one's society in such a manner that one has maximum control over one's own resources and maximum ability to employ them effectively when they are needed for the advancement of the national interest and the interests of world peace.

A country that has a budgetary deficit and an adverse trade balance both so fantastically high that it is rapidly changing from a major creditor to a major debtor on the world's exchanges, a country whose own enormous internal indebtedness has been permitted to double in less than six years, a country that has permitted its military expenditures to grow so badly out of relationship to the other needs of its economy and so extensively out of reach of political control that the annual spending of hundreds of billions of dollars on "defense" has developed into a national addiction — a country that, in short, has allowed its financial and material affairs to drift into such disorder, is so obviously living beyond its means, and confesses itself unable to live otherwise — is simply not in a position to make the most effective use of its own resources on the international scene, because they are so largely out of its control.

This situation must be understood in relationship to the exorbitant dreams and aspirations of world influence, if not world hegemony — the feeling that we must have the solution to everyone's problems and a finger in every pie — that continue to figure in the assumptions underlying so many American reactions in matters of foreign policy. It must also be understood that in world affairs, as in personal life, example exerts a greater power than precept. A first step along the path of morality would be the frank recognition of the immense gap between what we dream of doing and what we really have to offer, and a resolve, conceived in all humility, to take ourselves under control and to establish a better relationship between our undertakings and our real capabilities.

The second major positive imperative is one that also involves the husbanding and effective use of resources, but it is essentially one of purpose and policy.

Except perhaps in some sectors of American government and opinion, there are few thoughtful people who would not agree that our world is at present faced with two unprecedented and supreme dangers. One is the danger not just of nuclear war but of any major war at all among great industrial powers — an exercise which modern technology has now made suicidal all around. The other is the devastating effect of modern industrialization and overpopulation on the world's natural environment. The one threatens the destruction of civilization through the recklessness and selfishness of its military rivalries, the other through the massive abuse of its natural habitat. Both are relatively new problems, for the solution of which past experience affords little guidance. Both are urgent. The problems of political misgovernment, to which so much of our thinking about moral values has recently related, is as old as the human species itself. It is a problem that will not be solved in our time, and need not be. But the environmental and nuclear crises will brook no delay.

The need for giving priority to the averting of these two overriding dangers has a purely rational basis — a basis in national interest — quite aside from morality. For short of a nuclear war, the worst that our Soviet rivals could do to us, even in our wildest worst-case imaginings, would be a far smaller tragedy than that which would assuredly confront us (and if not us, then our children) if we failed to face up to these two apocalyptic dangers in good time. But is there not also a moral component to this necessity?

Of all the multitudinous celestial bodies of which we have knowledge, our own earth seems to be the only one even remotely so richly endowed with the resources that make possible human life — not only make it possible but surround it with so much natural beauty and healthfulness and magnificence. And to the degree that man has distanced himself from the other animals in such things as self-knowledge, historical awareness and the capacity for creating great beauty (along, alas, with great ugliness), we have to recognize a further mystery, similar to that of the unique endowment of the planet — a mystery that seems to surpass the possibilities of the purely accidental. Is there not, whatever the nature of one's particular God, an element of sacrilege involved in the placing of all this at stake just for the sake of the comforts, the fears and the national rivalries of a single generation? Is there not a moral obligation to recognize in this very uniqueness of the habitat and nature of man the greatest of our moral responsibilities, and to make of ourselves, in our national personification, its guardians and protectors rather than its destroyers?

This, it may be objected, is a religious question, not a moral-political one. True enough, if one will. But the objection invites the further question as to whether there is any such thing as morality that does not rest, consciously or otherwise, on some foundation of religious faith, for the renunciation of self-interest, which is what all morality implies, can never be rationalized by purely secular and materialistic considerations.

5

The above are only a few random reflections on the great question to which this paper is addressed. But they would seem to suggest, in their entirety, the outlines of an American foreign policy to which moral standards could be more suitably and naturally applied than to that policy which we are conducting today. This would be a policy founded on recognition of the national interest, reasonably conceived, as the legitimate motivation for a large portion of the nation's behavior, and prepared to pursue that interest without either moral pretension or apology. It would be a policy that would seek the possibilities for service to morality primarily in our own behavior, not in our judgment of others. It would restrict our undertakings to the limits established by our own traditions and resources. It would see virtue in our minding our own business wherever there is not some overwhelming reason for minding the business of others. Priority would be given, here, not to the reforming of others but to the averting of the two apocalyptic catastrophes that now hover over the horizons of mankind.

But at the heart of this policy would lie the effort to distinguish at all times between the true substance and the mere appearance of moral behavior. In an age when a number of influences, including the limitations of the electronic media, the widespread substitution of pictorial representation for verbal communication, and the ubiquitous devices of "public relations" and electoral politics, all tend to exalt the image over the essential reality to which that image is taken to relate — in such an age there is a real danger that we may lose altogether our ability to distinguish between the real and the unreal, and, in doing so, lose both the credibility of true moral behavior and the great force such behavior is, admittedly, capable of exerting. To do this would be foolish, unnecessary and self-defeating. There may have been times when the United States could afford such frivolity. This present age, unfortunately, is not one of them.

JOYCE CAROL OATES

On Boxing

FROM THE NEW YORK TIMES MAGAZINE

THEY ARE YOUNG welterweight boxers so evenly matched they might be twins — though one has a redhead's pallor and the other is a dusky-skinned Hispanic. Circling each other in the ring, they try jabs, tentative left hooks, right crosses that dissolve in midair or turn into harmless slaps. The Madison Square Garden crowd is derisive, impatient. "Those two! What'd they do, wake up this morning and decide they were boxers?" a man behind me says contemptuously. (He's dark, nattily dressed, with a neatly trimmed mustache and tinted glasses. A sophisticated fight fan. Two hours later he will be crying, "Tommy! Tommy! Tommy!" over and over in a paroxysm of grief as, on the giant closed-circuit television screen, middleweight champion Marvelous Marvin Hagler batters his challenger, Thomas Hearns, into insensibility.)

The young boxers must be conscious of the jeers and boos in this great cavernous space reaching up into the $20 seats in the balconies amid the constant milling of people in the aisles, the smells of hotdogs, beer, cigarette and cigar smoke, hair oil. But they are locked desperately together, circling, jabbing, slapping, clinching, now a flurry of light blows, clumsy footwork, another sweaty stumbling despairing clinch into the ropes that provokes a fresh wave of derision. Why are they here in the Garden of all places, each fighting what looks like his first professional fight? What are they doing? Neither is angry at the other. When the bell sounds at the end of the sixth and final round, the crowd boos a little louder. The Hispanic boy, silky yellow shorts, damp,

frizzy, floating hair, strides about his corner of the ring with his
gloved hand aloft — not in defiance of the boos, which increase
in response to his gesture, or even in acknowledgment of them.
It's just something he has seen older boxers do. He seems to be
saying "I'm here, I made it, I did it." When the decision is
announced as a draw, the crowd's derision increases in volume.
"Get out of the ring!" "Go home!" Contemptuous male laughter
follows the boys in their robes, towels about their heads, sweating, breathless. Why had they thought they were boxers?

How can you enjoy so brutal a sport, people ask. Or don't ask.
     And it's too complicated to answer. In any case, I don't
"enjoy" boxing, and never have; it isn't invariably "brutal"; I
don't think of it as a sport.
     Nor do I think of it in writerly terms as a metaphor for some-
thing else. (For *what* else?) No one whose interest in boxing
began in childhood — as mine did as an offshoot of my father's
interest — is likely to suppose it is a symbol of something beyond itself, though I can entertain the proposition that life is a
metaphor for boxing — for one of those bouts that go on and
on, round following round, small victories, small defeats, nothing determined, again the bell and again the bell and you and
your opponent so evenly matched it's clear your opponent *is*
you and why are the two of you jabbing and punching at each
other on an elevated platform enclosed by ropes as in a pen
beneath hot crude all-exposing lights in the presence of an indifferent crowd: that sort of writerly metaphor. But if you have
seen five hundred boxing matches, you have seen five hundred
boxing matches, and their common denominator, which surely
exists, is not of primary interest to you. "If the Host is only a
symbol," the Catholic writer Flannery O'Connor said, "I'd say
the hell with it."

Each boxing match is a story, a highly condensed, highly dramatic story — even when nothing much happens: then failure
is the story. There are two principal characters in the story,
overseen by a shadowy third. When the bell rings no one knows
what will happen. Much is speculated, nothing known. The boxers bring to the fight everything that is themselves, and every-

thing will be exposed: including secrets about themselves they never knew. There are boxers possessed of such remarkable intuition, such prescience, one would think they had fought this particular fight before. There are boxers who perform brilliantly, but mechanically, who cannot improvise in midfight; there are boxers performing at the height of their skill who cannot quite comprehend that it won't be enough; to my knowledge there was only one boxer who possessed an extraordinary and disquieting awareness, not only of his opponent's every move or anticipated move, but of the audience's keenest shifts in mood as well — Muhammad Ali, of course.

In the ring, death is always a possibility, which is why I prefer to see films or tapes of fights already past — already crystallized into art. In fact, death is a statistically rare possibility of which no one likes to think — like your possible death tomorrow morning in an automobile crash, or in next month's airplane crash, or in a freak accident involving a fall on the stairs — a skull fracture, subarachnoid hemorrhage.

A boxing match is a play without words, which doesn't mean that it has no text or no language, only that the text is improvised in action, the language a dialogue between the boxers in a joint response to the mysterious will of the crowd, which is always that the fight be a worthy one so that the crude paraphernalia of the setting — the ring, the lights, the onlookers themselves — be obliterated. To go from an ordinary preliminary match to a "Fight of the Century" — like those between Joe Louis and Billy Conn, Muhammad Ali and Joe Frazier, most recently Marvin Hagler and Thomas Hearns — is to go from listening or half-listening to a guitar being idly plucked to hearing Bach's "Well-Tempered Clavier" being perfectly played, and that too is part of the story. So much is happening so swiftly and so subtly you cannot absorb it except to know that something memorable is happening and it is happening in a place beyond words.

The fighters in the ring are time-bound — is anything so excruciatingly long as a fiercely contested three-minute round? — but the fight itself is timeless. By way of films and tapes, it has become history, art. If boxing is a sport, it is the most tragic of all sports because, more than any human activity, it consumes the very excellence it displays: Its very drama is this consumption. To expend oneself in fighting the greatest fight of one's life is to begin immediately the downward turn that next time may be a plunge, a sudden incomprehensible fall. *I am the greatest*, Muhammad Ali says. *I am the greatest*, Marvin Hagler says. You always think you're going to win, Jack Dempsey wryly observed in his old age, otherwise you can't fight at all. The punishment — to the body, the brain, the spirit — a man must endure to become a great boxer is inconceivable to most of us whose idea of personal risk is largely ego related or emotional. But the punishment, as it begins to show in even a young and vigorous boxer, is closely assessed by his rivals. After junior-welterweight champion Aaron Pryor won a lackluster fight on points a few months ago, a younger boxer in his weight division, interviewed at ringside, said: "My mouth is watering."

So the experience of seeing great fighters of the past — and great sporting events are always *past* — is radically different from having seen them when they were reigning champions. Jack Johnson, Jack Dempsey, Joe Louis, Sugar Ray Robinson, Willie Pep, Rocky Marciano, Muhammad Ali — as spectactors we know not only how a fight ends but how a career ends. Boxing is always particulars, second by incalculable second, but in the abstract it suggests these haunting lines by Yeats:

> Everything that man esteems
> Endures a moment or a day.
> Love's pleasure drives his love away,
> The painter's brush consumes his dreams;
> The herald's cry, the soldier's tread
> Exhaust his glory and his might:
> Whatever flames upon the night
> Man's own resinous heart has fed.
> — from "The Resurrection"

The referee, the third character in the story, usually appears to be a mere observer, even an intruder, a near-ghostly presence as fluid in motion and quick-footed as the boxers themselves (he is frequently a former boxer). But so central to the drama of boxing is the referee that the spectacle of two men fighting each other unsupervised in an elevated ring would appear hellish, obscene — life rather than art. The referee is our intermediary in the fight. He is our moral conscience, extracted from us as spectators so that, for the duration of the fight, "conscience" is not a factor in our experience; nor is it a factor in the boxers' behavior.

Though the referee's role is a highly demanding one, and it has been estimated that there are perhaps no more than a dozen really skilled referees in the world, it seems to be necessary in the intense dramatic action of the fight that the referee have no dramatic identity. Referees' names are quickly forgotten, even as they are announced over the microphone preceding a fight. Yet, paradoxically, the referee's position is one of crucial significance. The referee cannot control what happens in the ring, but he can frequently control, to a degree, *that* it happens: he is responsible for the fight, if not for the individual fighter's performance. It is the referee solely who holds the power of life and death at certain times; whose decision to terminate a fight, or to allow it to continue, determines a man's fate. (One should recall that a well-aimed punch with a boxer's full weight behind it can have an astonishing impact — a blow that must be absorbed by the brain in its jelly sac.)

In a recent heavyweight fight in Buffalo, 220-pound Tim Witherspoon repeatedly struck his 260-pound opponent, James Broad, caught in the ropes, while the referee looked on without acting — though a number of spectators called for the fight to be stopped. In the infamous Benny Paret–Emile Griffith fight of March 24, 1962, the referee Ruby Goldstein was said to have stood paralyzed as Paret, trapped in the ropes, suffered as many as 18 powerful blows to the head before he fell. (He died ten days later.) Boxers are trained not to quit; if they are knocked down they will try to get up to continue the fight, even if they can hardly defend themselves. The primary rule of the ring — to defend oneself at all times — is both a parody and a distillation of life.

Boxing is a purely masculine world. (Though there are female boxers — the most famous is the black champion Lady Tyger Trimiar with her shaved head and tiger-striped attire — women's role in the sport is extremely marginal.) The vocabulary of boxing is attuned to a quintessentially masculine sensibility in which the role of patriarch/protector can only be assured if there is physical strength underlying it. First comes this strength — "primitive," perhaps; then comes civilization. It should be kept in mind that "boxing" and "fighting," though always combined in the greatest of boxers, can be entirely different and even unrelated activities. If boxing can be, in the lighter weights especially, a highly complex and refined skill belonging solely to civilization, fighting seems to belong to something predating civilization, the instinct not merely to defend oneself — for when has the masculine ego ever been assuaged by so minimal a gesture? — but to attack another and to force him into absolute submission. Hence the electrifying effect upon a typical fight crowd when fighting emerges suddenly out of boxing — the excitement when a boxer's face begins to bleed. The flash of red is the visible sign of the fight's authenticity in the eyes of many spectators, and boxers are right to be proud — if they are — of their facial scars.

To the untrained eye, boxers in the ring usually appear to be angry. But, of course, this is "work" to them; emotion has no part in it, or should not. Yet in an important sense — in a symbolic sense — the boxers *are* angry, and boxing is fundamentally about anger. It is the only sport in which anger is accommodated, ennobled. Why are boxers angry? Because, for the most part, they belong to the disenfranchised of our society, to impoverished ghetto neighborhoods in which anger is an appropriate response. ("It's hard being black. You ever been black? I was black once — when I was poor," Larry Holmes has said.) Today, when most boxers — most good boxers — are black or Hispanic, white men begin to look anemic in the ring. Yet after decades of remarkable black boxers — from Jack Johnson to Joe Louis to Muhammad Ali — heavyweight champion Larry Holmes was the object of racist slurs and insults when he defended his title against the over-promoted white challenger Gerry Cooney a few years ago.

Liberals who have no personal or class reason to feel anger tend to disparage, if not condemn, such anger in others. Liberalism is also unfairly harsh in its criticism of all that predates civilization — or "liberalism" itself — without comprehending that civilization is a concept, an idea, perhaps at times hardly more than a fiction, attendant upon, and always subordinate to, physical strength: missiles, nuclear warheads. The terrible and tragic silence dramatized in the boxing ring is the silence of nature before language, when the physical *was* language, a means of communication swift and unmistakable.

The phrase "killer instinct" is said to have been coined in reference to Jack Dempsey in his famous early fights against Jess Willard, Georges Carpentier, Luis Firpo ("The Wild Bull of the Pampas"), and any number of other boxers, less renowned, whom he savagely beat. The ninth of eleven children born to an impoverished Mormon sharecropper and itinerant railroad worker, Dempsey seems to have been, as a young boxer in his prime, the very embodiment of angry hunger; and if he remains the most spectacular heavyweight champion in history, it is partly because he fought when rules governing boxing were somewhat casual by present-day standards. Where aggression must be learned, even cultivated, in some champion boxers (Tunney, Louis, Marciano, Patterson, for example), Dempsey's aggression was direct and natural: Once in the ring he seems to have wanted to kill his opponent.

Dempsey's first title fight in 1919, against the aging champion Jess Willard, was called "pugilistic murder" by some sportswriters and is said to have been one of boxing's all-time blood baths. Today, this famous fight — which brought the nearly unknown twenty-four-year-old Dempsey to national prominence — would certainly have been stopped in the first minute of the first round. Badly out of condition, heavier than Dempsey by almost sixty pounds, the thirty-seven-year-old Willard had virtually no defense against the challenger. By the end of the fight, Willard's jaw was broken, his cheekbone split, nose smashed, six teeth broken off at the gum, an eye was battered shut, much further damage was done to his body. Both boxers were covered in Willard's blood. Years later Dempsey's estranged manager Kearns confessed — perhaps falsely — that he had "loaded" Dempsey's gloves — treated his hand tape with a talcum substance that turned concrete-hard when wet.

For the most part, boxing matches today are scrupulously monitored by referees and ring physicians. The devastating knockout blow is frequently the one never thrown. In a recent televised junior-middleweight bout between Don Curry and James Green, the referee stopped the fight because Green seemed momentarily disabled: His logic was that Green had dropped his gloves and was therefore in a position to be hurt. (Green and his furious trainer protested the decision but the referee's word is final: No fight, stopped, can be resumed.) The drama of the ring begins to shift subtly as more and more frequently one sees a referee intervene to embrace a weakened or defenseless man in a gesture of paternal solicitude that in itself carries much theatrical power — a gesture not so dramatic as the killing blow but one that suggests that the ethics of the ring are moving toward those that prevail beyond it. As if fighter-brothers whose mysterious animosity has somehow brought them to battle are saved by their father. . . .

In the final moment of the Hagler-Hearns fight, the dazed Hearns — on his feet but clearly not fully conscious, gamely prepared to take Hagler's next assault — was saved by the referee from what might well have been serious injury, if not death, considering the ferocity of Hagler's fighting and the personal anger he seems to have brought to it that night. This eight-minute fight, generally believed to be one of the great fights in boxing history, ends with Hearns in the referee's protective embrace — an image that is haunting, in itself profoundly mysterious, as if an indefinable human drama had been spontaneously created for us, brilliantly improvised, performed one time and one time only, yet permanently ingrained upon our consciousness.

Years ago in the early 1950s, when my father first took me to a Golden Gloves boxing tournament in Buffalo, I asked him why the boys wanted to fight one another, why they were willing to get hurt. My father said, "Boxers don't feel pain quite the way we do."

Gene Tunney's single defeat in an eleven-year career was to a flamboyant and dangerous fighter named Harry Greb ("The Human Windmill"), who seems to have been, judging from boxing literature, the dirtiest fighter in history. Low blows, butting, fouls, holding and hitting, using his laces on an opponent's eyes

— Greb was famous for his lack of interest in the rules. He was world middleweight champion for three years but a presence in the boxing world for a long time. After the first of his several fights with Greb, the twenty-four-year-old Tunney had to spend a week in bed, he was so badly hurt; he'd lost two quarts of blood during the fifteen-round fight. But as Tunney said years afterward: "Greb gave me a terrible whipping. He broke my nose, maybe with a butt. He cut my eyes and ears, perhaps with his laces. . . . My jaw was swollen from the right temple down the cheek, along under the chin and part way up the other side. The referee, the ring itself, was full of blood. . . . But it was in that first fight, in which I lost my American light-heavyweight title, that I knew I had found a way to beat Harry eventually. I was fortunate, really. If boxing in those days had been afflicted with the commission doctors we have today — who are always poking their noses into the ring and examining superficial wounds — the first fight with Greb would have been stopped before I learned how to beat him. It's possible, even probable, that if this had happened I would never have been heard of again."

Tommy Loughran, the light-heavyweight champion from 1927 to 1929, was a master boxer greatly admired by other boxers. He approached boxing literally as a science — as Tunney did — studying his opponents' styles and mapping out ring strategy for each fight. He rigged up mirrors in his basement so that he could see himself as he worked out — for, as Loughran realized, no boxer ever sees himself quite as he appears to his opponent. But the secret of Loughran's career was that he had a right hand that broke so easily he could use it only once in each fight: It had to be the knockout punch or nothing. "I'd get one shot, then the agony of the thing would hurt me if the guy got up. Anybody I ever hit with a left hook, I knocked flat on his face, but I would never take a chance for fear if my left hand goes, I'm done for."

Both Tunney and Loughran, it is instructive to note, retired from boxing before they were forced to retire. Tunney was a highly successful businessman and Loughran a successful sugar broker on the Wall Street commodities market — just to suggest that boxers are not invariably illiterate, stupid, or punch-drunk.

One of the perhaps not entirely acknowledged reasons for the attraction of serious writers to boxing (from Swift, Pope, Johnson to Hazlitt, Lord Byron, Hemingway, and our own Norman Mailer, George Plimpton, Wilfrid Sheed, Daniel Halpern et al.) is the sport's systematic cultivation of pain in the interests of a project, a life-goal: the willed transposing of the sensation called "pain" (whether physical or psychological) into its opposite. If this is masochism — and I doubt that it is, or that it is simply — it is also intelligence, cunning, strategy. It is the active welcoming of that which most living beings try to avoid and to flee. It is the active subsuming of the present moment in terms of the future. Pain now but control (and therefore pleasure) later.

Still, it is the rigorous training period leading up to the public appearance that demands the most discipline. In this, too, the writer senses some kinship, however oblique and one-sided, with the professional boxer. The brief public spectacle of the boxing match (which could last as little as sixty seconds), like the publication of the writer's book, is but the final, visible stage in a long, arduous, fanatic, and sometimes quixotic, subordination of the self. It was Rocky Marciano who seems to have trained with the most monastic devotion, secluding himself from his wife and family for as long as three months before a fight. Quite apart from the grueling physical training of this period and the constant preoccupation with diet and weight, Marciano concentrated on only the upcoming fight, the opening bell, his opponent. Every minute of the boxer's life was planned for one purpose. In the training camp the name of the opponent was never mentioned and Marciano's associates were careful about conversation in his presence: They talked very little about boxing.

In the final month, Marciano would not write a letter. The last ten days before a fight he saw no mail, took no telephone calls, met no new acquaintances. The week before the fight he would not shake hands with anyone. Or go for a ride in a car. No new foods! No envisioning the morning after the fight! All that was not *the fight* was taboo: when Marciano worked out punching the bag he saw his opponent before him, when he jogged early in the morning he saw his opponent close beside

him. What could be a more powerful image of discipline —
madness? — than this absolute subordination of the self, this
celibacy of the fighter-in-training? Instead of focusing his energies and fantasies upon Woman, the boxer focuses them upon
the Opponent.

No sport is more physical, more direct, than boxing. No sport
appears more powerfully homoerotic: the confrontation in the
ring — the disrobing — the sweaty, heated combat that is part
dance, courtship, coupling — the frequent urgent pursuit by
one boxer of the other in the fight's natural and violent
movement toward the "knockout." Surely boxing derives much
of its appeal from this mimicry of a species of erotic love in
which one man overcomes the other in an exhibition of superior
strength.

Most fights, however fought, lead to an embrace between the
boxers after the final bell — a gesture of mutual respect and
apparent affection that appears to the onlooker to be more than
perfunctory. Rocky Graziano, often derided for being a slugger
rather than a "classic" boxer, sometimes kissed his opponents
out of gratitude for the fight. Does the boxing match, one almost wonders, lead irresistibly to this moment: the public embrace of two men who otherwise, in public or in private, could
not approach each other with such passion. Are men privileged
to embrace with love only after having fought? A woman is
struck by the tenderness men will express for boxers who have
been hurt, even if it is only by way of commentary on photographs: the startling picture of Ray (Boom Boom) Mancini after
his second losing fight with Livingstone Bramble, for instance,
when Mancini's face was hideously battered (photographs in
Sports Illustrated and elsewhere were gory, near-pornographic);
the much-reprinted photograph of the defeated Thomas
Hearns being carried to his corner in the arms of an enormous
black man in formal attire — the "Hit Man" from Detroit now
helpless, only semiconscious, looking precisely like a black
Christ taken from the cross. These are powerful, haunting, unsettling images, cruelly beautiful, very much bound up with the
primitive appeal of the sport.

Yet to suggest that men might love one another directly without the violent ritual of combat is to misread man's greatest

passion — for war, not peace. Love, if there is to be love, comes second.

Boxing is, after all, about lying. It is about cultivating a double personality. As José Torres, the ex-light-heavyweight champion who is now the New York State Boxing Commissioner, says: "We fighters understand lies. What's a feint? What's a left hook off the jab? What's an opening? What's thinking one thing and doing another . . . ?"

There is nothing fundamentally playful about boxing, nothing that seems to belong to daylight, to pleasure. At its moments of greatest intensity it seems to contain so complete and so powerful an image of life — life's beauty, vulnerability, despair, incalculable and often reckless courage — that boxing *is* life, and hardly a mere game. During a superior boxing match we are deeply moved by the body's communion with itself by way of another's flesh. The body's dialogue with its shadow-self — or Death. Baseball, football, basketball — these quintessentially American pastimes are recognizably sports because they involve play: They are games. One *plays* football; one doesn't *play* boxing.

Observing team sports, teams of adult men, one sees how men are children in the most felicitous sense of the word. But boxing in its elemental ferocity cannot be assimilated into childhood — though very young men box, even professionally, and numerous world champions began boxing when they were hardly more than children. Spectators at public games derive much of their pleasure from reliving the communal emotions of childhood, but spectators at boxing matches relive the murderous infancy of the race. Hence the notorious cruelty of boxing crowds and the excitement when a man begins to bleed. ("When I see blood," says Marvin Hagler, "I become a bull." He means his own.)

The boxing ring comes to seem an altar of sorts, one of those legendary magical spaces where the laws of a nation are suspended: Inside the ropes, during an officially regulated three-minute round, a man may be killed at his opponent's hands but he cannot be legally murdered. Boxing inhabits a sacred space predating civilization; or, to use D. H. Lawrence's phrase, before God was love. If it suggests a savage ceremony or a rite of atonement, it also suggests the futility of such rites. For what atonement is the fight waged, if it must shortly be waged again . . . ?

All this is to speak of the paradox of boxing — its obsessive appeal for many who find in it not only a spectacle involving sensational feats of physical skill but an emotional experience impossible to convey in words; an art form, as I have suggested, with no natural analogue in the arts. And of course this accounts, too, for the extreme revulsion it arouses in many people. ("Brutal," "disgusting," "barbaric," "inhuman," "a terrible, terrible sport" — typical comments on the subject.)

In December 1984, the American Medical Association passed a resolution calling for the abolition of boxing on the principle that it is the only sport in which the *objective* is to cause injury. This is not surprising. Humanitarians have always wanted to reform boxing — or abolish it altogether. The 1896 heavyweight title match between Ruby Robert Fitzsimmons and Peter Maher was outlawed in many parts of the United States, so canny promoters staged it across the Mexican border four hundred miles from El Paso. (Some three hundred people made the arduous journey to see what must have been one of the most disappointing bouts in boxing history — Fitzsimmons knocked out his opponent in a mere ninety-five seconds.)

During the prime of Jack Dempsey's career in the 1920s, boxing was illegal in many states, like alcohol, and like alcohol, seems to have aroused a hysterical public enthusiasm. Photographs of jammed outdoor arenas taken in the 1920s with boxing rings like postage-sized altars at their centers, the boxers themselves scarcely visible, testify to the extraordinary emotional appeal boxing had at that time, even as reform movements were lobbying against it. When Jack Johnson won the heavyweight title in 1908 (he had to pursue the white champion Tommy Burns all the way to Australia to confront him), the special "danger" of boxing was also that it might expose and humiliate white men in the ring. After Johnson's victory over the "White Hope" contender Jim Jeffries, there were race riots and lynchings throughout the United States; even films of some of Johnson's fights were outlawed in many states. And because boxing has become a sport in which black and Hispanic men have lately excelled, it is particularly vulnerable to attack by white middle-class reformers, who seem uninterested in lobbying against equally dangerous but "establishment" sports like football, auto racing, and thoroughbred horse racing.

There is something peculiarly American in the fact that, while boxing is our most controversial sport, it is also the sport that pays its top athletes the most money. In spite of the controversy, boxing has never been healthier financially. The three highest paid athletes in the world in both 1983 and 1984 were boxers; a boxer with a long career like heavyweight champion Larry Holmes — forty-eight fights in thirteen years as a professional — can expect to earn somewhere beyond $50 million. (Holmes said that after retirement what he would miss most about boxing is his million-dollar checks.) Dempsey, who said that a man fights for one thing only — money — made somewhere beyond $3,500,000 in the ring in his long and varied career. Now $1.5 million is a fairly common figure for a single fight. Thomas Hearns made at least $7 million in his fight with Hagler while Hagler made at least $7.5 million. For the first of his highly publicized matches with Roberto Duran in 1980 — which he lost on a decision — the popular black welterweight champion Sugar Ray Leonard received a staggering $10 million to Duran's $1.3 million. And none of these figures takes into account various subsidiary earnings (from television commercials, for instance) which in Leonard's case are probably as high as his income was from boxing.

Money has drawn any number of retired boxers back into the ring, very often with tragic results. The most notorious example is perhaps Joe Louis, who, owing huge sums in back taxes, continued boxing well beyond the point at which he could perform capably. After a career of seventeen years he was stopped by Rocky Marciano — who was said to have felt as upset by his victory as Louis by the defeat. (Louis then went on to a degrading second career as a professional wrestler. This, too, ended abruptly when 300-pound Rocky Lee stepped on the forty-two-year-old Louis's chest and damaged his heart.) Ezzard Charles, Jersey Joe Walcott, Joe Frazier, Muhammad Ali — each continued fighting when he was no longer in condition to defend himself against young heavyweight boxers on the way up. Of all heavyweight champions, only Rocky Marciano, to whom fame and money were not of paramount significance, was prudent enough to retire before he was defeated. In any case, the prodigious sums of money a few boxers earn do not account for the sums the public is willing to pay them.

Though boxing has long been popular in many countries and under many forms of government, its popularity in the United States since the days of John L. Sullivan has a good deal to do with what is felt as the spirit of the individual — his "physical" spirit — in conflict with the constrictions of the state. The rise of boxing in the 1920s in particular might well be seen as a consequence of the diminution of the individual vis-à-vis society; the gradual attrition of personal freedom, will, and strength — whether "masculine" or otherwise. In the Eastern bloc of nations, totalitarianism is a function of the state; in the Western bloc it has come to seem a function of technology, or history — "fate." The individual exists in his physical supremacy, but does the individual matter?

In the magical space of the boxing ring so disquieting a question has no claim. There, as in no other public arena, the individual as a unique physical being asserts himself; there, for a dramatic if fleeting period of time, the great world with its moral and political complexities, its terrifying impersonality, simply ceases to exist. Men fighting one another with only their fists and their cunning are all contemporaries, all brothers, belonging to no historical time. "He can run, but he can't hide" — so said Joe Louis before his famous fight with young Billy Conn in 1941. In the brightly lighted ring, man is *in extremis,* performing an atavistic rite or agon for the mysterious solace of those who can participate only vicariously in such drama: the drama of life in the flesh. Boxing has become America's tragic theater.

CYNTHIA OZICK

The First Day of School: Washington Square, 1946

FROM HARPER'S MAGAZINE

> This portion of New York appears to many persons the most delectable. It has a kind of established repose which is not of frequent occurrence in other quarters of the long, shrill city; it has a riper, richer, more honorable look than any of the upper ramifications of the great longitudinal thoroughfare — the look of having had something of a social history.
> — HENRY JAMES, Washington Square

I FIRST CAME DOWN to Washington Square on a colorless February morning in 1946. I was seventeen and a half years old and was carrying my lunch in a brown paper bag, just as I had carried it to high school only a month before. It was — I thought it was — the opening day of spring term at Washington Square College, my initiation into my freshman year at New York University. All I knew of NYU then was that my science-minded brother had gone there; he had written from the army that I ought to go there too. With master-of-ceremonies zest he described the Browsing Room on the second floor of the Main Building as a paradisal chamber whose bookish loungers leafed languidly through magazines and exchanged high-principled witticisms between classes. It had the sound of a carpeted Olympian club in Oliver Wendell Holmes's Boston, Hub of the Universe, strewn with leather chairs and delectable old copies of *The Yellow Book*.

On that day I had never heard of Oliver Wendell Holmes or

The Yellow Book, and Washington Square was a faraway bower where wounded birds fell out of trees. My brother had once brought home from Washington Square Park a baby sparrow with a broken leg, to be nurtured back to flight. It died instead, emitting in its last hours melancholy faint cheeps, and leaving behind a dense recognition of the minute explicitness of morality. All the same, in the February grayness Washington Square had the allure of the celestial unknown. A sparrow might die, but my own life was luminously new: I felt my youth like a nimbus.

Which dissolves into the dun gauze of a low and sullen city sky. And here I am flying out of the Lexington Avenue subway at Astor Place, just a few yards from Wanamaker's, here I am turning a corner past a secondhand bookstore and a union hall; already late, I begin walking very fast toward the park. The air is smoky with New York winter grit, and on clogged Broadway a mob of trucks shifts squawking gears. But there, just ahead, crisscrossed by paths under high branches, is Washington Square; and on a single sidewalk, three clear omens — or call them riddles, intricate and redolent. These I will disclose in a moment, but before that you must push open the heavy brass-and-glass doors of the Main Building and come with me, at a hard and panting pace, into the lobby of Washington Square College on the earliest morning of my freshman year.

On the left, a bank of elevators. Straight ahead, a long burnished corridor, spooky as a lit tunnel. And empty, all empty. I can hear my solitary footsteps reverberate, as in a radio mystery drama: they lead me up a short staircase into a big dark ghost-town cafeteria. My brother's letter, along with his account of the physics and chemistry laboratories (I will never see them), has already explained that this place is called Commons — and here my heart will learn to shake with the merciless newness of life. But not today; today there is nothing. Tables and chairs squat in dead silhouette. I race back through a silent maze of halls and stairways to the brass-and-glass doors — there stands a lonely guard. From the pocket of my coat I retrieve a scrap with a classroom number on it and ask the way. The guard announces in a sly croak that the first day of school is not yet; come back tomorrow, he says.

A dumb bad joke: I'm humiliated. I've journeyed the whole
way down from the end of the line — Pelham Bay, in the north-
east Bronx — to find myself in desolation, all because of a mud-
dle: Tuesday isn't Wednesday. The nimbus of expectation
fades. The lunch bag in my fist takes on a greasy sadness. I'm
not ready to dive back into the subway — I'll have a look
around.

Across the street from the Main Building, the three omens.
First, a pretzel man with a cart. He's wearing a sweater, a cap
that keeps him faceless — he's nothing but the shadows of his
creases — and wool gloves with the fingertips cut off. He never
moves; he might as well be made of papier-mâché, set up and
left out in the open since spring. There are now almost no
pretzels for sale, and this gives me a chance to inspect the construction of his bare pretzel-poles. The pretzels are hooked over
a column of gray cardboard cylinders, themselves looped
around a stick, the way horseshoes drop around a post. The
cardboard cylinders are the insides of toilet paper rolls.

The pretzel man is rooted between a Chock Full O' Nuts
(that's the second omen) and a newsstand (that's the third).

The Chock Full: the doors are like fans, whirling remnants of
conversation. *She will marry him. She will not marry him.* Fragrance
of coffee and hot chocolate. *We can prove that the senses are partial
and unreliable vehicles of information, but who is to say that reason is
not equally a product of human limitation?* Powdered doughnut
sugar on their lips.

Attached to a candy store, the newsstand. Copies of *Partisan
Review:* the table of the gods. Jean Stafford, Mary McCarthy,
Elizabeth Hardwick, Irving Howe, Delmore Schwartz, Alfred
Kazin, Clement Greenberg, Stephen Spender, William Phillips,
John Berryman, Saul Bellow, Philip Rahv, Richard Chase, Randall Jarrell, Simone de Beauvoir, Karl Shapiro, George Orwell!
I don't know a single one of these names, but I feel their small
conflagration flaming in the gray street: the succulent hotness
of their promise. I mean to penetrate every one of them. Since
all the money I have is my subway fare — a nickel — I don't
buy a copy (the price of *Partisan* in 1946 is fifty cents); I pass
on.

I pass on to the row of houses on the north side of the square. Henry James was born in one of these, but I don't know that either. Still, they are plainly old, though no longer aristocratic: haughty last-century shabbies with shut eyelids, built of rosy-ripe respectable brick, down on their luck. Across the park bulks Judson Church, with its squat squarish bell tower; by the end of the week I will be languishing at the margins of a basketball game in its basement, forlorn in my blue left-over-from-high-school gym suit and mooning over Emily Dickinson:

> There's a certain Slant of light,
> Winter Afternoons —
> That oppresses, like the Heft
> Of Cathedral Tunes —

There is more I don't know. I don't know that W. H. Auden lives just down *there*, and might at any moment be seen striding toward home under his tall rumpled hunch; I don't know that Marianne Moore is only up the block, her doffed tricorn resting on her bedroom dresser. It's Greenwich Village — I know *that* — no more than twenty years after Edna St. Vincent Millay has sent the music of her name (her best, perhaps her only, poem) into these bohemian streets: bohemia, the honeypot of poets.

On that first day in the tea-leafed cup of the town I am ignorant, ignorant! But the three riddle-omens are soon to erupt, and all of them together will illumine Washington Square.

Begin with the benches in the park. Here, side by side with students and their looseleafs, lean or lie the shadows of the pretzel man, his creased ghosts or doubles: all those pitiables, half-women and half-men, neither awake nor asleep; the discountable, the repudiated, the unseen. No more notice is taken of any of them than of a scudding fragment of newspaper in the path. Even then, even so long ago, the benches of Washington Square are pimpled with this hell-tossed crew, these Mad Margarets and Cokey Joes, these volcanic coughers, shakers, groaners, tremblers, droolers, blasphemers, these public urinators with vomitous breath and rusted teeth stumps, dead-eyed and self-abandoned, dragging their makeshift junkyard shoes, their buttonless layers of raggedy ratfur. The pretzel man with his toilet paper rolls conjures and spews them all — he is a loftier brother to these citizens of the lower pox, he is guardian of the garden of the jettisoned. They rattle along all the seams of Washington Square. They are the pickled city, the true and universal City-Below-Cities, the wolfish vinegar-Babylon that dogs the spittled skirts of bohemia. The toilet paper rolls are the temple columns of this sacred grove.

Next, the whirling doors of Chock Full O' Nuts. Here is the marketplace of Washington Square, its bazaar, its roiling gossip-parlor, its matchmaker's office and arena — the outermost wing, so to speak, evolved from the Commons. On a day like today, when the Commons is closed, the Chock Full is thronged with extra power, a cello making up for a missing viola. Until now, the fire of my vitals has been for the imperious tragedians of the *Aeneid*; I have lived in the narrow throat of poetry. Another year or so of this oblivion, until at last I am hammer-struck with the shock of Europe's skull, the bled planet of death camp and war. Eleanor Roosevelt has not yet written her famous column announcing the discovery of Anne Frank's diary. The term *cold war* is new. The Commons, like the college itself, is overcrowded, veterans in their pragmatic thirties mingling with the reluctant dreamy young. And the Commons is convulsed with politics: a march to the docks is organized, no one knows by whom, to protest the arrival of Walter Gieseking, the German musician who flourished among Nazis. The Communists — two or three readily recognizable cantankerous zealots — stomp through with their daily leaflets and sneers. There is even a Monarchist, a small poker-faced rectangle of a man with secretive tireless eyes who, when approached for his views, always demands, in perfect Bronx tones, the restoration of his king. The engaged girls — how many of them there seem to be! — flash their rings and tangle their ankles in their long New Look skirts. There is no feminism and no feminists: I am, I think, the only one. The Commons is a tide: it washes up the cold war, it washes up the engaged girls' rings, it washes up the several philosophers and the numerous poets. The philosophers are all existentialists; the poets are all influenced by *The Waste Land*. When the Commons overflows, the engaged girls cross the street to show their rings at the Chock Full.

Call it density, call it intensity, call it continuity: call it, finally, society. The Commons belongs to the satirists. Here, one afternoon, is Alfred Chester, holding up a hair, a single strand, before a crowd. (He will one day write stories and novels. He will die young.) "What is that hair?" I innocently ask, having come late on the scene. "A pubic hair," he replies, and I feel as Virginia Woolf did when she declared human nature to have "changed in or about December 1910" — soon after her sister Vanessa explained away a spot on her dress as "semen."

In or about February 1946 human nature does not change; it keeps on. On my bedroom wall I tack — cut out from *Life* magazine — the wildest Picasso I can find: a face that is also a belly. Mr. George E. Mutch, a lyrical young English teacher still in his twenties, writes on the blackboard: "When lilacs last in the dooryard bloom'd," and "Bare, ruined choirs, where late the sweet birds sang," and "A green thought in a green shade"; he tells us to burn, like Pater, with a hard, gemlike flame. Another English teacher — older and crustier — compares Walt Whitman to a plumber; the next year he is rumored to have shot himself in a wood. The initial letters of Washington Square College are a device to recall three of the seven deadly sins: Wantonness, Sloth, Covetousness. In the Commons they argue the efficacy of the orgone box. Eda Lou Walton, sprightly as a bird, knows all the Village bards, and is a Village bard herself. Sidney Hook is an intellectual rumble in the logical middle distance. Homer Watt, chairman of the English department, is the very soul who, in a far-off time of bewitchment, hired Thomas Wolfe.

And so, in February 1946, I make my first purchase of a "real" book — which is to say, not for the classroom. It is displayed in the window of the secondhand bookstore between the Astor Place subway station and the union hall, and for weeks I have been coveting it: *Of Time and the River*. I am transfigured; I am pierced through with rapture; skipping gym, I sit among morning mists on a windy bench a foot from the stench of Mad Margaret, sinking into that cascading syrup:

Man's youth is a wonderful thing: It is so full of anguish and of magic and he never comes to know it as it is, until it is gone from him

forever. . . . And what is the essence of that strange and bitter miracle of life which we feel so poignantly, so unutterably, with such a
bitter pain and joy, when we are young?

Thomas Wolfe, lost, and by the wind grieved, ghost, come back
again! In Washington Square I am appareled in the "numb
exultant secrecies of fog, fog-numb air filled with solemn joy of
nameless and impending prophecy, an ancient yellow light, the
old smoke-ochre of the morning . . ."

The smoke-ochre of the morning. Ah, you who have flung
Thomas Wolfe, along with your strange and magical youth,
onto the ash-heap of juvenilia and excess, myself among you,
isn't this a lovely phrase still? It rises out of the old pavements
of Washington Square as delicately colored as an eggshell.

The veterans in their pragmatic thirties are nailed to Need;
they have families and futures to attend to. When Mr. George
E. Mutch exhorts them to burn with a hard, gemlike flame, and
writes across the blackboard the line that reveals his own name,

> The world is too much with us; late and soon,
> Getting and spending, we lay waste our powers,

one of the veterans heckles, "What about getting a Buick, what
about spending a buck?" Chester, at sixteen, is a whole year
younger than I; he has transparent eyes and a rosebud mouth,
and is in love with a poet named Diana. He has already found
his way to the Village bars, and keeps in his wallet Truman
Capote's secret telephone number. We tie our scarves tight
against the cold and walk up and down Fourth Avenue, winding in and out of the rows of secondhand bookshops crammed
one against the other. The proprietors sit reading their wares
and never look up. The books in all their thousands smell
sleepily of cellar. Our envy of them is speckled with longing; our
longing is sick with envy. We are the sorrowful literary
young.

Every day, month after month, I hang around the newsstand
near the candy store, drilling through the enigmatic pages of
Partisan Review. I still haven't bought a copy; I still can't understand a word. I don't know what cold war means. Who is Trot-
sky? I haven't read *Ulysses*; my adolescent phantoms are rowing

in the ablative absolute with *pius* Aeneas. I'm in my mind's cradle, veiled by the exultant secrecies of fog.

Washington Square will wake me. In a lecture room in the Main Building, Dylan Thomas will cry his webwork syllables. Afterward he'll warm himself at the White Horse Tavern. Across the corridor I will see Sidney Hook plain. I will read the Bhagavad-Gita and Catullus and Lessing, and, in Hebrew, a novel eerily called *Whither?* It will be years and years before I am smart enough, worldly enough, to read Alfred Kazin and Mary McCarthy.

In the spring, all of worldly Washington Square will wake up to the luster of little green leaves.

EDWARD ROTHSTEIN

The Body of Bach

FROM THE NEW REPUBLIC

THERE WOULD SEEM to be very little mysterious about Bach. He has reached his 300th birthday with a reputation unmatched in the musical pantheon. He is neither neglected nor overrated; no revisions of the repertory are taking place; no discoveries are changing our understanding of his achievement. There is, simply, the music itself, extravagant in its range and invention: the *Goldberg Variations,* the *St. Matthew Passion,* the *B minor Mass,* the cantatas, the *Well-tempered Clavier,* the cello suites, the violin sonatas, assorted toccatas and suites and fugues and partitas.

The man behind the music also would seem to offer few secrets — no hints of syphilis as with his Romantic successors, no passionate letters like Beethoven's to his "Immortal Beloved," no arcane musical programs with autobiographical clues buried in scores as with Berlioz or Elgar or Berg. Bach simply looked at himself as a craftsman. "I was obliged to work hard," he said; "whoever is equally industrious will succeed just as well." We know him through that industry — a cantata written every week for two years, a set of collected works that took more than fifty years to edit. He was part of a dynasty of musicians who were so influential that in Eisenach the family name became generic; town musicians were called "die Baache." And Johann Sebastian embodied in his career the variety of that dynasty's social roles. He was a virtuoso organist, a court composer, a church composer, a teacher, a producer of secular concerts. The facts about his life are known through those roles, in public documents, city records, petitions, announcements, resignations. The private man is seemingly irrelevant: he worked hard, married twice, and in domestic harmony fathered twenty children.

But there is something missing in this apparently clear portrait. We are used to enshrining composers as gods in a temple of art, divorcing earthly facts from our understanding of the music. But in no other composer is the disparity between the man and his work so immense. Bach's life is considered stupefyingly ordinary, but his music is divine, dealing in essence rather than in accident, in being rather than in appearance. Indeed, who can listen to the *D sharp minor Fugue* in Book I of the *Well-tempered Clavier* and not feel, in the ways in which a single theme is contemplated, combined with itself, inverted, expanded, contracted, and dissected, that this work has transcendent concerns? Even the turns of the melodic theme, which hint at something vulnerable, even melancholy, ultimately become aspects of architecture rather than of sentiment. Albert Schweitzer, who wrote one of the more profound studies of the composer, put it this way: "The artistic personality exists independently of the human, the latter remaining in the background as if it were something almost accidental. Bach's works would have been the same even if his existence had run quite another course." As a man, he remains mundane; his music, meanwhile, dwells in the eternal.

It is remarkable how consistent this view of Bach has been. Even during the years of Bach's supposed eclipse just after his death, when his works were not performed and were compared unfavorably with Handel's, he still had a profound impact on music's greatest practitioners — on Mozart, Haydn, Beethoven, and even Chopin. Bach's son, Carl Philipp Emanuel, made money by renting unpublished scores of his father's works; his wife continued the tradition, and so did Bach's granddaughter.

And, soon enough, devotion to Bach as transcendent artist entered the heart of German musical and intellectual life. On hearing the *Well-tempered Clavier* for the first time on June 21, 1827, Goethe felt, he wrote, "as if the eternal harmony were communing with itself, as might have happened in God's bosom shortly before the creation of the world. It was thus that my inner depths were stirred, and I seemed neither to possess nor

close. "There will always be Harlequins, Mommie," he says. "But
they won't be the same. Not without Louis L'Amour."

Now several hundred friends of Calvino, writers, editors, publishers, press, local dignitaries fill up the cemetery. I hold Chichita's hand a long moment; she has had, someone said, two
weeks of coming to terms not so much with death as with the
nightmare of dying.

The last chapter of *Palomar* begins, "Mr. Palomar decides that
from now on he will act as if he were dead, to see how the world
gets along without him." So far, not too good, I thought. Mexico
has fallen down and his daughter is late to the burial. On the
plus side, there is no priest, no service, no words. Suddenly, as
a dozen television cameras switch on, the dark shiny wooden
box, containing Calvino, appears in the atrium. How small the
box is, I think. Was he smaller than I remember? Or has he
shrunk? Of course, he is dead but, as he wrote, "First of all, you
must not confuse being dead with not being, a condition that
occupies the vast expanse of time before birth, apparently sym-
metrical with the other, equally vast expanse that follows death.
In fact, before birth we are part of the infinite possibilities that
may or may not be fulfilled; whereas, once dead, we cannot
fulfill ourselves either in the past (to which we now belong entirely but on which we can no longer have any influence) or in
the future (which, even if influenced by us, remains forbidden
to us)."

With a crash, the pallbearers drop the box into the shallow
bathtub. Palomar's nose is now about four inches beneath the
earth he used to examine so minutely. Then tiles are casually
arranged over the coffin; and the box is seen no more. As we
wait for the daughter to arrive, the heat is disagreeable. We look
at one another as though we are at a party that has refused to
take off. I recognize Natalia Ginzburg. I see someone who looks
as if he ought to be Umberto Eco, and is. "A person's life consists
of a collections of events, the last of which could also change the
meaning of the whole. . . ." I notice, in the crowd, several dozen
young schoolchildren. They are fans of Calvino's fairy tales;
plainly, precocious consumers of "texts" and proto-theorists.

Then daughter and buckets of cement arrive simultaneously. One of the masons pours cement over the tiles; expertly, he smooths the viscous surface with a trowel. Horrible cement. "Therefore Palomar prepares to become a grouchy dead man, reluctant to submit to the sentence to remain exactly as he is; but he is unwilling to give up anything of himself, even if it is a burden." Finally, the cement is flush with the ground; and that's that.

I am standing behind Chichita, who is very still. Finally, I look up from the gray oblong of fresh cement and there, staring straight at me, is Calvino. He looks anguished, odd, not quite right. But it is unmistakably Mr. Palomar, witnessing his own funeral. For one brief mad moment we stare at each other; then he looks down at the coffin that contains not himself but Italo. The man I thought was Italo is his younger brother, Floriano.

I move away, before the others. On the drive back to Rome, the sun is bright and hot; yet rain starts to fall. Devil is beating his wife, as they say in the South. Then a rainbow covers the entire eastern sky. For the Romans and the Etruscans, earlier inhabitants of the countryside through which we are driving, the rainbow was an ominous herald of coming change in human affairs, death of kings, cities, world. I make a gesture to ward off the evil eye. Time can now end. But " 'If time has to end, it can be described, instant by instant,' Palomar thinks, 'and each instant, when described, expands so that its end can no longer be seen.' He decides that he will set himself to describing every instant of his life, and until he has described them all he will no longer think of being dead. At that moment he dies."[2] So end "my last meditations on Nature," and Calvino and Nature are now one, or One.

---

[2]Now that Calvino's work is done, one must praise the faithful William Weaver for his elegant translations over many years.

Julia

FROM THE AMERICAN SCHOLAR

TO COME ACROSS A CHARACTER like Julia in a Warwickshire village was a strange, contradictory experience; on the one hand purely surprising, yet on the other entirely natural, since she was as believable, as solid, as inevitable as Dogberry or Mistress Quickly. And yet she resembled neither of these so much as she resembled a female version of the great Falstaff himself. Or perhaps, with her unquenchable oddity, she would have had to be invented, if she had been a fictitious character, by some connoisseur of the quirkiness of humanity rather than a writer of Shakespeare's centrality. One could imagine meeting her in the pages of *Tristram Shandy*. Yet her historical period, the scene of her adventures, was substantially the same as those of George du Maurier's *Trilby* or even Murger's *Vie de Bohème*.

After that rapid fire of literary allusions, entirely appropriate in introducing a person so highly charged with imagination, so accustomed to seeing her own life as a collection of legends that she never troubled to narrate, let us draw breath and come at the subject more factually. Julia's origins were Birmingham Irish. She had grown up in Shirley, where her father had kept, I think, a livery stable. I seem to remember someone saying that Julia as a girl used to help to break in horses; if so, this might have brought her into contact with circus and fairground people and perhaps started her on that lifelong association, in one form and another, with show business and the performing arts.

At all events, when I got to know her in the early to middle 1940s, she must have been over sixty; so that the version of her history most generally accepted, that she had been an artist's model in Paris at the turn of the century, squared perfectly well with chronology. (I say "generally accepted" because it was the version current among most people who knew her, though where they got it I am not sure, since Julia herself never mentioned her own past history except very rarely in a brief aside.) But she certainly knew Paris, and her memories of it seemed to be from that epoch and from the angle of vision, so to speak, that would be natural to a Birmingham girl who was modeling for a living and mixing with a bohemian, largely English-speaking, set. She referred now and then to Parisian buildings and institutions, but always gave them their names in English — "Oh, yes, that was in a little street over by the Red Windmill."

A girl from a Shirley livery stable who became a favorite of the artists' community in the Paris of 1900 must be presumed to have had something to offer, and perhaps the young Julia had been a beauty. When I first saw Julia I was nineteen, an age at which one does not think of people over forty as having physical lives at all, or even much in the way of a physical appearance beyond what will serve to tell one apart from another. They are, to the eyes of an adolescent as to the eyes of a child, rather like life-size animated dolls: always clothed, needless to say, and always in very much the same *kind* of clothes; and always moving, sitting, or standing in characteristic attitudes. Their individuality comes partly from the way they move their limbs and even more from the sound of their voices. If you hear a young person talking about an older one — a schoolboy, say, relating some encounter with a master — the voice will always be mimicked, and nearly always in grotesque caricature.

So, at nineteen, I did not think of Julia as "looking like" anything in particular, and certainly not as being beautiful or ugly. Her voice, which was cheerful and penetrating, was somewhat battered (what people called a "whiskey voice," which she had certainly taken steps to earn) but had clarity in its middle range, and must at one time have been melodious. In build she was of medium height for a woman, and, though by this time rather dumpy, she was supple and active enough. What strikes me, looking back, was that her head and face *were*, in fact, beautiful, with that beauty which is not affected by age because it is a matter of bone structure and carriage and expression. Her iron-gray hair was wound round her head in some sort of long plait, giving a helmet-like impression that carried a hint of the classical; she could have posed for a statue of Minerva. As for her face, its features were good; the nose in particular, straight and delicate, gave her refinement, a touch of the human thoroughbred.

I forgive my nineteen-year-old self, however, for not taking much notice of Julia's face, because one eye was covered by a large black patch, looped round her head with elastic. I suppose she found this more comfortable than a glass eye, and certainly the socket behind it was empty. So one tended, on catching sight of her face, to have one's attention drawn straight to the patch; and what remained of her girlish beauty, for surely it had once been fresh and vivid, went unnoticed.

As for how she came by the patch, once again her milieu had an accepted story: the eye had been shot out at the gaming table in Monte Carlo. Later I heard another version that laid the scene in, I think, Dieppe; a reckless, distraught gambler had pulled out a revolver and taken a shot at someone, the bullet had ricocheted and entered Julia's eye, whereupon Julia's escort had pulled out his own revolver and shot the man dead on the spot. Heady stuff, not normally associated with Warwickshire village life — the splendid, sinewy raw material of legend.

Meanwhile, what put me, at nineteen, into Julia's orbit? What gave me contact with the inner circle of her aides-de-camp, those privileged to impart to one another succulent fragments of her legend? The answer is simple: she kept "theatrical lodgings." This, I fancy, is a trade that has pretty well disappeared from the earth. In Victorian times the lower reaches of the acting profession lived a life that one would not have expected any human being to stand for, as long as there was a ditch to dig. Every town of any size had a theater; most theaters were played by little fit-up companies that performed for one week — six evening shows and at least one matinee — and, on the Sunday morning, packed up and traveled on. Each Sunday, the country must have been threaded in every direction by touring theatrical companies, stage managers loading props in the guard's van, producers gloomily adding up the budget, bravely joking and chattering and keeping up each other's spirits as they waited on foggy platforms or clattered past silent goods yards. On arrival, there was no time to look for somewhere to stay. The theater would have the addresses of landladies in the neighboring streets — because there was no time, either, for long journeys to and from the suburbs — who let rooms to "theatricals," one lot going and another lot coming, in the way the tide fills and washes out of a rock pool. The English theater, and its red-nosed half sister, Twice-Nightly Variety, were made possible for a hundred years by this army of theatrical landladies, many or most of whom were superannuated dancers or singers, or the widows of jugglers or conjurors or female impersonators. They have departed — unsung, as far as I know, and unhonored — into the shades of history.

I am the more glad to have known, in Julia, a particularly fine, though late-blooming, specimen of the type. Not that she let rooms by the week. Her cottage was at Shottery, very near Anne Hathaway's, and Stratford-on-Avon dealt with no weekly touring fit-up companies. Her clientele were Shakespearean actors and actresses, who took their rooms for "the season." But they represented the most modest level of the company, mostly employed to carry a spear or make part of a colorful whirling crowd; or they were wardrobe staff, or they painted scenery or did general odd jobs. I remember, for instance, a boy who worked in the wardrobe department, cutting out costumes and allowed occasionally to put in a suggestion as to their design. I never knew anyone, male or female, as deeply devoted to clothes as this youth. There was a gleam of pure happiness in his eye as he talked of the wonderful outfits they contrived. He told me once about the dress they had made for that year's leading lady (it was Diana Wynyard): "A lovely creation," he called it, "in stinging cerise." I went to the theater and hardly attended to the play. Every time Diana Wynyard made an entrance, a voice in my head intoned, "a lovely creation in stinging cerise."

At Julia's, one met small-part actors, young ones who hoped they were on the way up and old ones who feared they were on the way down, and stage-management staff, and even people like me; for my friends and I used to get over from Oxford when we could, and during these years, I saw some sort of production of all Shakespeare's major plays. The Stratford Memorial Theatre, though even then a national institution, was not so grand in those days as it has since become; it had some help from public funds, but not on the gargantuan scale it has since come to expect, and in the winter it closed down for months on end. Closed down as a Shakespearean theater, that is; it showed variety and pantomime, and I have stayed at Julia's with red-nosed comics, girl tap dancers, and one young man who went on to become solidly established as a player of the mouth organ (sorry, harmonica). Then there was the pair of male lovers who kept a market garden. (Did their establishment not contain any living accommodation? Why were they at Julia's? Or did they just come for meals?) And there was the middle-aged man with the withered hand and the courteous, cultivated manner, who appeared to live mainly on, and for, gin, and was said to disappear on three- or four-day blinds, at the end of which some policeman would gather up his unconscious body from a gutter. There was the young actor who always referred to everyone at the theater, male or female, as "a screaming bitch" and shortly afterwards crossed the Atlantic and embarked on a well-publicized affair with a Hollywood actress, which made the headlines in the cheap Sunday papers for month after month. And the slightly less-young actor who, worried about his fast-dwindling hair, had heard or read somewhere that nettle stings brought the moribund roots back to life. He used to go out of the front door, walk a few steps to where there was a thick bed of nettles, go down on his hands and knees, and sting his bald dome stoically at least once a day. I have seen him on the stage since, but whether wigged or not I could not tell.

Over this motley, shifting empire Julia presided, and it must be said that one thing her boarders had in common was unwavering loyalty to her. Every human being encounters dislike and hostility sometimes, but if anyone disliked Julia he must have kept well away from Stratford, for I never met or heard of him. By the sheer force of her character, starting with no material advantages — for after all she was just a rather battered woman on the far side of middle age, in a shabby dress and an eye patch, who kept a boardinghouse — she established total authority in her circle. And she did it, as I say, without making enemies. She simply drew you into her world; and once you were in her world, you paid homage to her because she was queen of it.

And what was Julia's world? It was, I can see now, a very Celtic dimension. She had the gift of surrounding ordinary humdrum life with an atmosphere of celebration. She loved fantasy and humor, and her chief instrument for projecting them was verbal. Her vocabulary was made up of dozens of ritual phrases. Nothing was called by its ordinary name. In particular the basic facts of existence were given labels that colored them with a mocking humor. To die was "to pass down the tramcar." Somebody with bad lungs was "coughing his soul-case up." The lavatory out in the backyard was "the Palace of Varieties" or more simply "the Palace."

This verbal gossamer became entangled with everything. A perfectly ordinary woman called Mrs. Nichols, who lived nearby, was always "My Lady Nicotine." (The reference is to a now-forgotten book by J. M. Barrie.) If she expressed her intention of going down to The Bell to have a whiskey, it was always "a little whixey-itis." If this sounds arch, I can only say that in its effect it was nothing of the kind. Julia was far too earthy to be arch. Though, speaking of earthiness, I believe it is a fact worth recalling that I never heard her use a single one of the official rude words. The content of what she said may have come from the world of Émile Zola's Parisian back streets and Murger's studios, but the vocabulary would not have offended a Victorian governess.

At first, Julia must have seen me as one more faceless lodger coming in and going out with the tide, but our relationship became closer when she realized that I shared her gift for fanciful talk. On one of my earliest visits, the cottage must have been crowded, because I was sleeping on a camp bed in the kitchen, and was awakened in the early morning by a young cat, barely out of kittenhood, treading warily and delicately over me. Frail, skinny, pacing very scrupulously on long white legs, the little cat reminded me, as I said to Julia at breakfast time, of "a ballerina who was new to the job." Julia instantly seized on the phrase; the cat was known as "the ballerina" for the rest of its life, and I became in her mind an identifiable person.

For me, Julia's cottage, number something, Hathaway Hamlet, Shottery — it torments me that I cannot remember the number, and if I go back to look now, the changed appearance of the place confuses me and I am not sure which door was Julia's — the cottage, I say, held a very special place at the center of my affections and of my imaginative world. What appealed to me was the blend of the rural with the artistic, intellectual, bohemian. I was well enough accustomed to country life, and already my love of the countryside had formed its deep roots, but I had made very few close relationships with actual country people, whose talk of crops and the weather and subsidies tended necessarily to exclude me. I knew a number of families who ran small farms on the borders of Staffordshire and Shropshire; I liked and respected them, and they were kind to me; but this was not the sort of ground from which real friendships grow. At Julia's I found a rural environment, a thatched cottage among a cluster of such cottages at the end of a tree-lined lane — and inside the cottage, talk of the theater and books and music, and gossip about wonderfully exciting people, and, yes, even lovely creations in stinging cerise.

Perhaps it all sounds silly and juvenile, but as the French poet remarked, *Tant pis, c'est moi.* That vision of life has remained with me always as an ideal. You can tell everything about a person by finding out his or her notion of happiness. All of us, I think, carry about in the back of our minds a vision of what the truly happy life would be, if we could only attain it. The degree to which this vision is blurred or precise will vary greatly from one mind to another, but I believe it is always there. My vision of happiness has always been a life in which there is the excitement of ideas, the divine rage of art and the self-forgetfulness of the artist, set amid quiet fields and gardens and trees, with a river winding somewhere nearby. I have the temperament of an artist, the absolute need to live my life in a continuum of art and ideas as well as of experiences; but in my century, these things have nearly always had to be sought in the big cities of the world, where noise and haste and crowded pavements give a hysterical edge to life and therefore increasingly to art.

It was not always so. Goethe's Weimar, Mozart's Salzburg, were small, meadowy towns. Shakespeare's London, though it had its dark and dangerous places, must have had quiet lanes where the country people drove their flocks exactly as they did in Stratford. How big was the Florence of Dante or even the Paris of Villon? Great art, great ideas, have flowered from small towns that grew like trees, with their roots in the soil and their branches spread to the sky. I know historically, from the kind of examples I have just given, that this wise and fortunate balance was possible, that it has been a reality in human life; and I know personally, within my own life experience, what it felt like; because that was what life at Julia's felt like.

Sometimes one sees a fisherman's cottage right down on the beach, so close to the sea that one might think the next high wave would engulf it; but of course the wisdom and local knowledge of the builder has put it forever just out of reach of the biggest rollers. Julia's cottage, and Hathaway Hamlet generally, were in this position vis-à-vis the perpetually incoming tide of tourists and sightseers. No one who has been on so much as a day trip to Stratford will need to be told that Anne Hathaway's cottage is situated in Shottery, about a mile from the center of town, to be reached either by walking across the fields or going round by the road. The coaches and cars go round by the road, and in those days the road that ran past the cottage was a cul-de-sac; people stopped, got out, and did the official visit, or merely stared at the building from the roadway and crossed it off their list, and drove back the way they had come. The fifty yards surrounding Anne's birthplace marked the end of that particular tourist run. If the visitors had gone another two hundred yards down the road, they would have come upon this cluster of thatched and half-timbered dwellings, all the same period as Anne's, and no doubt their cameras would have been clicking and whirring. But they never did. The next destination was waiting, the next item to be crossed off the list, and the tide, after each toppling wave, receded.

Apart from that one manifestation of the sight-seeing trade, life in Shottery, in the 1940s and early 1950s, was very quiet and untroubled. House prices and rents were still low. The village inn, The Bell, was still an ordinary country pub.

Needless to say, things are very different now. To mention only two changes in particular, the road running past Anne Hathaway's is no longer a dead end; it runs on and links up with one of the main roads in and out of Stratford, so that there is always the sound of traffic; and the Bell Inn has expanded for a mass clientele who would leave no room for a Julia sitting comfortably at the bar with her whixey-itis. Hathaway Hamlet, for its part, has obviously become the estate agent's dream it was always destined to be. Sometimes, now, I walk past that cluster of thatched roofs, protected these days by trim hedges and with its outline changed by new garages. There are the cottages, obviously each worth in today's market a king's ransom, and no doubt full of exquisite antique furniture. It is no one's fault, of course; impersonal forces have done their work, and the good people who live in Hathaway Hamlet today have committed no crime in falling in love with these cottages and buying them, nor in maintaining them at what is now the appropriate level of chic. But something has gone from the world.

I knew Julia well for, I suppose, seven or eight years. During that time my vision of her naturally became clearer and more rounded. I was growing up, and she was revealing more of herself. My first impressions of her were one-dimensional, as a richly funny character, full of quirks and peculiarities, hovering several feet above ordinary mundane life in the same way that Falstaff does. But Falstaff, in the end, is punctured and brought down to earth; and Julia ultimately revealed, to my wondering young eyes, that she was a real woman and not a character from some rich, bubbling picaresque novel; that she had, like everyone else, a relationship with the ordinary world in all its dailiness and predictability.

It was, of course, a relationship of adversaries. The ordinary daily world is not friendly to those who live outside its enclosures. At worst it persecutes them into isolation, madness, and death. At best it denies them the solid satisfactions that are its own comforts and compensations. Julia had (evidently) parted company with the conventional world at the very beginning of

her life, and the world had, as usual, exacted its price. She had
been made to suffer. I never, of course, learned the history of
these sufferings, but as I grew to know her better, I had occasional glimpses into the depths of her resentments, resentments
that could only have arisen from pain, exclusion, humiliation.
She hated, for instance, anything to do with established religion.
I must have been staying at the cottage one Christmas, because,
although I don't remember anything else about it, I remember
sitting in front of the fire on Christmas Eve, listening on the
radio to the carol service from King's College, Cambridge. At
least, I started to listen to it; but Julia, who was moving about
attending to various household tasks, began to show signs of
discomfort and nervous impatience. The clerical tones, the soaring voices of the choirboys, seemed to cause her a distress similar to that suffered by a person who can't bear a cat in the room
and suddenly sees one come in. "Bosh and bad luck!" she hissed,
flicking venomously at the radio with a duster as she went past.
"Bosh and bad luck, that is!" She did not actually seize the radio
and switch it off, but I could see she was longing to, so I did it
for her. To this day I listen on Christmas Eve to that carol
service from King's, and to this day I hear Julia's "bosh and bad
luck" — the two have fused in my mind into an antiphonal
whole.

Then, a year or two later, I was again sitting by the cottage
fireside in the afternoon, and Julia began talking about a man
she had loved. I remember very few facts about this man and
her relationship with him. Perhaps she gave me very few. But
she had loved him and they had had wonderful times together.
"He had an old Riley car, and we used to go away for holidays,
driving about wherever we took a fancy to go." Was the man
married? Was there some external reason why he and Julia
could not settle down into a regular union, or was it just tem-
peramental? At any rate: "One Christmas he said to me, 'My
father wants me to go to Communion with him. And I can't.' I
said, 'Why not?' and he said, 'Because of you.' So I said, 'Well,
if that's how you feel, you'd better get on with it.' " And that, I
was left to gather, had been their parting.

So it came to me, in glimpses, a vision of the thorns that had beset Julia's path, how she had had her heart broken, been denied this and excluded from that.

I thought a good deal about Julia's lover, and his old Riley, and his churchgoing father. But the real food for thought came one chilly summer evening when, with the light fading behind the small leaded panes, Julia unexpectedly launched into a long string of stories, each one the case history of some person whose life had been spoiled by respectability, domesticity, marriage. She seemed to have known case after case of people, usually men but sometimes women too, who had lived under such tension in the prison-house of social conformity that they had ended up by going to pieces or doing desperate things. I sat, appalled, silently listening. "They showed me all round their little new home, all set up with this and that and the flowers in the garden and a car in the garage. And I thought, 'He's in his squirrel cage. And he'd give his soul to get out of it.'"

I shall never forget that evening: Julia's voice, drained now of its laughter and self-mockery, lowered to a flat and emphatic timbre, adding story to story of frustration and suffering. Every word entered my ear like a stab. For I, too, was in my squirrel cage.

In recalling, here, my visits to Hathaway Hamlet I have consistently made use of the first person singular: *I* did this, *I* found that. Actually it was nearly always *We*. I had the company, most of the time, of the wife I married when I was twenty-two and parted from finally when I was thirty. I do not want to discuss this relationship beyond remarking that nothing in the whole awful mess was particularly my wife's fault. For me to get married at twenty-two was a monumental act of folly, and it was her misfortune (as well as, to a significant extent, her doing) that I should have involved her in that folly.

Sometimes I look back on that wedding day in July 1947, and try to reconstruct the state of mind that had driven me through all the stages — the proposal, the ring, the banns, culminating finally in that dazed walk down the aisle. It took place in St. Gile's Church, Northampton, a few yards from Northampton General Hospital where John Clare found asylum during the long years of his madness; but he was not madder than I was. "I am; but who I am none cares or knows." Looking back, I feel that that line applied as well to me on that July morning as it ever did to him. What could I have been thinking of? What kind of vision had I, if I had any at all, of the fifty more years I expected to live? I have lived nearly forty of them, and, looking back, all I can say is that I see as little into the mind of that young man as if he were someone else, someone I never met or heard of.

The wedding ceremony — it took about ten minutes, in the almost empty church — seemed to snap this spell. At once, standing in the vestry, I knew the monstrous folly of what I had done. But it was too late. The register lay open for our names; the pen was handed to me with the ink wet on the nib. We signed, and a decade of disaster for both of us was under way.

Of the effect on my partner's life, I can say nothing, except that I think of her with total compassion. The effect on my life was, first, to ruin my twenties. My psychic maladjustment found expression in physical illness, and when I look back on that decade I see doctors' waiting rooms and hospital wards. Nor did the distortion stop there, because in my thirties, or at any rate the first half of them, I wasted a lot of energy having the sort of "good time" I ought to have had ten years earlier and got out of the way.

Sometimes I wonder whether my trance-like state, the incredible lack of self-knowledge combined with zombie fatalism, did not result from some kind of deep exhaustion. Between seventeen and twenty-one I not only filled my head with an enormous amount of information, I also reoriented my life and therefore to some extent my personality. After growing up in Stoke-on-Trent, and having no chance to absorb any but the notions of Stoke-on-Trent, I was pitchforked into Oxford at seventeen, and immediately recognized it as the natural setting for my life and endeavors. But there is a snag in that word *natural*. If Oxford was my natural place, then Stoke-on-Trent had been artificial, and since it had so totally molded me, I had to break out of that mold, not with any overt feelings of hostility and rejection (if asked at any time of my life, I would always have said I liked Stoke, and so I did in very many ways) but with a long, dragging, unconscious effort, like the effort of a plant to turn round to a stronger source of light.

The quarrel, if such it was, is long since healed, and my two towns now seem to me each to have given me about half of my personality as it is today. But *something* must have put me into that drugged state, and perhaps it was that the long effort of adaptation had left me without the energy to steer a course through the maze of conflicting experiences that life in one's twenties always is.

I can see my wife now on that evening in Julia's cottage, sitting on a chair in the corner, a small dark figure with head bent, listening. And I can see myself, pale and wan, sitting aghast as Julia knocked out the props, one by one, from

The old and bitter world where they marry in churches.

Julia, who had always been a builder of shelters, who had always fashioned beautiful and whimsical structures of fantasy and good humor in which one could pretend to be living one's life, was for that hour relentlessly destructive, heaping up story on story about people who had tried to ignore the needs of their emotions and instincts, tried to make themselves snug little shelters for the sake of safety and respectability and then found that the shelters were cages against which they must hurl themselves till something broke, they or the cage or both. . . . I had gone, so often and so eagerly, to Hathaway Hamlet as a glorious playground, and now suddenly it was a house of correction.

I found growing up a long and painful process, so long that perhaps in the end I shall go down to the grave with the process still not completed. But I do at least know when it started: that rain-chilled evening, sitting wordless by the empty fireplace as Julia poured the cold torrent of her anger against settled people and their settled ways.

Biographical Notes
Notable Essays of 1985

Biographical Notes

JULIAN BARNES is the author of *Metroland, Before She Met Me,* and *Flaubert's Parrot.* He was recently awarded the 1986 E. M. Forster Award by the American Academy and Institute of Arts and Letters. His next novel, *Staring at the Sun,* will be published by Knopf in 1987.

DONALD BARTHELME has published many collections of short stories, among them *Come Back, Dr. Caligari; Unspeakable Practices, Unnatural Acts; City Life; Guilty Pleasures; Sadness; Amateurs; Great Days;* and *Overnight to Many Distant Cities.* He has also written two novels, *Snow White* and *The Dead Father.*

JOSEPH BRODSKY, exiled from the Soviet Union in 1972, is Five College Professor of Literature at Mount Holyoke College. His collection of poems, *A Part of Speech,* was published in 1980; and a collection of essays, *Less Than One,* came out in 1986. He is a MacArthur Prize Fellow and a member of the American Academy of Arts and Letters. A new collection of poetry, *Homage to Urania,* will be published in 1987.

ALEXANDER COCKBURN has been an Irish citizen resident of the United States since 1973. He writes regular columns for *The Nation* and *The Wall Street Journal,* and contributes to many magazines. He is currently writing books about the press and about automobiles.

GERALD EARLY is currently finishing a book entitled *The Culture of Bruising: Essays Towards a Definition of Literature, Prizefighting, and the Modern World.*

KAI ERIKSON has written *Wayward Puritans: A Study in the Sociology of Deviance* and *Everything in Its Path: Destruction of Community in the*

Buffalo Creek Flood. He is editor of *The Yale Review* and professor of sociology and American studies at Yale University.

ROBERT FITZGERALD, poet and translator of the *Odyssey*, the *Iliad*, and the *Aeneid*, was Boylston Professor of Rhetoric and Oratory Emeritus at Harvard. A collection of his selected prose, including essays on his friends James Agee, Randall Jarrell, and Flannery O'Connor will be published by New Directions in 1987. Robert Fitzgerald died in January 1985.

WILLIAM H. GASS is the author of seven books of fiction and nonfiction, including *Omensetter's Luck, In the Heart of the Heart of the Country, On Being Blue,* and *The World Within the Word.* He is the David May Distinguished University Professor in the Humanities at Washington University in St. Louis. His recent collection of essays, *Habitations of the Word,* won the 1986 National Book Critics Circle Award for Criticism.

STEPHEN JAY GOULD teaches biology, geology, and the history of science at Harvard University. He is the author of *Ontogeny and Phylogeny, The Mismeasure of Man,* and four collections of essays: *Ever Since Darwin, The Panda's Thumb, Hens' Teeth and Horses' Toes,* and *The Flamingo's Smile.* A MacArthur Prize Fellow, he writes a monthly scientific essay for *Natural History* magazine.

ANNE HOLLANDER is an independent scholar and writer living in New York City. Her book *Seeing Through Clothes* is about the representation of clothing in art. Her essays and reviews have appeared in *The American Scholar, The New Republic, The New York Review of Books, The New York Times Book Review, Vogue, Connoisseur,* and *Raritan.* She is currently writing a book about painterly and graphic sources for film.

GEORGE F. KENNAN, formerly a career Foreign Service officer and ambassador to Russia and Yugoslavia, is now a retired professor at the Institute for Advanced Study in Princeton. He is the author of a number of books on American foreign policy and diplomatic history, including *The Nuclear Delusion, The Decline of Bismarck's European Order,* and *The Fateful Alliance.*

JOYCE CAROL OATES is the author most recently of *Marya: A Life* and *Raven's Wing,* a collection of short stories. Her essay "On Boxing" will be published in an expanded version, with photographs by John Ranard, in 1987. She teaches at Princeton University and helps edit *The Ontario Review.*

CYNTHIA OZICK is the author of two novels, *Trust* and *The Cannibal*

Galaxy, and several collections: *The Pagan Rabbi and Other Stories, Bloodshed and Three Novellas*, and *Levitation: Five Fictions*. She has published *Art & Ardor: Essays* and is currently at work on a novel.

EDWARD ROTHSTEIN is the music critic for *The New Republic* and a senior editor at the Free Press, Macmillan Inc. He was a music critic for *The New York Times* and did graduate work in mathematics, literature, and philosophy at Brandeis and Columbia universities and at the Committee on Social Thought at the University of Chicago. His essays on literature, science, and culture have appeared in *The New York Review of Books, Commentary, The American Scholar, Musical Quarterly*, the *Washington Post*, and other publications. He is at work on a study of the friendship between Gershom Scholem and Walter Benjamin.

FREDERICK TURNER is the author of three books, the most recent of which is *Rediscovering America: John Muir in His Time and Ours*. He is at work on a book about the making of the American literary landscape. A reformed professor, he is now a free-lance writer living in Santa Fe, New Mexico.

GORE VIDAL was born in West Point and is the author of twenty novels, including the American chronicle (*Burr, 1876, Washington, D.C.*, and *Lincoln*), five plays, and five collections of essays, the most recent of which, *The Second American Revolution*, won the National Book Critics Circle Award for Criticism in 1982. He is currently at work on a novel, *Manifest Destiny*.

JOHN WAIN has published many volumes of fiction, poetry, essays, and literary criticism. His novels include *Hurry on Down, A Winter in the Hills*, and *Young Shoulders*. He is the editor of *Everyman's Book of English Verse* and the author of a prizewinning biography, *Samuel Johnson*. The first installment of his autobiography was *Sprightly Running*; his new book, *Dear Shadows*, will be published this year.

Notable Essays of 1985

SELECTED BY ROBERT ATWAN

MAX APPLE
Rocket Redux. *New York Times Sports Magazine*, September 29.

WILL BAKER
Sourdoughs, Filibusters, and a One-Eared Mule. *The Georgia Review*, Summer.

JAMES BALDWIN
Freaks and the American Ideal of Manhood. *Playboy*, January.

JOHN BAYLEY
The Order of Battle at Trafalgar. *Salmagundi Magazine*, Fall / Winter.

RALPH BEER
Holding to the Land. *Harper's Magazine*, September.

SVEN BIKERTS
Notes from a Confession. *The Agni Review*, No. 22.

DAVID BLACK
Walking the Cape. *Harper's Magazine*, June.

ROY BLOUNT, JR.
Salute to John Wayne. *The Atlantic*, February.

HAROLD BRODKEY
Reading, the Most Dangerous Game. *New York Times Book Review*, November 24.

HAYDEN CARRUTH
The Intentional Alligator. *The Georgia Review*, Summer.

ALAN CHEUSE
The Crossing-the-Street Dilemma. *Ms.*, January.

ELEANOR CLARK
A Sahara Silhouette. *Partisan Review*, No. 4, 1984 / No. 1, 1985.

ROBERT S. CLARK
Letter from Dresden. *Hudson Review*, Winter.

HARRY CREWS
Fathers, Sons, Blood. *Playboy*, January.

ANNIE DILLARD
Singing with the Fundamentalists. *The Yale Review*, Winter.

STANLEY ELKIN
My Tuxedo: A Meditation. *Chicago*, May.

JOSEPH EPSTEIN
A Fat Man Struggles to Get Out. *American Scholar*, Summer.

IAN FRAZER
Bear News. *The New Yorker*, September 9.

THOMAS FRICK
Nietzsche's Typewriter. *The Agni Review*, No. 22.

NADINE GORDIMER
Guarding "The Gates of Paradise." *New York Times Magazine*, September 8.

STEPHEN JAY GOULD
The Median Isn't the Message. *Discover*, June.

STEPHEN GREENBLATT
China: Visiting Rites. *Raritan*, Spring.

VICKI HEARNE
Lo, Hear the Gentle Pit Bull. *Harper's Magazine*, June.

DAVID HELLERSTEIN
The Middle Dominions. *The North American Review*, June.

WILLIAM HOWARTH
E. B. White at The New Yorker. *The Sewanee Review*, Fall.

WILLIAM HUMPHREY
Birds of a Feather. *Sports Illustrated*, October 14.

SAMUEL HYNES
Remembering Okinawa. *TriQuarterly*, Winter.

LAURA (RIDING) JACKSON
Is There a World for Literature? — Is There Literature for a World? *Chelsea*, No. 44.

RONALD JAGER
The Higher Ecology. *Harper's Magazine*, May.

STUART JOHNSON
"Dallas" / Dallas. *Southwest Review*, Winter.

FRANCES W. KAYE
Remembering Snow Geese. *Prairie Schooner*, Spring.

ALFRED KAZIN
New York: The Writer in the Powerhouse. *The New York Review of Books*, October 10.

FRANK KERMODE
The Decline of the Man of Letters. *Partisan Review*, No. 3.

DAVID LEAVITT
The New Lost Generation. *Esquire*, May.

GEORGE LEONARD
The White Roach. *Esquire*, November.

BARRY LOPEZ
The Passing of the Birds. *Orion*, Autumn.

MICHAEL MARTONE
Pulling Things Back to Earth. *The North American Review*, June.

ED MCCLANAHAN
The Day the Lampshades Breathed. *Conjunctions*, No. 8.

KENNETH A. MCCLANE
A Death in the Family. *The Antioch Review*, Spring.

EDWARD MENDELSON
Baedeker's Universe. *The Yale Review*, Spring.

STEPHEN MENICK
Children of Rumm. *The Iowa Review*, Vol. XV, No. 2.

JEFFREY MEYERS
The Quest for Hemingway. *The Virginia Quarterly Review*, Summer.

EUGENE MIRABELLI
Looking and Not Looking: Pornographic and Nude Photography. *Grand Street*, Autumn.

N. SCOTT MOMADAY
Discovering the Land of Light. *New York Times Magazine* (Part 2), March 17.

ELTING E. MORISON
Being an American. *The Yale Review*, Spring.

KATHLEEN NORRIS
Gatsby on the Plains: The Small-Town Death Wish. *North Dakota Quarterly*, Fall.

ROBERT NOZICK
Theological Explanations. *Ploughshares*, Vol. II, No. 4.

SHAUN O'CONNELL
Boggy Ways: Notes on Irish-American Culture. *The Massachusetts Review*, Summer / Autumn.

JAROSLAV PELIKAN
Humanism: Two Definitions and Two Defenses. *Southern Humanities Review*, Summer.

SAMUEL PICKERING, JR.
Upstairs. *The Kenyon Review*, Spring.
Man of Letters. *The Virginia Quarterly Review*, Winter.

ROGER POOLE
Travels of Kierkegaard. *Raritan*, Spring.

MARILYNNE ROBINSON
Bad News from Britain. *Harper's Magazine*, February.

ANTONIO BENITEZ ROJO
The Repeating Island. *New England Review / Bread Loaf Quarterly*, June.

OLIVER SACKS
The President's Speech. *The New York Review of Books*, August 18.
The Twins. *The New York Review of Books*, February 28.

SCOTT R. SANDERS
Stone Towns and the Country Between. *Indiana Review*, Spring.
Quarriers. *Northwest Review*, No. 3.

TOBIAS SCHNEEBAUM
Savages of the Brazza River. *Pequod*, Nos. 19, 20, 21.

JANET ADAM SMITH
Tom Possum and the Roberts Family. *The Southern Review*, October.

SUSAN SONTAG
On Mapplethorpe. *Vanity Fair*, July.

HARRY STEIN
Fighting the Good Fight. *Esquire*,
    August.

ANTHONY STORR
The Sanity of True Genius. *The
    Virginia Quarterly Review*, Winter.

CALVIN TRILLIN
Right of Way. *The New Yorker*, May 6.

JOHN UPDIKE
At War with My Skin. *The New Yorker*,
    September 2.

ALICE WALKER
Father: For What You Were. *Essence*,
    May.

GERALD WEISSMANN
Springtime for Pernkopf. *Hospital
    Practice*, October 15.

PETER WILD
Captivity: The Second Time Around.
    The North Dakota Quarterly, Fall.

DON ZACHARIA
My Legacy. *The Kenyon Review*,
    Winter.

to need ears, still less eyes, or any other sense." Wagner presented Bach as a musical savior of the German people itself:

> If we would comprehend the wonderful originality, strength, and significance of the German mind in one incomparably eloquent image, we must look keenly and discerningly at the appearance, otherwise almost inexplicably mysterious, of the musical marvel Sebastian Bach. . . . Look at this head, hidden in its absurd French full-bottomed wig, look at this master, a miserable cantor and organist in little Thuringian towns whose names we hardly know now, wearing himself out in poor situations, always so little considered that it needed a whole century after his death to rescue his works from oblivion; even in his music taking up with an art-form which externally was the complete likeness of his epoch, dry, stiff, pedantic, like perruques and pigtails in notes; and see now the world the incomprehensibly great Sebastian built up out of these elements!

The amazement and worship endure even in the most scholarly musicological circles of this century. Bach has always been at the center of the "authenticity" movement, which attempts to reconstruct the instruments, ensembles, and performance practice of Bach's time. Arguments over "authentic performance" can resemble disputations over holy texts; they have split the musical community along more than scholarly lines. "You play Bach your way," the harpsichordist Wanda Landowska commented to a colleague, "I will play him his way."

Behind these invocations of the sacred there was, however, a man whose life and character must have been bound up in his music. Even the physical traces of Bach are suggestive. His skeleton was found in 1894 in an oak coffin, with its skull bearing — in Schweitzer's words — a "prominent lower jaw, high forehead, deep-set eyesockets, and marked nasal angle." He continues: "Among the interesting peculiarities of Bach's skull may be mentioned the extraordinary toughness of the bone of the temple that encloses the inner organ of hearing, and the quite remarkable largeness of the fenestra rotunda." The skull bears some resemblance to the only two portraits of Bach that have been authenticated. Both were probably painted by Elias Gottlieb Haussmann, the later (1748) a copy of the earlier (1746). A few years before his death the composer is shown holding, angled against his stomach, the score of a puzzle canon: the canon challenges the player to figure out how and when and where a version of the theme is to be played against itself. Bach's right hand is fleshy, feminine, delicately proffering the sheet of paper, while the rest of his body takes no cognizance of his presented art. He stares directly out at the viewer, bewigged in perruques and pigtails, his face as well fed as his belly, the mouth in a pose of slight tension, neither a smile nor a sneer, possessing some degree of self-satisfaction. His left eyebrow is raised, as if in inquiry, his right brow slightly lowered. It is not quite what we expect of the composer either of the canon or the great *Passions*. The body is so solidly there, the eyes so surely presenting a claim, their glance so skeptical — and so ambiguous — that the gentility of the musical offering seems posed, unconvincing, artificial.

Was that the pose in which he made his true "Musical Offering" to King Frederick II, based on a theme that the king composed? With a slight irony, and more than a slight ego? When Bach visited Potsdam, the king had presented him with a theme on which to improvise. Most immodestly, Bach improvised extravagantly, and just two months later had engraved two fugues, ten canons, and a trio sonata based upon the king's theme. This is surely the gesture of a man at once making an effusive offering while raising his eyebrow in pride over his invention and his powers. As in the portrait, this is not a man out of touch with his surroundings. Bach is very much in control, choosing to write his puzzle canons, knowing full well how they will be received, and how anomalous such taut structures are in a world beginning to love sentimental novels.

There is also something in the composer's thick neck and corpulent chest covered in white silk and a gold-buttoned coat that suggests a physical body that can be sensed even in Bach's most abstract music — in its dance rhythms, surprising accents, and swirl of figuration. Bach was, in fact, hot-tempered and stubborn. He was censured for getting into a sword fight after calling one of his players a "nanny-goat bassoonist." His taste for wine is evident in the substantial sums that appear on many of his accounts. But in Haussmann's portrait there is also that feminine hand, so split apart in manner from the physically commanding pose of the man. Indeed, in dealing with those in authority, those who controlled the means of patronage, Bach presented that most fleshy delicate hand, the pinky lightly floating in deference. Bach *served* all his life. Servile epistolary salutations were, for example, conventions of the time, but Bach never missed an opportunity to exploit the style when approaching patrons. There is this remarkable opening to an argumentative missive:

> Their Magnificences, the Most Noble, Most Reverend, Most Distinguished, Respected and Most Learned Members of the Most Worshipful Royal and Electoral Saxon Consistory at Leipzig, My Most Honored Masters and High and Mighty Patron. YOUR MAGNIFICENCES, MOST NOBLE, MOST REVEREND, MOST DISTINGUISHED, RESPECTED AND MOST LEARNED, MOST HIGHLY ESTEEMED MASTERS AND HIGH PATRONI!

But after that very salutation comes the stern and skeptical glance, a demand, an appeal, a complaint — a man discontent with his place and his role.

The letter following that fawning address was, in fact, to Bach's masters at Leipzig, the city where Bach spent most of his mature musical life, from 1723 to 1750. There he produced his great sacred works, including five complete cycles of cantatas, the *Mass* and *Passions*, and the great fugues and canons of his late years. It was the place, in other words, where the transcendental Bach took shape, after he had written most of his organ and keyboard masterpieces. As Kantor of the Thomaskirche and Director Musices, he was the most important musician in Leipzig, responsible for the music in the four principal churches, and for the town's musical life. These were the years of musical grandeur, in which Bach, one would assume, had the religious and public support of Leipzig behind him.

Still, as any number of his letters to the Leipzig Council indicate, the situation was in fact far different. Before going to Leipzig, Bach was remarkably content at Köthen, where he was a court composer to a prince who loved music. Then the prince married a rather unmusical woman. Sensing the change in his status, Bach made inquiries in other towns. Kuhnau, who held the position at Leipzig, had died. Telemann, then the most renowned musician in Germany, was first offered the position; next in line was Christoph Graupner, who was something of an alumnus. Only when they both declined was Bach considered. To the councillors Bach was a mediocrity and, conversely, the position was a compromise for Bach. From his place at the center of court life with a sensitive prince, he moved to Leipzig, where he had to answer to several dozen civic and church superiors, who included the fifteen members of the city council who hired him, the ecclesiastical authority of the consistory, which supervised the church services, and the rector of the school itself, within which Bach had to teach Latin along with music. Bach was paid less than a quarter of what he had received at Köthen, living expenses were higher, and he was dependent upon "freelance" playing at funerals and weddings. (Bach later complained that a "healthy wind was blowing" one year in Leipzig so he made almost nothing from funerals.)

Bach's new position also demanded rising at four or five in the morning to maintain discipline in the school until the students retired at eight in the evening. He was expected to write and prepare music for all the church services; he composed a cantata every week for the first two years. Moreover, as soon as he arrived in Leipzig, Bach was embroiled in a dispute over whether he would have charge of the music at St. Paul's, the university church. Bach needed the income and pressed his case. In 1725 he went over his superiors' heads and wrote three petitions to the Elector of Saxony, pleading a tightly argued case. This did not make for good relations with the council; Bach lost his appeal, and the composer found commissions passing him by, leading to other conflicts. In 1729, just after his first performance of the *St. Matthew Passion*, the council ignored both Bach's selections of new pupils and his musical priorities. At a council meeting, according to the minutes, Bach was called "incorrigible." The council decided "he must be reproached and admonished."

Eschewing his usual salutation, Bach sent a memo to the council, biting in its graciousness and titled: "Short but most necessary draft for a well-appointed church music; with certain modest reflections on the decline of the same." The climactic conflict, lasting more than two years, came in 1734, when Johann August Ernesti was appointed rector of the school. One historical account, dating from 1776, describes how the men became bitter enemies: "Bach began to hate those students who devoted themselves completely to the *humaniora* and treated music as a secondary matter, and Ernesti became a foe of music. When he came upon a student practicing on an instrument he would exclaim, 'What? You want to be a beer-fiddler too?'" Finding deaf ears at the council with more than four lengthy complaints and responses, Bach again appealed over their heads, "To His Most Serene Highness, the Mighty Prince and Lord, Frederick Augustus, King in Poland," etc., etc.

These confrontations, which occurred earlier in Bach's career as well, show a keen sense of political hierarchy in Bach's language, along with a peremptory dismissal of political manners in his actions. When it came to musical matters, there was no compromise. Yet Bach came to Leipzig at a moment when music was becoming less and less important in schools and the community, ironically, because of the dawn of the Enlightenment, which Ernesti represented. Bach's role was peculiar; he was even dependent at the end of his life on contributions from the community, because he essentially had no social position. When he died, one member of the council cautioned against replacing him with anyone resembling a "Kapellmeister." His successor gave his first performance in a concert hall, not a church.

Christoph Wolff, the distinguished Bach scholar, points out that Bach understood these matters quite well. In the cantata of homage to the municipal council (BWV 216a), Mercury, the god of commerce, declares his gift to the council: "My trade, which here / I firmly plant, / shall provide you with / the greatest part of your lustre." That trade, and the world of the bourgeoisie that developed in its wake, did indeed leave the Kantor and Director Musices looking somewhat quaint. Haussmann's portrait captures the paradox, in Bach's face and body and hand, the gracious offer of music, and the ironic awareness that the music was posing more than a trivial puzzle to its listeners.

The biggest puzzle is that this most contentious man working at this peculiar historical moment produced such works as the *St. Matthew Passion* and the *B minor Mass* — music that seems to speak without ambiguities about faith and belief, in a tone of voice and with a technical assurance that make the music seem not just pre-modern, but otherworldly. There would seem to be scarcely a hint of Bach treating the religious realm as he did the political, of offering praise out of duty rather than belief, or of demonstrating the raised eyebrow and ambiguous lips of the Haussmann portrait. There is a certainty in Bach's harmonies. However much they meander into painful realms, the foundation is never left behind.

Moreover, the texts themselves are never subordinate to technical aspects of the music. In fact, they determine the music's central figurations. In the common practice of the period, the music *paints* the texts being set, illustrating them, commenting upon them, knowing its own laws are subordinate to the word. This means that words like "descent" are illustrated with descending melodic lines. Relations between meaning and musical sign can become still more intricate. Sometimes the music intentionally bears mystical or numerological meanings — a bass line, for example, repeated thirteen times, underscoring the tragedy of the "Crucifixus" in the *Mass*. And always in the vocal music, there are the chorales — the heart of Lutheran music — which Bach harmonizes and reharmonizes, treating them with as much care as if they too were sacred texts. Scores also bear dedicatory abbreviations, wholly sincere, like "S.D.G." ("Soli Deo Gloria," To god alone be praise) or "J.J." ("Jesu juva," Help me, Jesus). Bach writes that even so rudimentary an element of music as the figured bass — the fundamental bass line to be filled in by the player — merits such attention. In instructing his pupils, he wrote: "Like all music, the figured bass should have no other end and aim than the glory of God and the recreation of the soul; where this is not kept in mind there is no true music, but only an infernal clamor and ranting."

What then of the clamor and ranting that comes of Bach's own life? And what are its echoes in the music itself? Theodor Adorno noted that if we treat Bach simply as an archaic man of faith, we have missed the most important aspect of his music: it is a product of its time, anticipating the Enlightenment even as it seems to nestle itself in formal rigors.

Even the work that would seem furthest from the Enlightenment — the *B minor Mass* — acknowledges the new age by attempting to swerve away from it. The *Mass* was written over a period of twenty years; its Credo is now believed to be one of Bach's final works. It is deliberately archaic, orthodox, exaggerating aspects of formality and faith. Bach divided the Credo text into nine sections, grouped into a trinity of three parts each. There is also a formal symmetry around the center group of three, with the Crucifixus lying at its heart. That tripartite center is framed by two arias: "Et in unum Deum" (I believe in one Lord Jesus Christ) and "Et in Spiritum sanctum" (And I believe in the Holy Ghost). Each chorus is suffused with numerical symbolism and pictorial references, so that in "Et incarnatus," for example, the pulsing three tones of the bass line shift upon the words "and was made man"; the breathing sighs of the violins descend, and become incarnated, musically, in that low-pitched earthly realm, like the described movement of the Holy Ghost. Such a musical symbol is not subliminal. It can, in performance, elicit a gasp, as if the music itself had incarnated a spiritual idea and was presenting it, not for appreciation, but as the simple truth.

This gives the Credo an orthodoxy and a seriousness far more extreme than the most impassioned cantatas. But even in this case, the effect of the music is far different from a simple assertion of faith. As the arias and the instrumental solos make clear, there is an *interior* world being presented as well. The communal fugues and proclamations of the choruses are contrasted with the meditative arias of personal belief that frame the central section of the Credo. "Et in unum Deum" is a duet in which the proclamation of belief in one god becomes a sensuous intertwining of imitative voices; similarly, the oboe duet in "Et in Spiritum" is lyrically intimate. The choruses of the central section — the Incarnation, Crucifixion, and Resurrection — also convey a sense of human drama, sounding hushed and eerie at first and finally blazing forth with communal force.

All is so tightly controlled here that the tensions between individual and community, will and authority, sentiment and law, feeling and faith — all the tensions so evident elsewhere in Bach's music — are muted. The cantatas, though, celebrate those tensions, placing them at the core of Bach's religious music. The erotic arias between the soprano soul and bass Christ in *Cantata No. 140*, the variations on the single chorale theme in *Cantata No. 4*, the sharp contrasts between choral fugues and mellifluous arias in nearly all of the cantatas, show Bach moving constantly between the public demands of faith and its interior trials. In these works, as in the *Passions*, the style becomes almost operatic, dramatic, very different from earlier sacred works. The subject in much of Bach's sacred music is man — man in the particular — represented religiously in the figure of Christ. This shares certain elements with Pietism — the movement that attacked Lutheran orthodoxy, stressing personal and mystical devotion. There are anticipations of similar attitudes in other Baroque composers such as Heinrich Schütz, now celebrating his quadricentennial. But this religious emphasis on the individual links Bach more to the world that came after him than to the world that came before.

This is true even in the most serious secular works. The *Goldberg Variations*, as Glenn Gould pointed out, does not guide the listener through a structure or a narrative that develops in a certain direction. Instead, said Gould, it seems, despite its intricate architecture, to be "a community of sentiment" possessing "a fundamental coordinating intelligence which we [label] ego." It is the path of an individual will at play in the realm of musical structure. Bach is so sure of musical law that it grants him freedom. The canons at each interval are as ecstatic in spirit as the regularly appearing dance movements. And the *Variations'* piety is limited: the return of the magisterial theme at the end is preceded by a "quodlibet" — a playful interweaving of popular songs of the period, *"Ich bin so lang nicht bei dir g'west"* (Long have I been away from you) and *"Kraut und Rüben haben mich vertrieben"* (Cabbage and turnips have put me to flight). It has even been suggested that these songs refer to the theme itself. First heard at the beginning of the work, it returns an hour later; its foundations — its bass line and harmonies — have been transmuted and transformed, put in flight with sophisticated techniques that Bach may have modestly considered as commonplace as cabbages and turnips.

Bach's musical style, in fact, may almost be defined as the play of an ego in a highly structured world. Such, for example, is the texture of the fugue, which seems to govern every note Bach penned. His fugues construct musical orders in which each individual voice is playfully free — maintaining its identity but capable of the most fantastical diversions — while having its position verified and reinforced by other voices. The fugue establishes a community of like minds and distinct parts, very different from the polyphony of the Renaissance, where the focus is less on individual voices than on the overall texture. It also contrasts with earlier Baroque fugues, where propriety and sobriety govern the behavior of the voices. Bach's achievement is to make each voice seem completely independent, while showing again and again their links, and even identities, with other free voices. Bach turned the Baroque fugue into a sign of the Enlightenment.

The fugue as used by Bach presents an order known not through faith, but through persistent examination and exploration. His themes are not mere organizations of musical material; instead they venture forth into the fugue fully formed, with shape and character and tensions all their own. Bach, it was said, could glance at a theme and, as if judging its character, tell immediately how it should be treated in a fugue — whether there should be stretti (multiple entrances overlapped in a short time), inversion (the theme played upside down), retrogression (the theme played backward), and so on.

The theme's character is defined as a character by no other composer before Bach. The fugue thus becomes reflective as well as rational. A single voice explores and creates its own musical universe. The fugue as a style can be seen as a prelude, historically, to its own extinction in a style of "feeling," where one voice finds itself thoroughly alone, without such mirrorings and reflections and architectural structures; it wanders through sentiment and fantasy. The fugue and the canon began to seem archaic in the rococo world of Bach's sons. The canon could even seem, as C. P. E. Bach told Charles Burney, a "certain proof to him of a total want of genius." But C. P. E. Bach's successors in the Romantic era understood quite clearly the powers of canon and fugue. The most autobiographical music of the nineteenth century invokes the fugue in attempts to turn personal feeling into something more metaphysical, as in Beethoven's last piano sonatas or the finale to Liszt's piano sonata.

There is indeed something metaphysical about Bach's concern with the fugue: the belief that the world and the self are images of each other, that the word and music and the world are linked in their structure and their substance. Hence the nearly mystical concern with musical signs and symbols, from the most mundane illustration of joy with dotted rhythms to the use of themes with notes corresponding to the letters of Bach's name.

There is no way in this metaphysical vision to separate the world of daily life from a transcendent spiritual realm. So Bach did not think it all peculiar to include in a book of music composed and collected for his wife, Anna Magdalena, a poem (attributed to him) about a most mundane pleasure. It is entitled "Edifying Thoughts of a Tobacco Smoker":

> Whene'er I take my pipe and stuff it
> And smoke to pass the time away,
> My thoughts, as I sit there and puff it,
> Dwell on a picture sad and gray;
> It teaches me that very like
> Am I myself unto my pipe.

Like the pipe, he is made of but earth and clay; like the pipe, which glows leaving ash, so will his fame pass and his body turn to dust.

> Thus o'er my pipe, in contemplation
> Of such things, I can constantly
> Indulge in fruitful meditation,
> And so, puffing contentedly,
> On land, on sea, at home, abroad,
> I smoke my pipe and worship God.

Similar speculation suffuses Bach's musical universe. In his compositions, with their word-painting and affects and symbolism, metaphoric and metaphysical links are made between the most mundane and the most spiritual. The world is full of echoes and allusions. Nothing is arbitrary. Into this world comes the ego, the musical subject, Bach himself, whose work is craft rather than art because he does not create a world, he attempts to mirror it. In doing so, of course, he also catches part of himself. His presence slightly disrupts that metaphysical mirror because he begins to sense in his own peculiar position something awry — earthly hierarchies and authorities not quite matching the heavenly. So there is a double perspective: Bach serves, but he also serves himself. "J.J." (Help me, Jesus), he writes, but he also inscribes his own name musically in his final work. He is the voice in the fugues, the solitary individual ironically sensing his own freedom while remaining linked to a larger order. We can see him in the Haussmann portrait questioning, daring, stern and patient, and we can imagine him relishing his glass of port as well as his own skills, smoking his pipe and worshiping God.

FREDERICK TURNER

Visions of the Pacific

FROM SOUTHWEST REVIEW

1

A FEW MONTHS short of my forty-third birthday I finally saw the
Pacific. Clearing the southerly jumble of San Francisco — Daly
City, the airport, and all — my wife and I in our rented car
curved west toward a still unseen coast, and suddenly coming
out from behind a high headland, there it lay, a grand glittering
disc. Our view from above took in so much that I thought I
could truly discern the beginnings of the globe's curve where
sea met sky like the edge of a scimitar.

Flying west the day previous, I had been hoping to see the
continent's end as I passed above the flat, rectilinear stretches
of the midlands, the ever-bigger rivers choked in March with
brown chunks of spring-loosened ice, the gradual rise of the
land westward through snow-flecked tablelands and mesas, and
then at last the mountains, high, white, solemn. I had been
hoping that light would last into California and show me with
its sharpened, dying rays that golden sea. But somewhere in
Nevada the last of the light went in an amethyst haze and left
me still unfulfilled of that sight.

Oh, I had seen oceans before. Midwestern though I was by
birth, I had for years known the American Atlantic. I had come
to know, too, the hot green of the Gulf. Once I bobbed, effort-
less, in an Aegean swell as another sunset made Poseidon's temple at Sounion radiant, and Byron's name, scratched into a
column, grew black in final definition. A small fishing boat with

red sails stood off, its men shaking their hands at me to warn of sharks. But still I had no Pacific to me, and so my Americanness seemed privately incomplete. I was still back in the 1840s before we had become a Pacific as well as an Atlantic nation. But now in this very morning moment I caught up with history.

Immediately my thoughts went to Steinbeck, whose *Red Pony* had defined California for me ever since I read it in late childhood. In particular I thought of the old grandfather of "The Leader of the People" who tells the wondering boy Jody that there is a line of old men along the Pacific shore, hating the sea because it had stopped them, put a halt to that big, crawling beast that had purely followed instinct in going ever westward until there was no west left. If then I pondered the curiousness of this phenomenon — men hating the Pacific because it stopped their restlessness, made them sink roots — I don't remember that, only the image itself. I was young enough at the time to skip over the implications here and fasten on an actual line of black-clad old men along a shore that looked very much like my Lake Michigan's, their faces set, furious, reddened like the violent flesh tones in the illustrations to the volumes of *Book Trails,* my first significant books. Through subsequent years other California images had been superimposed—blondes, beach boys, the Rose Bowl—but beneath these there yet resided that primitive one of the old men and the ocean. Especially the ocean, implacable as Steinbeck had suggested it, inattentive to history and human strivings. And so, seeing it now, I saw again grandfather and the black and red men, balked at its frothy verge.

But as the highway accommodatingly kept company with the shoreline, other images intruded on the old men. Like an archaeologist of memory, I now saw beyond Steinbeck to the California excavations of recent years, digs that went down, not for gold, but for bones, artifacts, ashes, that sedimentary speech that, enunciating an old mortality, announces our own. Here was a view of this land and sea that had nothing fundamentally to do with Steinbeck's story of the westering, however personally compelling this remained. Thousands of years before the long advance over the terrain I'd just flown across men came up out of the Pacific in long rattan or reed crafts, oared, sailed, guided by their instincts, too, but in this instance to go eastward toward the rising sun. Asians, Phoenicians, Polynesians in their turn came here on scarcely imaginable errands, the light ever before them, beckoning, the shadows behind them, arrowlike in their wakes.

Of their crafts no single bit survives. Perishable like the crews who manned them, they have disappeared, and we cannot anywhere dig so deep as to exhume a prow of ancient intention, discover forgotten design: no Sutton Hoo seems awaiting us along these shores. But some stone anchors have been found and a few fragmentary Chinese manuscripts exist to tell of that ancient reality in light of which the old men ranged along the shore seemed boys indeed.

Nor was even this enough. For there were those on these Pacific shores who could have watched the gradual bobbing advance of the argonauts in their reed boats. Wanting to style ourselves "discoverers," first here and first surely to assess the meanings of here, where here was, we refused to countenance the antiquity of the native presence in the New World. Black-clad and red with the mistakes of the Old World, we were for many years old in our enslavement to one version of history. We were stuck on the figure of twelve thousand years ago as the earliest date for humans in the New World: this was our flattened vision of history beyond which it seemed imprudent and even dangerous to go, as if we too were sailors in Colón's crew, frightened by seas of wider speculation. Then we thought larger, thought twenty thousand, a barrier broken by carbon-14. Now an understanding of the phenomenon of racemization — the steady, inexorable breakdown of amino acids in bone — says seventy thousand, or more. In this yawning perspective the strange new expanse that greeted the restless eyes of the whites looks more like an old highway, long known in its tides and trades by dark precursors of whom the garrulous old grandfather knew nothing.

But then of course Steinbeck wasn't writing a history text; he was writing a story about what it felt like to have made that perilous passage, to have come out of the last deserts, down out of the blue air of the Sierra, through the foothills, and into the broad and fecund green of the Sacramento and San Joaquin valleys beyond which lay the end of the enterprise. And this is what the tale's grandfather has in mind as well: not history, a dry recital of the facts of westering, but what it felt like to have done it. "I tell those old stories," he says to Jody, "but they're not what I want to tell. I only know how I want people to feel when I tell them."

In this sense, it makes no real difference what the history of California's Pacific is. Maitland was right when he observed that the essential matter of history was not what happened but what people thought and said about it. This is why the Pacific coast is littered with the name "Balboa," for in the Western white imagination, anyway, the Pacific means Balboa, its discoverer.

So it was he I thought of last and longest as we continued southward toward destinations bearing names the Spaniards bestowed upon all this newness, the sun swinging out from the land, arcing westward over the waves toward Cipangu and Cathay, as bright with its old promise as when Balboa beheld it shining on the billowy green expanse he saw from a jungle hilltop.

2

Peter Martyr, that gossipy guy who hung around the royal court and talked with many involved in Spain's New World enterprises, said Balboa was a fencing master born on the Portuguese border at Jerez de los Caballos. He was tall and well-knit, Martyr said, possessed of a steady disposition. Martyr didn't say whether he had imagination, but events show plainly that he did, a fatal gift in his case. He was one of that number pulled overseas by the wake of Colón's 1498 landfall at Paria, where the Admiral finally encountered evidence appearing to speak plainly of those Eastern kingdoms so long sought: monkeys, deer, pearls. And so when Colón returned with these exotic items there was a rush. Gentlemen with neither training nor aptitude nor any understanding of the lands and stakes involved obtained licenses from the crown to go out and return rich. Don Roderigo de Bastidas, a wealthy notary from Triana, obtained one, his patent authorizing him to bring back precious metals and gems, slaves, mixed breeds, monsters, serpents, spices, and drugs. Vasco Núñez de Balboa shipped with him and in 1501 saw the eastern portion of the Panamanian isthmus before the ships, peppered by the borings of sea worms, turned back to the outpost of Haiti. Bastidas went back to Spain, apparently with enough riches and adventures to fill out the rest of life. Balboa, yet unfulfilled of either, stayed on.

For seven years we hear nothing of him. The island was a pestilential place now — dying Indian slaves, dying Spaniards, dwindling resources and prospects, the mines nearly dead, too. Occasional *entradas* into the island's heart resulted in no new treasure finds, no kingdoms, only the continuing savaging of the natives. On Haiti now there was a line of haters along the once-golden shore, hating the land they stood on, hating the sea that divided them from home, or the Indies, or anywhere else but where they were.

In 1509 Alonso de Ojeda, a seasoned if cruel and imprudent conquistador, and Diego de Nicuesa got licenses to explore and colonize the lands from the north coast of present-day Colombia up through what are now Panama, Costa Rica, and Nicaragua. Ojeda went out from Haiti in November, Nicuesa following with reinforcements a few days later. Balboa, bored, hopelessly sunk in debt, gloomily watched them spread their sails for adventure. He had wished to go, but a colonial law wisely prohibited debtors from leaving on such expeditions without having made settlement with their creditors, and Balboa could make no such arrangement. So, he was apparently doomed to wear out more time on Haiti.

A few days later, the lawyer Martín Fernándo de Enciso, Ojeda's second in command, pulled out with more men and supplies. When his ship was well out to sea Balboa, the absconding defalcator, suddenly emerged from a barrel where he had been stowed by a friend. Standing on the canting deck, blinking in the tropic light, the hero entered the history of the New World. He had with him only his sword and his fierce dog, Leoncillo. The lawyer was furious, fearing he would be held accountable for Balboa's debts. But there was nothing to be done now, and soon enough as laws, customs, and most of civilization's stays fell apart, rotten, under the relentless pressure of the unfeatured jungles there would be many in the company who would thank God that there had been nothing to do with Balboa but keep him.

From the first the entire expedition was a fatal bungle. At the future site of Cartagena, Ojeda foolishly provoked the wrath of the natives and so lost seventy men, including the famed pilot, Juan de la Cosa: in an omen of the venture, a party searching for survivors of this clash came upon Cosa tied to a tree, his body aquiver with arrows, raving on toward a poisonous death, a destination plotted for him since first he shipped for the unknown with Colón in 1492. Ojeda himself was badly wounded, too, and survived only because he commanded his surgeon (under pain of death) to cauterize his wound with two red-hot iron plates.

In such a state, already battered and fearful, the company arrived on the eastern shore of the Gulf of Uraba where the chastened Ojeda established a tiny outpost he called San Sebastián after that arrow-martyred saint whose protection he now devoutly sought. A few months later, Enciso yet to arrive with much-needed relief and prospects here bleaker by the day, Ojeda gave up and went back to Haiti, broken by his encounter with the wilderness of the New World. There he took holy orders and died a monk in the order of St. Francis.

A tough, limited man was left in charge of the wretched outpost, but though limited, Francisco Pizarro had what it took to keep things together until the terrifically tardy Enciso finally arrived, running his ship into a shoal reef as he did so and busting it to flinders. Then, taking rapid survey of the condition of his command, it was clear to the lawyer that he was not equal to this: the country bristling with jungle and swamps, unknown more than a hundred paces beyond the festering clearing; the natives armed and filled with venom against the invaders; and the men themselves, what few were left, reduced to eating roots and palm buds, fearful, mutinous. "Let us," so an old chronicle quotes one of them, "leave these deadly shores, where the sea, the land, the heavens, and men repulse us." They would not be likely to take orders from a man of law. Only Balboa could fully function here.

Where others lapsed into sweaty sickness, their quilted stuffs stained with fever, or squatted in the bush, helpless in yellow

disease; sat listless as demasted vessels; fell into hopeless plot-
tings; Balboa, alone, singular, saw into possibilities, saw beyond
these sorry beginnings, the muddy little clearing with its leaky
huts, pathetic mockup of Spain's heirarchical order. The man
had an itch, and this hot wilderness, limitless in potential for
him, inflamed it. He plunged to his work now, taking charge of
the expedition, by common consent the ablest man among
them.

He informed Enciso he had been to the westward shore of
the Gulf and that there the natives did not use poisoned arrows.
So the company loaded their remnant stores into two brigantines, crossed to the western shore (still westering) and there,
under the leadership of the ex-stowaway, successfully attacked
a native village. Pursuing its fleeing inhabitants upriver, the
Spaniards stumbled across a cache of gold: anklets, coronets,
bracelets in the amount of 10,000 *castellanos* (which Washington
Irving later computed to be $53,259 in U.S. dollars). The new
outpost they established was christened *Nuestra Señora de la An-
tigua del Darien* in accordance with a vow of Enciso's; but everybody called it simply Darien. So began the white march to the
Pacific.

Within a few months the strong man had eliminated the last
of his local opposition, had deported the ineffectual Enciso, and
had himself proclaimed *alcalde* (mayor) of Darien. Vision, it is
said, is the sure knowledge of what to do next, and whatever
may be said of the quality of Balboa's vision — ruthless, vain-
glorious — he had it: knew the proper proportions of conquest
here, the conciliatory gestures, the obdurate cruelty, the divisive
alliances that rendered inconsequential the numerical superiority of the neighboring tribes. He was not a man of many words
(they came haltingly to him when he had to engage in formal
discourse, as his letters to Ferdinand show) but a force armed
with a vision of something beyond where he now found himself,
a future kingdom to conquer, a city to find and sack, and above
all, those golden gables of the Far East. With a special certainty
he began the penetration of the isthmus to what he may already
have suspected, or at least hoped, might lie on its southern side.
And always, the savage Leoncillo ranged along with him and
drew an archer's pay for its work against native adversaries.

It was after he had bullied a chieftain named Comogre into an alliance that the way to the other side and its hidden sea was cleared. Comogre's son, aghast at the cupidity of the invaders, bitingly remarked that if gold was the stuff for which they had forsaken all — homes, families, country — there was another sea to the south and beside it a kingdom of fabulous wealth with more gold than even such as they could ever use. The description of what would prove to be the Pacific and in time the kingdom of the Incas (though that would be Pizarro's story, not Balboa's) was greeted with unrestrained joy, some of the blackened adventurers even weeping at the prospect of such plunder.

Speedily the company returned to Darien where Balboa set about preparations for the march south. They left September 1, 1513, 190 Spaniards and 800 Indians, their way smoothed at first by Balboa's previous intimidation of the nearer tribes. But as they went farther south from the known they began to encounter those who had not heard of the invincibility of the whites and so opposed them. Particularly warriors owing allegiance to one Quarequá who put up a fierce resistance and lost 600 of their number. Of this, the last major engagement of the march to the Pacific, it was said that some of these warriors fought in the battle dress of women and "shared the same passion." These were subsequently thrown to the dogs, led by Leoncillo, who tore them to pieces under the watchful eyes of Christians acting under authority of the Laws of Burgos, which specified the execution of sodomites. Later, the Flemish engraver, Theodore de Bry, depicted this scene, Balboa, center, in elegant dress, pointing out the intricacies of the operation while in the foreground the dogs rend and tear the almost naked bodies.

On the twenty-fifth of the month, Balboa was told by one of his guides that the sea could be glimpsed from a nearby summit. Accompanied only by the dog, as if no other was so fit to share the moment with him, he scaled the slope and stood at last "Silent, upon a peak in Darien," the poet's conflation of him with "stout Cortez" a brilliant mistake. Looking down through the dense tangle he saw it. Had he been attentive to the whole moment, as probably he was not, he might have heard behind him the heavy suspiration of his native bearers and his cursing comrades, toiling upward together. Many of these latter had shipped for no better reasons than their leader, but probably none was so alive to the potential of this moment as the man who now stood, perhaps in pose, on the summit while the others struggled up around him crying, "The sea! The sea!" And it is this moment, of course, that is commemorated in history and in those dozens of "Balboa"s that dot California's shores.

Four days thereafter, having encountered local obstacles — pathless jungle, steep slopes, natives — the company arrived at the sea's edge about the hour of vespers, and Balboa, in helmet and breastplate, a drawn sword in one hand and the Spanish flag in the other, waded into the mild surge and took formal possession.

3

There can be a quality to a seaside morning that is like no other, soft, dreaming, circumambient. Waking up into it, you become aware that in sleep a sort of serene privacy has included you, and you are blessed for the day. At Santa Cruz, where we stopped on the Pacific, there was such a quality to this morning as I sat on the glassed-in porch of a seaside cottage, scratching words about Balboa across the rough fiber of notebook pages. The smoke of morning coffee lifted into the profoundly silent air, and at the end of the gently sloping street I could see morning standing out on the Pacific, pearly gray and touched with the faintest underblush of pink.

Like the old conquistador who had to endure an interval between his first view of the Pacific and his actual contact with it, I had yet to touch it. I had seen sunset flame out across its hushed waves, had seen it turn to ink as the first stars spangled, and now, still dry and sandless, I put down my pen and sauntered down to the sea.

Already a few young mothers with children had spread out their gear on the small beach that lay behind a stone jetty, but the town's college kids, whose missions kept them abroad far into the night, were not yet in evidence. I cast off my sandals and stepped to the water's edge where a small boy played with two toy boats, one a tug, the other a stately seagoing craft with canvas sails. Launching his caravel, he saw it quickly capsized by the merest wavelet, its sails suddenly sodden and lank. But the tug bobbed like a barrel, righting itself after each roll, its enamel paint brightened again and again. Wading past him then, I heard the brine's hiss about my knees, saw the green swell coming up about me. The clouds in the distance were like sails. I stretched my arms out over the water, taking my own sort of possession, thinking as I did so, not only of that old and vain action, but of the meanings of "possession," which include the act of possessing and also the state of being possessed: to be held, swept up, enrapt, as now I was by this sea. Musing there in this mild embrace, the boy, his boats, the beach, all held before me as I turned back, I wondered again what it was in "The Leader of the People" that had so taken me those many years ago, whether I had even so early responded to a hidden threnodic note in the fiction. Whether at the time I first read it the true power of it was that I sensed that it was really about the failure to realize paradise, the grand newness of everything here proving unequal to men's baseless dreams, the whole of the New World forfeit to the lust for the Ever Elsewhere. Or was this rather a superimposition of later thoughts, as the older man is compelled by his own tides to revise the boy he once was?

Whatever the case, that threnodic note is there for me now in Steinbeck's story. It stands out plainly, and if it is not the story's major theme, neither does it seem hidden, a minor strain.

In this context it seems arguable that threnody or the elegiac is the dominant tone of all our literature. If the story of the formative white encounters with the New World is the story of tragic disillusionment and the singular discoverers — Colón, Balboa, Cortés, Dalfinger, Raleigh, La Salle — tragic heroes flawed by their inability to become possessed by the lands they claimed, then it might be inevitable that our literature would somehow express this. To me, it does so.

Of course, there are literary monuments that clearly do not and are just as clearly in the American grain. Franklin's autobiography, Crèvecoeur, and the early Whitman come quickest to mind; Poe, Dickinson, James, Hemingway do not seem in the American elegiac mode. Nor do the prominent writers (many

of them ethnic) of the years since World War II, as if that event
and its atomic conclusion had sealed off the past and its themes
forever. But then, think of how many of our great, seminal
works and writers do express the elegiac mode, beginning with
Governor Bradford's *Of Plimouth Plantation* and its celebrated
description of New England's wall of winter woods, the soul of
that bleak, featureless wilderness that seemed the very antithesis
of human hope. Cooper's Leatherstocking stories, Hawthorne's
tales and romances of innocence and paradise lost, Melville's
South Sea romances, Emerson (that desperate optimist), calling
two centuries after the fact of first encounter for Americans to
develop an original relationship with their lands; Thoreau, the
post–Civil War Whitman, Parkman, Twain's great idyll of a
boy's escape back into the wild heart of New World nature —
and the failure of that escape; *The Great Gatsby, In the American
Grain, U.S.A.* Even in the years since World War II the elegiac
mode occasionally surfaces once again, and when it does, the
result is often a work of a peculiar, haunting resonance: *Hender-
son the Rain King, At Play in the Fields of the Lord, Little Big Man,*
Roethke's "North American Sequence," even the film *Alice's Restaurant.* And all this is not to mention (more than passingly) the
elegiac mode of some of the most arresting works of the Latin
American literature of our time as in Carlos Fuentes' *Terra Nos-
tra,* much of Neruda, and Gabriel García Márquez.

There is something brooding, somber here, the memory of
bright hopes dashed by first encounters with magnificent lands
and seascapes, paradise poisoned by dreams saved from a fan-
tastic pettiness only by their size and tragic consequences, of
death and utter disappointment, of blighted seaboards and
blasted rain forests, of entire native cultures, fragile as feathers,
that disappeared. Traveling the jungles of South America, passing the hopeless little outposts of civilization staffed by characters out of Conrad, Claude Lévi-Strauss wrote that "our
adventurings into the heart of the New World have a lesson to
teach us: that the New World was not ours to destroy, and yet
we destroyed it; and that no other will be vouchsafed to us."
That is the burden of our New World history and literature, the
beginnings of which are to be found in Seville, in the Archives
of the Indies, in those bundles of manuscripts, the frozen, still-

burning records of what was done here, of the ends of enterprise, of caciques, conquistadores, the threatening wilderness
that was all around. Seizing Balboa's bundle, we think to lay
hands on the story of a great discovery and find instead an all
but unutterable blackness within . . .

4

When first he heard of the Pacific no less than when he first
beheld it, the thought of the East's gabled treasure houses
blazed in Balboa's head. So when he and his company arrived
on the Pacific's shores and a native chieftain described the do-
mesticated animal of the rumored kingdom somewhere over the
water to the southeast, molding its likeness in the sea's wet clay,
Balboa saw a dromedary, there being yet no way to conceptual-
ize a llama. And at that moment, precursors to Steinbeck's old
men, there came to be a line of men on the Pacific hating it
because it stopped them.

And would continue to hate it for the maddening weeks that
stretched themselves out, end to end, into months and even
years. For Ferdinand, while he had appointed Balboa *adelantado*
(governor) of the "South Sea," had placed him under the command of a new provincial governor sent out in 1514, Pedro
Arias de Avila (Pedrarias). That rendered Balboa powerless to
enact his vision of the new water as a highway eastward while
the vicious old Pedrarias fumbled and stewed at this command
post of Acla.

Pedrarias was in truth the very embodiment of that fierce
negativity the Old World brought to its discovery of the New.
The man carried a coffin with him on his travels, had it installed
in his quarters. In a long career in foreign places, he spread
death about him as though that coffin contained a fatal pesti-
lence that he would loose on the Africans and now on the Indians. So soon had he established his command at Acla did he
order such insanely cruel attacks on the natives of the isthmus
that shortly the flimsy truces managed by Balboa were all un-
done, and it was hazardous for whites to travel anywhere beyond their outposts. Nor was life within these much more
bearable. At Acla and at Darien ragged beggars crowded the

lanes and squares. Unburied bodies sprawled swollen in ditches and in mass graves never closed because they were constantly in use. Hidalgos and men-at-arms hung about in irritable idleness, itching to go for gold. And the roads leading out of these places were lined with rows of severed native heads, gaping, shrivelled, sightless on pike points, the work of Pedrarias' cousin, Gaspar de Morales, who imagined such things might prove good and continuing examples to enemies.

At last the old man, sick, torn between his growing fear of the terrible place he had made this and the mounting evidence of wealth to be had from the lands of the South Sea, commanded Balboa to transport materials for brigantines overland from Acla to the sea and there construct the ships. He would sail those sweet waters to the Pearl Islands and perhaps from there to the empire of the Great Khan himself: who could say how small a stretch of sea divided the Spaniards from their goal?

Balboa, competent as ever even under so rash a commander, accomplished the transport of the materials (no small matter there) and built the ships, though in the process most of his native laborers died. Alas, the sea worms had been at the new ships the while, and on a trial voyage to the nearest of the Pearl Islands, their hulls like honeycombs, they sank into the opalescent waters: nails, screws, rigging all lost. It all had to be done over, and Balboa did it, finishing the work in October 1518.

Why then does he linger down there for two months and more, the contract fulfilled, the ships apparently seaworthy? Why does he not return to his commander at Acla? Rumor comes up from the south shore, traveling those very paths Balboa had blazed, telling Pedrarias his man is preparing to desert the poisoned outpost, sail for the East, leaving history and its consequences behind and heading prowlike into the ahistory of the future.

The wily death-bringer accepts the rumor's truth, sends back a honeyed message to Balboa, politely requesting his return to Acla where they will discuss details of that South Sea voyage they are to make together. Meanwhile, he dispatches Francisco Pizarro and a heavily armed detail southward across the isthmus to intercept Balboa on his return journey or else apprehend him on the southern shore.

Now there is a fatal lapse in Balboa's thinking, the grand vision lacking a certain critical attention to detail. Or is it, as he would soon claim, that he is innocent of the traitorous charge, meant no mutiny? Whatever the case, he turns back toward Acla, obedient to the summons — and is shortly met by Pizarro, that ruthless one-dimensional figure, who takes him prisoner without ceremony.

Back they go, Balboa clanking in irons, away from the sea, the beach, fair breezes, waiting ships, away from light and vision, along paths already a bit overgrown as if in league with worms against all such paltry human designs: to the rotten little town with its huts, its sickness, its yet unhatched plots. And there in the village square Balboa's vision is summarily terminated. Along with his alleged co-conspirators, whom Balboa had caused to see themselves wrapped in strange silks — doubtless the only genuine vision they had ever had — Balboa is executed. In the streaming tropic gloom while the condemned beg for mercy, or swear their innocence and undying allegiance, call on the Virgin, and even Pedrarias' executioner whimpers a bit in the fading light, the sudden enormity of his task weighing on him like conscience, Balboa's head is toppled, weightless, from his shoulders, rolls briefly in the jungle mud, the eyes blinking once or twice like one who is startled. Inside a near hut, waiting for this end, Pedrarias nurses his unabated terrors and a running ulcer on his scrotum.

To the south, under patient skies and punctual, unrecking tides, the brigantines of Balboa swing emptily at anchor, their hulls still innocent of the deep waters of what one day will be known as Balboa's Pacific.

GORE VIDAL

On Italo Calvino

FROM THE NEW YORK REVIEW OF BOOKS

ON THE MORNING of Friday, September 20, 1985, the first equi-
noctial storm of the year broke over the city of Rome. I awoke
to thunder and lightning; and thought I was, yet again, in
World War II. Shortly before noon, a car and driver arrived to
take me up the Mediterranean coast to a small town on the sea
called Castiglion della Pescáia where, at one o'clock, Italo Calvino, who had died the day before, would be buried in the
village cemetery.

Calvino had had a cerebral hemorrhage two weeks earlier
while sitting in the garden of his house at Pineta di Roccamare,
where he had spent the summer working on the Charles Eliot
Norton lectures that he planned to give during the fall and
winter at Harvard. I last saw him in May. I commended him on
his bravery: he planned to give the lectures in English, a language that he read easily but spoke hesitantly, unlike French
and Spanish, which he spoke perfectly; but then he had been
born in Cuba, son of two Italian agronomists; and had lived for
many years in Paris.

It was night. We were on the terrace of my apartment in
Rome; an overhead light made his deep-set eyes look even
darker than usual. Italo gave me his either-this-or-that frown;
then he smiled, and when he smiled, suddenly, the face would
become like that of an enormously bright child who has just

worked out the unified field theory. "At Harvard, I shall stammer," he said. "But then I stammer in every language."

Unlike the United States, Italy has both an educational system (good or bad is immaterial) and a common culture, both good and bad. In recent years Calvino had become the central figure in Italy's culture. Italians were proud that they had produced a world writer whose American reputation began, if I may say so, since no one else will, in these pages when I described all of his novels as of May 30, 1974. By 1985, except for England, Calvino was read wherever books are read. I even found a Calvino coven in Moscow's literary bureaucracy; and I think that I may have convinced the state publishers to translate more of him. Curiously, the fact that he had slipped away from the Italian Communist party in 1957 disturbed no one. Then, three weeks short of Calvino's sixty-second birthday, he died; and Italy went into mourning, as if a beloved prince had died. For an American, the contrast between them and us is striking. When an American writer dies, there will be, if he's a celebrity (fame is no longer possible for any of us), a picture below the fold on the front page; later, a short appreciation on the newspaper's book page (if there is one), usually the work of a journalist or other near-writer who has not actually read any of the dead author's work but is at home with the arcana of Page Six; and that would be that.

In Calvino's case, the American newspaper obituaries were perfunctory and incompetent: the circuits between the English departments, where our tablets of literary reputation are now kept, and the world of journalism are more than ever fragile and the reception is always bad. Surprisingly, *Time* and *Newsweek*, though each put him on the "book page," were not bad, though one thought him "surrealist" and the other a "master of fantasy"; he was, of course, a true realist, who believed "that only a certain prosaic solidity can give birth to creativity: fantasy is like jam; you have to spread it on a solid slice of bread. If not, it remains a shapeless thing, like jam, out of which you can't make anything." This homely analogy is from an Italian television interview, shown after his death.

The New York Times, to show how well regarded Calvino is in these parts, quoted John Updike, our literature's perennial apostle to the middlebrows[1] (this is not meant, entirely, unkindly), as well as Margaret Atwood (a name new to me), Ursula K. LeGuin (an estimable sci-fi writer, but what is she doing, giving, as it were, a last word on one of the most complex of modern writers?), Michael Wood, whose comment was pretty good, and, finally, the excellent Anthony Burgess, who was not up to his usual par on this occasion. Elsewhere, Mr. Herbert Mitgang again quoted Mr. Updike as well as John Gardner, late apostle to the lowbrows, a sort of Christian evangelical who saw Heaven as a paradigmatic American university.

Europe regarded Calvino's death as a calamity for culture. A literary critic, as opposed to theorist, wrote at length in *Le Monde*, while in Italy itself, each day for two weeks, bulletins from the hospital at Siena were published, and the whole country was suddenly united in its esteem not only for a great writer but for someone who reached not only primary school children through his collections of folk and fairy tales but, at one time or another, everyone else who reads.

After the first hemorrhage, there was a surgical intervention that lasted many hours. Calvino came out of coma. He was disoriented: he thought that one of the medical attendants was a policeman; then he wondered if he'd had open-heart surgery. Meanwhile, the surgeon had become optimistic; even garrulous. He told the press that he'd never seen a brain structure of such delicacy and complexity as that of Calvino. I thought immediately of the smallest brain ever recorded, that of Anatole France. The surgeon told the press that he had been obliged to do his very best. After all, he and his sons had read and argued over *Marcovaldo* last winter. The brain that could so puzzle them must be kept alive in all its rarity. One can imagine a comparable

---

[1] Although the three estates, high, middle, and lowbrow, are as dead as Dwight Macdonald, their most vigorous deployer, something about today's literary scene, combined with Calvino's death, impels me to resurrect the terms. Presently, I shall demonstrate.

surgeon in America: only last Saturday she had kept me and my sons in stitches; now I could hardly believe that I was actually gazing into the fabulous brain of Joan Rivers! On the other hand, the admirer of Joan Rivers might have saved Calvino; except that there was no real hope, ever. In June he had had what he thought was a bad headache; it was the first stroke. Also, he came from a family with a history of arterial weakness. Or so it was said in the newspapers. The press coverage of Calvino's final days resembled nothing so much as that of the recent operation on the ancient actor that our masters have hired to impersonate a president, the sort of subject that used to delight Calvino — the Acting President, that is.

As we drove north through the rain, I read Calvino's last novel, *Mr. Palomar.* He had given it to me on November 28, 1983. I was chilled — and guilty — to read for the first time the inscription: "For Gore, these last meditations about Nature, Italo." "Last" is a word artists should not easily use. What did this "last" mean? Latest? Or his last attempt to write about the phenomenal world? Or did he know, somehow, that he was in the process of "Learning to be dead," the title of the book's last chapter?

I read the book. It is very short. A number of meditations on different subjects by one Mr. Palomar, who is Calvino himself. The settings are, variously, the beach at Castiglion della Pescàia, the nearby house in the woods at Roccamare, the flat in Rome with its terrace, a food specialty shop in Paris. This is not the occasion to review the book. But I made some observations; and marked certain passages that seemed to me to illuminate the prospect.

Palomar is on the beach at Castiglion: he is trying to figure out the nature of waves. Is it possible to follow just one? Or do they all become one? *E pluribus unum* and its reverse might well sum up Calvino's approach to our condition. Are we a part of the universe? Or is the universe, simply, us thinking that there is such a thing? Calvino often writes like the scientist that his parents were. He observes, precisely, the minutiae of nature: stars, waves, lizards, turtles, a woman's breast exposed on the beach. In the process, he vacillates between macro and micro.

The whole and the part. Also, tricks of eye. The book is written in the present tense, like a scientist making reports on that ongoing experiment, the examined life.

The waves provide him with suggestions but no answers: viewed in a certain way, they seem to come not from the horizon but from the shore itself. "Is this perhaps the real result that Mr. Palomar is about to achieve? To make the waves run in the opposite direction, to overturn time, to perceive the true substance of the world beyond sensory and mental habits?" But it doesn't quite work; and he cannot extend "this knowledge to the entire universe." He notes during his evening swim that "the sun's reflection becomes a shining sword on the water stretching from shore to him. Mr. Palomar swims in that sword. . . ." But then so does everyone else at that time of day, each in the same sword which is everywhere and nowhere. "The sword is imposed equally on the eye of each swimmer; there is no avoiding it. 'Is what we have in common precisely what is given to each of us as something exclusively his?' " As Palomar floats he wonders if he exists. He drifts now toward solipsism: "If no eye except the glassy eye of the dead were to open again on the surface of the terraqueous globe, the sword would not gleam any more." He develops this, floating on his back. "Perhaps it was not the birth of the eye that caused the birth of the sword, but vice versa, because the sword had to have an eye to observe it at its climax." But the day is ending, the wind-surfers are all beached, and Palomar comes back to land: "He has become convinced that the sword will exist even without him."

In the garden at Roccamare, Palomar observes the exotic mating of turtles; he ponders the blackbird's whistle, so like that of a human being that it might well be the same sort of communication. "Here a prospect that is very promising for Mr. Palomar's thinking opens out; for him the discrepancy between human behavior and the rest of the universe has always been a source of anguish. The equal whistle of man and blackbird now seems to him a bridge thrown over the abyss." But his attempts to communicate with them through a similar whistling leads to "puzzlement" on both sides. Then, contemplating the horrors of his lawn and its constituent parts, among them weeds, he precisely names and numbers what he sees until "he no longer thinks of the lawn: he thinks of the universe. He is trying to apply to the universe everything he has thought about the lawn. The universe as regular and ordered cosmos or as chaotic pro-liferation." The analogy, as always with Calvino, then takes off (the jam on the bread) and the answer is again the many within the one, or "collections of collections."

Observations and meditations continue. He notes, "Nobody looks at the moon in the afternoon, and this is the moment when it would most require our attention, since its existence is still in doubt." As night comes on, he wonders if the moon's bright splendor is "due to the slow retreat of the sky, which, as it moves away, sinks deeper and deeper into darkness or whether, on the contrary it is the moon that is coming forward, collecting the previously scattered light and depriving the sky of it, concen-trating it all in the round mouth of its funnel." One begins now to see the method of a Calvino meditation. He looks; he de-scribes; he has a scientist's respect for data (the opposite of the surrealist or fantasist). He wants us to see not only what he sees but what we may have missed by not looking with sufficient attention. It is no wonder that Galileo crops up in his writing. The received opinion of mankind over the centuries (which is what middlebrow is all about) was certain that the sun moved around the earth but to a divergent highbrow's mind, Galileo's or Calvino's, it is plainly the other way around. Galileo applied the scientific methods of his day; Calvino used his imagination. Each either got it right; or assembled the data so that others could understand the phenomenon.

In April 1982, while I was speaking to a Los Angeles audience with George McGovern, Eugene McCarthy, and the dread phys-ical therapist Ms. Fonda Hayden, "the three 'external' planets, visible to the naked eye . . . are all three 'in opposition' and therefore visible for the whole night." Needless to say, "Mr. Palomar rushes out on to the terrace." Between Calvino's stars and mine, he had the better of it; yet he wrote a good deal of political commentary for newspapers. But after he left the Com-munist party, he tended more to describe politics and its delu-sions than take up causes. "In a time and in a country where everyone goes out of his way to announce opinions or hand down judgements, Mr. Palomar has made a habit of biting his tongue three times before asserting anything. After the bite, if he is still convinced of what he was going to say, he says it." But then, "having had the correct view is nothing meritorious; statistically, it is almost inevitable that among the many cockeyed, confused or banal ideas that come into his mind, there should also be some perspicacious ideas, even ideas of genius; and as they occurred to him, they can surely have occurred also to somebody else." As he was a writer of literature and not a theorist, so he was an observer of politics and not a politician.

Calvino was as inspired by the inhabitants of zoos as by those of cities. "At this point Mr. Palomar's little girl, who has long since tired of watching the giraffes, pulls him toward the penguins' cave. Mr. Palomar, in whom penguins inspire anguish, follows her reluctantly and asks himself why he is so interested in giraffes. Perhaps because the world around him moves in an unharmonious way, and he hopes always to find some pattern to it, a constant. Perhaps because he himself feels that his own advance is impelled by uncoordinated movements of the mind, which seem to have nothing to do with one another and are increasingly difficult to fit into any pattern of inner harmony."

Palomar is drawn to the evil-smelling reptile house. "Beyond the glass of every cage, there is the world as it was before man, or after, to show that the world of man is not eternal and is not unique." The crocodiles, in their stillness, horrify him. "What are they waiting for, or what have they given up waiting for? In what time are they immersed? . . . The thought of a time outside our existence is intolerable." Palomar flees to the albino gorilla, "sole exemplar in the world of a form not chosen, not loved." The gorilla, in his boredom, plays with a rubber tire; he presses it to his bosom by the hour. The image haunts Palomar. " 'Just as the gorilla has his tire, which serves as tangible support for a raving, wordless speech,' he thinks, 'so I have this image of a great white ape. We all turn in our hands an old, empty tire through which we would like to reach the final meaning, which words cannot achieve.' " This is the ultimate of writers' images; that indescribable state where words are absent not because they are stopped by the iron bars of a cage at the zoo but by the limitations of that bone-covered binary electrical system which, in Calvino's case, broke down September 19, 1985.

Suddenly, up ahead, on a hill overlooking the sea, is Castiglion della Pescáia. To my left is the beach where Palomar saw but sees no longer the sword of light. The sea has turned an odd disagreeable purple color, more suitable to the Caribbean of Calvino's birth than the Mediterranean. The sky is overcast. The air is hot, humid, windless (the headline of today's newspaper, which has devoted six pages to Calvino's life and work: *Cataclisma in Messico*). I am forty minutes early.

The cemetery is on a hill back of the town which is on a lower hill. We park next to a piece of medieval wall and a broken tower. I walk up to the cemetery which is surrounded by a high cement wall. I am reminded of Calvino's deep dislike of cement. In one of his early books, *La Speculazione Edilizia*, he described how the building trade had managed, in the 1950s, to bury the Italian Riviera, his native Liguria, under a sea of "horrible reinforced cement"; "il boom," it was called. To the right of the cemetery entrance a large section of wall has been papered over with the same small funeral notice, repeated several hundred times. The name "Italo Calvino," the name of Castiglion della Pescáia, "the town of Palomar," the sign says proudly; then the homage of mayor and city council and populace.

Inside the cemetery there are several walled-off areas. The first is a sort of atrium, whose walls are filled with drawers containing the dead, stacked one above the other, each with a photograph of the occupant, taken rather too late in life to arouse much pity as opposed to awe. There are plastic flowers everywhere; and a few real flowers. There are occasional small chapels, the final repository of wealthy or noble families. I have a sense of panic: They aren't going to put Italo in a drawer, are they? But then to the right, at the end of the atrium, in the open air, against a low wall, I see a row of vast floral wreaths, suitable for an American or Neapolitan gangster, and not a drawer but a new grave, the size of a bathtub in a moderately luxurious hotel. On one of the wreaths, I can make out the words "Senato" and "Communist . . . ," the homage of the Communist delegation in the Italian Senate. Parenthetically, since Italy is a country of many political parties and few ideologies, the level of the ordinary parliamentarian is apt to be higher than his American or English counterpart. Moravia sits in the European parliament. Sciascia was in the chamber of deputies. Every party tries to put on its electoral list a number of celebrated intellectual names. The current mayor of Florence was, until recently, the head of the Paris opera: according to popular wisdom, anyone who could handle that can of worms can probably deal with Florence.

Over the wall, the purple sea and red-tiled whitewashed houses are visible. As I gaze, moderately melancholy, at Palomar country, I am recognized by a journalist from Naples. I am a neighbor, after all; I live at nearby Ravello. Among the tombs, I am interviewed. How had I met Calvino? A few drops of warm rain fall. A cameraman appears from behind a family chapel and takes my picture. The state television crew is arriving. Eleven years ago, I say, I wrote a piece about his work. Had you met him *before* that? Logrolling is even more noticeable in a small country like Italy than it is in our own dear *New York Times*. No, I had not met him when I wrote the piece. I had just read him, admired him; described (the critic's only task) his work for those who were able to read me and might then be inclined to read him (the critic's single aim). Did you meet him later? Yes, he wrote me a letter about the piece. In Italian or English? Italian, I say. What did he say? What do you think he said? I am getting irritable. He said he liked what I'd written.

Actually, Calvino's letter had been, characteristically, interesting and tangential. I had ended my description with "Reading Calvino, I had the unnerving sense that I was also writing what he had written; thus does his art prove his case as writer and reader become one, or One." This caught his attention. Politely, he began by saying that he had always been attracted by my "mordant irony," and so forth, but he particularly liked what I had written about him for two reasons. The first, "One feels that you have written this essay for the pleasure of writing it, alternating warm praise and criticism and reserve with an absolute sincerity, with freedom, and continuous humor, and this sensation of pleasure is irresistibly communicated to the reader.

Second, I have always thought it would be difficult to extract a unifying theme from my books, each so different from the other. Now you — exploring my works as it should be done, that is, by going at it in an unsystematic way, stopping here and there; sometimes aimed directly without straying aside; other times, wandering like a vagabond — have succeeded in giving a general sense to all I have written, almost a philosophy —'the whole and the many,' etc. — and it makes me very happy when someone is able to find a philosophy from the productions of my mind which has little philosophy." Then Calvino comes to the point. "The ending of your essay contains an affirmation of what seems to me important in an absolute sense. I don't know if it really refers to me, but it is true of an ideal literature for each one of us: the end being that every one of us must be, that the writer and reader become one, or One. And to close all of my discourse and yours in a perfect circle, let us say that this One is All." In a sense, the later Palomar was the gathering together of the strands of a philosphy or philosophies; hence, the inscription "my last meditations on Nature."

I let slip not a word of this to the young journalist. But I do tell him that soon after the letter I had met Calvino and his wife, Chichita, at the house of an American publisher, and though assured that there would be no writers there but us, I found a room ablaze with American literary genius. Fearful of becoming prematurely One with them, I split into the night.

Two years ago, when I was made an honorary citizen of Ravello, Calvino accepted the town's invitation to participate in the ceremony, where he delivered a splendid discourse on my work in general and on *Duluth* in particular. Also, since Calvino's Roman flat was on the same street as mine (we were separated by — oh, the beauty of the random symbol! — the Pantheon), we saw each other occasionally.

For the last year, Calvino had been looking forward to his fall and winter at Harvard. He even began to bone up on "literary theory." He knew perfectly well what a mephitic kindergarten our English departments have become, and I cannot wait to see what he has to say in the three lectures that he did write. I had planned to arm him with a wonderfully silly bit of lowbrow criticism (from *Partisan Review*) on why people just don't like to read much anymore. John Gardner is quoted with admiration: " 'In nearly all good fiction, the basic — all but inescapable — plot form is this: a central character wants something, goes after it despite opposition (perhaps including his own doubts), and so arrives at a win, lose or draw.' " For those still curious about high, middle, and lowbrow, this last is the Excelsior of lowbrow commercialities, written in letters of gold in the halls of the Thalberg building at MGM but never to be found in, say, the original *Partisan Review* of Rahv and Dupee, Trilling and Chase. The PR "critic" then quotes "a reviewer" in *The New York Times* who is trying to figure out why Calvino is popular. "If love fails, they begin again; their lives are a series of new beginnings, where complications have not yet begun to show themselves. Unlike the great Russian and French novelists" (this is pure middlebrow: *which* novelists, dummy! Name names, make your case, *describe*), "who follow their characters through the long and winding caverns [!] of their lives, Calvino just turns off the set after the easy beginning and switches to another channel." This sort of writing has given American bookchat (a word I coined, you will be eager to know) a permanently bad name. But our PR critic, a woman, this year's favored minority (*sic*), states, sternly, that all this "indeterminancy" is not the kind of stuff real folks want to read. "And Calvino is popular, if at all, among theorists, consumers of 'texts' rather than of novels and stories." I shall now never have the chance to laugh with Calvino over this latest report from the land to which Bouvard and Pécuchet emigrated.

At the foot of cemetery hill, a van filled with police arrives. Crowds are anticipated. The day before, the President of the Republic had come to the Siena Hospital to say farewell. One can imagine a similar scene in the United States. High atop the Tulsa Tower Hospital, the Reverend Oral Roberts enters the hushed room. "Mr. President, it's all over. *He* has crossed the shining river." A tear gleams in the Acting President's eye. "The last round-up," he murmurs. The tiny figure at his side, huge lidless eyes aswim with tears, whispers, "Does this mean, no more Harlequin novels?" The Acting President holds her